Risking Truth

Reshaping the World through Prayers of Lament

SCOTT A. ELLINGTON

PICKWICK *Publications* · Eugene, Oregon

RISKING TRUTH
Reshaping the World through Prayers of Lament

Pickwick Publications
A Division of Wipf and Stock Publishers
199 W. 8th Ave., Suite 3
Eugene, OR 97401

ISBN 13: 978-1-55635-263-8

Princeton Theological Monograph Series 98

Cataloging-in-Publication data:

Ellington, Scott A.

Risking truth : reshaping the world through prayers of lament / Scott A.
Ellington.

xiv + 200 p.; 23 cm. Includes bibliographical references.

Princeton Theological Monograph Series 98

ISBN 13: 978-1-55635-263-8 (alk. paper)

1. Laments in the Bible. 2. Laments—History and criticism. 3. Suffering—
Religious aspects—Christianity. 4. Bible. O.T. Psalms—Criticism, interpretation, etc.
5. Bible. O.T. Job—Criticism, interpretation, etc. 6. Bible. O.T. Jeremiah—Criticism,
interpretation, etc. I. Title. II. Series.

BT732.7 E50 2008

Manufactured in the U.S.A.

For Linda

Contents

Acknowledgments

No one writes alone. In thinking through the many questions raised during the course of this study, I have enjoyed and been stimulated by the writings of numerous men and women for whom Israel's prayers in the face of God's silence are more than simply an object of study or an academic exercise. The lament prayers do not so much invite reflection as they encourage a journey into the darkness along side of those who first prayed them. The authors who have had the most to offer are invariably those who have had the courage to make such a journey. Though hardly a popular topic, I have come to appreciate the extent to which biblical laments resonate with some of our most profound and life-changing experiences.

I am indebted to those friends and colleagues who have been generous with their time and guidance as they have helped me to ask some tough questions about the nature of God and our relationship with him. I appreciate the contributions of David Clines, Rickie Moore, and Kathleen O'Connor in helping me to define some of the parameters of this study. The staff of the John Burlow Campbell Library has offered invaluable assistance with gathering the necessary research materials for this work. I am also grateful for the many pastoral insights that Ron Harvard has generously shared with me.

I am particularly indebted to John Goldingay, who helped set the direction of my initial inquiries into Israel's laments and who has continued to offer encouragement and guidance. Professor Goldingay has the gift of asking penetrating and provocative questions that invite a deeper look and a fresh perspective in considering Israel's prayers. I am also thankful for the assistance and constant encouragement of Walter Brueggemann who fostered my initial interest in the laments and who has shared freely from his extensive knowledge. Professor Brueggemann, in addition to being vastly creative in his own writings, possesses the gift of sparking creativity in those around him. Both men have a love for the text that is infectious and without their unwavering encouragement and assistance as dialogue partners, this book could not have been written.

Lastly I wish to express my love and appreciation for all that my wife Linda has done to help bring this book to completion. From the many long hours spent reading and proofing the manuscript to her unwavering support throughout the writing process, Linda has been my greatest encouragement.

Introduction

Risking Truth

Prayers of lament arise from experiences of loss. To hear a diagnosis of cancer, to be permanently disabled in an automobile accident, to be fired from a job, to be betrayed by a spouse, or to lose everything and be forced to live in the streets are all experiences that can overturn our world. They threaten to rob us of our sense of security, of the goodness of life, and of the justice of God. They can strip us of dignity and can plant in our hearts the conviction that we have been betrayed by our own frailties, by those around us, and most importantly by God. In the context of biblical prayers of lament God is the particular problem. In the midst of the crisis fervent prayers crying out to God and seeking his deliverance are met with divine silence. At the heart of biblical laments are the twin experiences of profound loss and the silence of God.

Inherent in the title of this study is the recognition that the act of lament adds to the experience of loss an element of risk. Simply to lose everything involves no particular risk. There is no risk taken in a fatalistic acceptance of loss over which we have no control or in the automatic assumption that all suffering is somehow deserved or in the conviction that God is powerless to transform the situation. Simply surrendering to and accepting such loss negates the need for the prayer of lament. To lament, though, is to refuse to accept things as they are, to protest God's continued silence, and to press God for deliverance.

To lament is to embark on a journey of double risk. First of all, to lament in the face of loss is to admit openly that things have gone horribly wrong. It requires that we turn loose of the ordered world that anchors reality and gives meaning and structure to life. To lament is to cast into doubt, to challenge, and perhaps even finally to reject the "standing answers" that heretofore have provided a framework in which to understand God. Lament reaches toward the hiddenness of God, rejecting every pious platitude that insists that everything is as it should be and raising fundamental questions about God's faithfulness and justice.

Not surprisingly, there is tremendous resistance to risking a stable world, particularly in moments of crisis when that stability and assurance are most needed, so that denial, rationalization, or a rejection of the testimony of experience may be preferable to the risk of accepting the evidence of loss at face value. So strong is the need to hold on to a stable rendering of reality that the one suffering may even be willing to commit intellectual, moral, and emotional suicide in order to preserve an ordered world, regardless of its flaws. The protection of stability may even require the sacrifice by their community of the one who is cast down. Job's friends were quick to realize that if God would do such things to one who truly is blameless and upright then no one is safe. They recognized that Job's questions posed an immediate threat to their own sense of safety. The prayer of lament takes the risk of dismantling a stable, albeit dysfunctional, rendering of reality, with no assurance of being able to offer something enduring in its place.

A second risk taken in the act of lament is that of newness. This perhaps sounds strange. Why would a victim of suffering and loss choose to stay in the crumbling remnants of an old and obviously failed world when he or she could launch out on a journey of discovery into a new and potentially better one? The answer lies in part with the truth that in order to seek newness one must first abandoned the old world, and with it any vestiges of order and refuge that it provided. In the film *Castaway*, the central character risks death by building a crude raft and striking out into the open sea, rather than choosing to live and die safe but alone on a small island. To risk newness requires a leap into the abyss. Such newness is only a possibility, never a certainty. To abandon the old life and move toward the possibility of newness is an act of tremendous courage and risk because, should newness fail to materialize, then the refugee must face a death that has been stripped of all meaning.

To risk both the loss of the old and the uncertainty of the new requires an act of faith and courage; it requires the act of lament. While newness *may* come and life *may* be restored, stability and certainty once put to death can never be fully raised to life again. And to accept the risk of potential newness is to realize that, even if new life is granted, things can never again be as they were and that the future is never guaranteed.

Outline of the Study

In the chapters that follow we will explore the various functions of lament in the lives of the diverse communities that produced the Bible. With its extended use in a wide variety of contexts, biblical prayers of lament respond to a diverse range of needs and fulfill a range of purposes. Chapter one will examine the core dynamic that defines the prayer of lament, the tension between belief and experience. When an experience of profound suffering and loss is met by the silence and apparent absence of God, essential tenets in our beliefs about God are challenged. Prayers of lament function to adjudicate the tension created between beliefs about God and experiences of God's silence and abandonment that call those beliefs into question. As the one praying both affirms his or her most basic beliefs and testifies to experiences that contradict those beliefs, the stage is set for both experience and belief to be transformed by a fresh encounter with God. Should, however, God remain silent, the possibility exists that belief will not be transformed but destroyed.

Chapter two will consider the nature of the God to whom prayers of lament are offered. The twentieth century has witnessed a theological shift in our thinking about God. Classic articulations of theism required that God be unchanging and unaffected by his creation in order to safeguard his perfection. As a result, God was not thought of as suffering, experiencing emotion, or being in any way influenced by his creation. In the last century, though, the understanding of God as one who suffers both with and for his creation has gained acceptance. The God to whom lament is offered both experiences suffering and laments for the suffering of creation. Various biblical writers also struggle, though, with the realization that at times God causes suffering in his creation and may be experienced as an enemy.

Chapter three will focus on a central element of those prayers of lament found in the Psalter. The context of community prayer in the Psalms underscores an important feature of psalms of lament. Those prayers frequently reach beyond the present circumstance of distress and appeal to memories of God's presence and action to save in the past. The psalm writers draw on memories of God's deliverance in the past and testify to fresh experiences of God in the present. The story of Israel's relationship with God is a central resource in the psalms of lament and their writers frequently appeal to and seek to participate directly in that story.

In chapter four the prayers of Job center on the problematic of trusting a God who punishes the righteous and fails to protect the innocent. The prayers that Job offers drive an exploration of the distinction between seeking for God's justice in the execution of his laws and seeking an encounter with God that transcends those laws. It is the particular contribution of the writer of Job to observe that the fact of continuing to address speech to God can at times eclipse the importance of the content of speech about God.

Chapter five considers the purpose of lament prayers in the prophetic tradition. Jeremiah is representative of those exilic prophets whose vocation demands of them that they first experience and then express the suffering of another. Jeremiah and the prophet of Lamentations are tasked with participating in the suffering both of God and of Israel. Their prayers probe the boundaries of a covenant relationship in which the suffering of God shapes directly his exercise of justice.

Chapter six seeks out the sporadic uses of lament in the New Testament. Lament prayers are most often alluded to or partially reported in the Gospel accounts. Lament takes on a canonical role in the New Testament. In the gospel of Matthew in particular, prayers of lament both provide structure for the unfolding Messianic mission and serve to hasten the advent of the Kingdom of God. Laments both accompany and give shape to Matthew's proclamation of the gospel.

Chapter seven will draw together the varied and diverse applications of the prayer of lament in the Bible in order to describe more clearly its theological functions in scripture and to suggest ways that it continues to be relevant in the life of the community of faith today. A central conviction arising from this study is that prayers of lament fulfill a variety of important functions in the Bible and are vital to the life of the community of faith.

1

Why Should We Cry Out?

On January 26, 2004, the day after Christmas, an earthquake deep beneath the floor of the Indian Ocean gave birth to a tsunami that devastated coastal areas in and around Indonesia, Sri Lanka, Thailand, and India. The death toll approached 300,000 and, because of the remoteness and poverty of some of the affected areas, a final death count can only be estimated. Literally in a matter of moments the lives of many hundreds of thousands of people were struck by overwhelming tragedy and loss. Houses, churches and temples, hospitals, schools, and even entire villages were obliterated. Families were torn apart and people perished by the tens of thousands regardless of age, religion, race, wealth, or social position.

When Safety Vanishes

STABILITY AND SAFETY ARE THINGS THAT WE PRIZE VERY HIGHLY IN life. We will pay a heavy price to obtain them and an even heavier price to keep them once we have them. We will go to extremes, will even fight wars, in order to protect a safe and prosperous life for ourselves and for our families. We will turn a blind eye to our own faults and sins, while villainizing those who threaten our safety. We will turn away from the suffering of others and find ways to justify insulating ourselves from a chaotic world that threatens to rob us of our sense of security. In the developed nations today we have experienced great prosperity and an unusual degree of security, so much so that we have come to think of such things as normal and even as our God-given right. Small wonder that we resist so energetically anything that threatens to undo the lives that we have built for ourselves.

Ultimately, though, we cannot shield ourselves from loss. Uncertainty, change, injury, and death are constants in the world that no amount

I

of wealth or technology can fully guard against. The spread of nuclear technology among diverse nations and powers, continued vulnerability to terrorist attacks, the shift of populations from poor to wealthy nations, the mounting strain on our environment as we exhaust its natural resources, and the threat of new diseases and super-viruses are just a few of the things that threaten our sense of well-being. Ultimately we are unable sufficiently to control our national borders, our economies, our livelihoods, our homes, or even our own bodies. Loss threatens each of us and can completely transform our lives in an instant.

In the Bible, safety and security are found not in military strength or wealth or technological advantage, but in a relationship with God. Yahweh, the God of Israel, is exalted as the creator of the world and is the sovereign ruler of the nations. The forces of nature are in the palm of his hand and he controls wind and fire, flood and earthquake. God is the mighty warrior who takes up arms, vanquishing enemy armies. He is the healer who cleanses lepers and raises the dead to new life. He is the loving parent who provides food for the destitute. He is the righteous judge who delivers the weak and powerless. Proverbs 21:31 puts it succinctly: "The horse is prepared against the day of battle: but safety is of the LORD." For those who live in a relationship with Yahweh, he is both the provider and the guarantor of life. The loss of security, then, threatens their sense of an ordered world and touches directly on their relationship with God.

For the writers of the Bible the experience of loss elicits prayers of lament. Such prayers are born from devastation when safety is replaced by turmoil. We find them in those places where our defenses against chaos have been breached and our resources for coping overwhelmed. Feelings of pain, fear, confusion, and outrage drive lament prayers. They are the fruit not of quiet reflection, but of pressing need.

Lament does not arise from perplexity over theological uncertainties. It is anguish and not theological curiosity that energizes the cries of "How long oh Lord?" and "Why have you abandoned me?" Theological reflection, if present at all in lament, is so only in a derivative sense. The prayer of lament seldom asks "Why do tsunamis take the life of babies?" but rather "Why did this tsunami kill my baby?" Lament is the product of life experiences and not of detached contemplation. It is not concerned with objectivity, but rather with verbalizing pain. The crisis that confronts the one praying a lament is more than the potential loss of a theological understanding of God, it is the weakening or loss of trust in God. It is not just that tragedy has struck, but that in the midst of that tragedy the God who has been a loving source of protection and prosperity in the past seems suddenly to have fallen silent, so that he will not provide, not protect, and not heal. Loitering behind many of the biblical laments is the basic question "Can this God still be trusted?"

Praying the prayer of lament is a risky business. Lament is risky, first of all, because it abandons all pretense of excuse, denial, or cover-up. Like the little boy in Hans Christian Anderson's story *The Emperor's New Clothes*, lament proclaims loudly and, for some, embarrassingly that the world is not as it was thought to be and that the emperor is, in fact, naked. Such prayers simply will not constrain themselves to conventional, acceptable, safe language in their address to God. Laments rightly diagnose the fundamental problem as a crisis of relationship with God. Yes the enemy attacked, yes the floodwaters rose, yes the disease wasted, but the real problem is that God both permitted these things to happen and then stood silently by as his people cried out to him for help. Lament declares boldly that everything is not all right, that God has not delivered, and that he has hidden his face from his people. The prayer of lament does not indulge itself in rationalization and excuse, but offers an honest and impassioned expression of the experience of God's hiddenness in the midst of chaos. In short, in order to lament one must first turn loose of illusory certainty.

Lament challenges every theology of guaranteed safety and every doctrine of assured outcomes. Goaded by pain, such prayers do not shrink from exposing the cracks in our most sacred ideas about God. No question is illegitimate and no expression of doubt is off-limits. Nor does this questioning of the sacred take place in a corner, confined to the heart of the sufferer, but spills out in groans, pleas, and shouts before God and the assembled congregation. Lament will neither deny pain nor give place to theology, but risks truthful communication that could potentially lead to a loss of trust and the dismantling of our theologies of God. But more than just our confidence in God and our theology are risked by the act of lament. By challenging God to answer and to act, the prayer of lament places at risk the very foundations of an ongoing relationship with God. By putting God "on the spot," lament runs the risk that he will neither answer nor move, that his silence will endure. Open lament risks exposing a new reality, that the God who brought his people out of Egypt and into the land of the promise no longer is a God who saves.

Lament is also, though, an act of hope. It will not accept as final the mere testimony of eyes and ears. It refuses to answer the silence of God in kind. Like a small child, lament keeps endlessly repeating "Mommy! Mommy! Mommy!" in that irritating tone of children that simply cannot be ignored. While lament may explore dark places and journey to extreme frontiers in a relationship with God, by its very nature it refuses to step back from that relationship into silence. The prayer of the lament stakes all on the conviction that God hears and will answer. Ultimately, while the prayer of lament involves a degree of risk, to remain silent in the face of God's silence is to accept and embrace the certainty of hopelessness.

In this book we will focus on the biblical writer's exploration of their faith in God and relationship with God in light of experiences that cast doubt on much of what they believed to be true about him. In lament the contradiction between what we believe to be true about God and the ways that we experience him in daily life reaches its zenith. Prayers of lament provide the primary tools with which the people of Israel can explore and redefine their relationship with God in the midst of chaos. They do this by placing at risk both belief and experience. It is in and through the prayers of lament that the tension between belief and experience is most effectively adjudicated. Lament allows us to resume the journey of faith in the midst of profound loss and divine silence. Were we to either forsake our beliefs or deny our experience, it would be impossible to continue the journey. The cry of lament is not an embarrassing lapse of faith on Israel's part, but is a courageous act of risk-taking. Indeed to remain silent or, worse yet, to mouth praises into the silence, is a betrayal of faith, finding sufficiency as it does in a God who is distant and past. Lament is a profound and potent expression of faith.

The Place of Lament in the Life of the Church

Growing up in the church as a child, I was introduced to stories from the Old Testament that stirred my imagination and shaped my earliest notions of God. Upon leaving my children's Sunday School class, though, a marked change took place. The Old Testament stories, which revealed God so vividly and which had such a central role in the nurturing of my faith as a child, took on more of a peripheral character in the teaching I received as an adult Christian. It was almost as if I were expected to "outgrow" the God of the Old Testament. Occasional sorties into the Old Testament were made, plundering proof-texts for the purpose of supporting some point more adequately and fully expressed in the New Testament, but rarely was the Old Testament explored in any depth for its own unique contributions to Christian faith and understanding. Only in seminary did I "rediscover" the Old Testament and come to know it as the Bible of the New Testament writers. The notion that the Old Testament had somehow been made redundant by the New was gradually replaced with an appreciation for the extent to which the New Testament is founded on, depends upon, and flows out of the Old.

Almost entirely absent from the pages of the New Testament are the faith community's wrestlings with the problems of innocent suffering, the prosperity of the wicked, and the silence of God in times of need.[1] Prayers of lament, so common in the Old Testament, are much more rare in the New and this has led some to assume that the suffering of Christ on our behalf has replaced our need for such prayers. A theology that sees the Old Testament as essentially supplementary in nature and largely eclipsed by the revelation of Christ will disdain the biblical resources given to the church for responding to God in the extremities of life. It is my desire to explore the uses that Israel made of lament and to consider its place in the shaping of our ideas and beliefs about God today.

Lament is found throughout the Old Testament, from the foundational stories of the Pentateuch, to the worship of the Psalm writers, to the reflections of the sages, to the oracles of the prophets. Experiences of suffering and of God's silence in the face of that suffering elicited from Israel a cry. In our highly individualistic societies today, it bears pointing out that that cry was not a private matter for the prayer closet, but was offered in the context of public worship, teaching, and preaching. The silence of God in the face of human suffering was of concern to the community as a whole.

But how are we of the new covenant to appropriate such prayers? While we do not find adopting prayers of praise and thanksgiving problematic, the same cannot be said about prayers of lament. How

---

1. Though, as we shall see in chapter six, lament continues to play an important role in the New Testament, especially in Matthew's gospel.

do prayers of lament fit into the life of the modern (and increasingly postmodern) church? Should they have the same form as the laments of Israel? Should the victory of Christ over sin, sickness, and death alter their content? When confronted with suffering and divine silence, how should we speak to God?

Our Loss of Lament

Ours is an age and a culture, at least in North America, in which many have forgotten how to lament in the ways that mirror biblical prayer. By that I do not mean that we have forgotten how to cry, because no amount of affluence and technology has been able to guarantee our safety and security so that we have no occasion for tears. No matter how great our take-home pay, how high the fences around our homes, how extensive our insurance coverage, or how thorough the security measures at our national borders, tragedy, crisis, and loss know where we live and can easily find us. Technological advances, while solving many problems, curing many diseases, and generally making our lives easier in many ways (though perhaps also making them more frantically active), have at the same time introduced a host of new concerns, from the destruction of the environment to an explosive growth in the human population to the breeding of super viruses to the perpetuation of an ever increasing gap between poor and rich, and have so far failed to realize visions of a utopian world. In spite of continual advances in our society, we still feel pain and loss, and indeed we fear both perhaps as never before.

Ironically, the rise of wealth and technology has often been accompanied by the demise of community. Restaurants have replaced dining room tables as the setting for our mealtime communion and an impressive array of gadgets and gizmos tempt us away from conversations with neighbors across backyard fences and family evenings enjoyed with the help of nothing more substantial than a deck of cards. The craft of communication atrophies in the face of such an onslaught. Not only do we in the developed world still suffer, but more than ever before we do so alone, unaccustomed to sharing those things in our lives that matter most. But tears of pain and sorrow at the experience of loss are not in and of themselves lament.

Nor have we forgotten how to protest and complain. Indeed, our affluence and many comforts seem to have increased our sense of discontent and our impatience with anything that frustrates our wishes, even for a moment. A higher standard of living has brought with it a greater sense of entitlement. The consumer mentality which so defines the Western society in which we live feeds upon itself, so that yesterday's privilege becomes today's right and what is new and wonderful today will not even be acceptable as a starting point tomorrow. Complaint and protest are quick to form on our lips any time that our ever-increasing expectations are not met with ever-increasing speed and ease. But complaint and protest are not in and of themselves lament either.

If pain and protest alone are not sufficient to constitute biblical lament, what is its basis? Biblical lament, while it does include tears, pleas, complaints and protests, is something more. It is the experience of loss suffered within the context of *relatedness*. A relationship of trust, intimacy, and love is a necessary precondition for genuine lament. When the biblical writers lament, they do so from within the context of a foundational relationship that binds together the individual with members of the community of faith and that community with their God. That biblical lament is offered to God is clear, but perhaps less obvious is the essential role that the community plays. The prayer of lament is not a private thing, but is offered "out loud," "standing up," and "in church." Lament is not the property of the individual, but belongs to the community that presents itself before God. This is true even for those individual laments in which the writer struggles with being cut off from the worshipping community, for these prayers are valued, repeated, and recycled in the community's worship. The covenant relationship between God and his people provides the context for prayers of lament that define, shape, limit, release, and direct the voices of lament that we find in the Bible. When severed from this relational context, lament cannot serve for us its essential function. Cries of pain and protest that do not arise from the community's covenant relationship with God have no foundation on which to stand in approaching God for an answer. They become nothing more than a raging against the storm or a weeping in the darkness, an act of defiance against a hostile deity or a hopeless gesture that carries with it no expectation of being heard. But Israel through their laments sought to understand and explore the dynamics of the covenant relationship. Covenant assumes a God who is both available to hear and responsive. Covenant prayers assume a partner in conversation. They are dialogical in nature. Lament is lament only when it is addressed to someone.

Eugene Petersen reminds us that prayer is neither offered in a vacuum nor is it without a history. Speaking of the prayers found in the Psalter, Petersen affirms that "God's word precedes these words: these prayers don't seek God, they respond to the God that seeks us."[2] Prayers to God do not arise *ex nihilo*, "from nothing", but are part of an on-going dialogue and an unfolding relationship. Thus, the lament prayers offered in the Bible shape and are shaped by the larger community of faith and by a God who is in an ongoing and growing relationship with the ones praying.

Prayers of lament, though, are occasioned not by conversation with God, but by his silence. Their cry of abandonment calls for the end of that silence. The book of Exodus, which contains Israel's core salvation story, opens with the absence of God. Donald Gowan highlights the predominance of human plans and actions in light of the absence of God's visible working as the Exodus story begins. Chapters one and two describe the schemes and strategies of Pharaoh, the midwives, Moses' mother and sister, Pharaoh's daughter, and Moses himself.[3] At the close of chapter two, God has done nothing apart from rewarding the midwives, and Moses is living in exile in the land of Midian. Human attempts to bring about salvation have had little effect. The absence of God is ended and the direction of the story is dramatically altered, though, by a cry of lament.

> The Israelites groaned under their slavery, and cried out. Out of the slavery their cry for help rose up to God. God heard their groaning, and God remembered his covenant with Abraham, Isaac, and Jacob. God looked upon the Israelites, and God took notice of them. (Exod 2:23b–25)

Though never contextless, lament is the first word spoken on the way to salvation and newness. In lament, the initiative is seized and the silence is shattered not by God, but by his covenant partners.

Because biblical lament is fundamentally relational in nature, the cause of lament is redefined in terms of that relationship. William Soll

2. Petersen, *Answering God*, 5.

3. Gowan, *Theology in Exodus*, 1–24.

observes that, "lament is not merely an articulation of unhappiness; it seeks in the midst of unhappiness, to recover communion with God."[4] That which occasions the lament initially may be sickness, famine, an economic crisis, an attack by enemies, or any number of other problems, but in and of themselves these pose no permanent threat. The real force of the lament is not the initial crisis, but that which follows it, namely, the silence, hiddenness, or absence of God. Over and over the psalmist cries out for God to "hear," "turn," "arise," "see," "remember," and "answer," because as soon as he does so sickness, famine, and the sword lose all power to harm. When at last the Lord "hears," the enemies that afflict the psalm writer are inevitably "put to shame." The focus of the writer's prayer in the midst of the crisis is not "Why has this happened to me?" but "Why do you hide your face, O Lord?" "Why are you so far from hearing me?" and "How long, O Lord?"

That which occasions the crisis in relationship is often unclear. Samuel Balentine's study of biblical accounts of the hiding of God's face concludes that it cannot be reliably connected with any identifiable human cause. While it is true that in the prophetic writings the hiding of God's face is often the result of human sin, in the Psalms of lament this is frequently not the case. Balentine argues that hiddenness, just as much as presence, is integral to the nature of God.

> God's hiddenness is not primarily related to his punishment for disobedience. It is not basically a reflection of man's inability to understand or even to perceive God's presence in the world. It is manifest in both these ways, but is not restricted to them. It is rather an integral part of the nature of God which is not to be explained away by theological exposition of human failures or human limitations. God is hidden just as he is present; he is far away just as he is near. Once this fact is given due consideration, then it is possible to understand the Old Testament's witness to the absence of a present God: 'Truly thou art a God who hidest thyself. O God of Israel, the Savior (Isa. 45:15).'[5]

Balentine's observations underscore the relational nature of lament. The prayer of lament becomes the means for exploring the mystery of divine hiddenness and it is the character of God and not human character that

---

4. Soll, "The Israelite Lament," 79.
5. Balentine, *The Hidden God*, 175–76.

is the focus of such prayer. In the prayer of lament, we reach into the hiddenness of God.

Biblical lament at its core is about the threat of the breakdown of relationship between the one praying and his or her covenant partner. The seeming rejection of the psalmist by God leads others to reject him or her as well. "Many are saying to me, 'There is no help for you in God'" (Ps 3:2). "You have caused friend and neighbor to shun me; my companions are in darkness" (Ps 88:18). "When shall I come and behold the face of God? . . . These things I remember, as I pour out my soul: how I went with the throng, and led them in procession to the house of God, with glad shouts and songs of thanksgiving, a multitude keeping festival" (Ps 42:2, 4). There can be no place in the community of faith for the one whom God himself has truly rejected. Lament is offered in the face of diminished relationship and has implications for the entire community's relationship with God.

In summary, then, the Old Testament offers us the primary biblical exploration of the hiddenness of God in times of need, the pervasiveness of evil in the good world that God created, and the suffering of the innocent out of all proportion of any sins that they have committed. Such circumstances in the lives of the people of Israel did not occasion stoic silence or a confession of sin or claims that such sufferings should be seen as beneficial, but elicited cries of plea and protest. Lament is a cry over a relationship in crisis.

Biblical laments often bear little resemblance to the prayers of the contemporary Christian church.[6] First of all, in a frequently positivistic society such as our own, biblical lament has been largely withdrawn from the vocabulary of Christian prayer and from the liturgy of Christian worship. Lament psalms are increasingly being excluded from prayer books and set readings because of their negative and, at times, vengeful tone.[7] Scarce indeed, in many of our churches, are the reading, preaching, praying, or teaching of prayers of lament, particularly those

---

6. In an interesting study of the life stories behind numbers of inspirational praise hymns that have arisen from circumstances of great suffering, Henry Gariepy documents the fact that many great hymns that have their origin in suffering result not in lament, but in victory and assurance of salvation. *Songs in the Night.* Christian hymnbooks are not always modeled on the Psalter, with its balancing of both praise and lament.

7. Kaufman has documented this trend in "Undercut by Joy."

that lack a hasty resolution or positive outcome. It is difficult to imagine a sermon or even a scripture reading from Psalm 88:

> Your wrath has swept over me;
>   your dread assaults destroy me.
> They surround me like a flood all day long;
>   from all sides they close in on me.
> You have caused friend and neighbor to shun me;
>   my companions are in darkness. (Ps 88:16–18)

At the very least, such texts raise awkward questions about whether the offering should be taken up before or after the scripture reading.

This tendency to avoid laments is even prevalent in the traditionally conservative churches that hold a high view of the inspiration and authority of scripture. Thus, ironically, those traditions that value the reading of the Bible most highly are themselves guilty of reading it selectively. Walter Brueggemann has argued that the removal of lament from the vocabulary of the church is a social and political, rather than a spiritual or doctrinal, choice. Lament, he suggests, is unwelcome among those who are materially well off and whose continued prosperity and comfort depend on the maintenance of the status quo.[8] Brueggemann asserts that there is a connection between the delegitimation and suppression of lament in the liturgy and teaching of a church, and its increased material prosperity and investment in mainstream society. Lament sounds so dreary, negative, and unspiritual to those who do not wish to be reminded either of their own vulnerability to suffering or of the suffering of those around them who are less fortunate.

There is also something in the self-help, I-can-do-it, lift-myself-up-by-my-own-boot-straps mentality of Western societies that chaffs at the forthright admission of helplessness inherent in lament. Lament presupposes a frank admission that we both need God and are powerless to save ourselves. As if that were not bad enough, lament also acknowledges by its very nature that, having openly declared our impotence and dependence, we are now uncertain about the relationship to which we have committed ourselves. Lament requires that we freely admit our helplessness and that we embrace uncertainty. It believes, but cannot know for sure, that God will answer.

---

8. Brueggemann, "The Costly Loss of Lament."

The prayer of lament has also fallen on hard times for doctrinal reasons. Some Christian teachings elevate faith in God's presence and action to the point of dismissing lament as an expression of a lack of faith. This has been a particular hallmark of the rapidly growing Pentecostal and Charismatic movements that have placed such strong emphasis on experiences of God's presence and power. For some it is difficult to reconcile a God who heals, responds to prayer, and is experienced as present with a God who can also be experienced as hidden, absent, and silent. Indeed, how can we even talk about the absence or hiddenness of God in a post-Pentecost church that attests to the perpetual indwelling of God's spirit in every Christian? From this perspective the paradox in God's nature alluded to by Isaiah seems incomprehensible: "Truly, you are a God who hides himself, O God of Israel, the Savior" (Isa 45:15). But if, as Balentine has argued, it is in the nature of God to be both present and hidden, then we cannot expect experiences of his hiddenness to disappear with the coming of Pentecost. Prayers of lament, far from being contrary to faith, are instrumental in the expression of faith. Lament remains our primary access to the God who hides himself in our midst.

When Truths Collide

Biblical lament is the point of impact of two truths: belief and experience. Belief is that which we have reasoned through and come to hold as true about God and our relationship with him in the calm and ordered times of life. It is in part a reflection on experiences, but is more structured and detached. Belief is more prescriptive than descriptive. It defines normalcy for us. The vagueness and ambiguity of individual experiences is smoothed over in the formulation of beliefs. Belief is by its very nature reductionist. Experience, on the other hand, is more immediate, less tidy, and must be integrated into a belief system through a process of interpretation. It never quite fits our beliefs as perfectly as it should. The difference between a belief and an experience is the same as the difference between designing an aircraft and flying it. Blueprints, mathematical analyses, and computer simulations can never fully prepare the test pilot for the day when she climbs into the cockpit of the prototype and leaves the ground.

When our beliefs collide with contradictory experiences, those experiences may be radically reinterpreted or even ignored entirely in order to sustain our beliefs. But there is a price to be paid for such alterations to experience, as cognitive dissonance grows between what we believe about God and the ways that we have access to him through experience. The belief that God hears and responds to prayers for healing when they are offered in faith, for example, is strained each time such prayers go unanswered. When the weight of contrary experiences grows sufficiently ponderous, basic beliefs will be reevaluated and even changed. The amount of contrary experience needed to shift a belief depends on the amount of freight carried by that belief. Some beliefs, such as the conviction that it never snows in southern Florida, would require relatively little in the way of experience to change: one good blizzard would do it! Other beliefs, such as our understanding of who God is and how he acts, are far more resistant to change. The belief that God is both sovereign and good has, through the centuries, withstood the onslaught a vast array of experiences to the contrary. The prayer of lament arises from an experience that challenges belief: a tragic event is followed by God's subsequent lack of response to prayer, thus raising questions and doubts about the nature of God's relationship with his people. Lament places a strong affirmation of belief, that God is a God who hears and delivers, over against an experience of God's silence and hiddenness in times of need.

The tension between belief and experience is essential to biblical lament. It is as that dialectic is held before God that the possibility of genuine newness is realized. But such prayers are also risky. By putting the relationship in such a precarious posture, the praying community both invites an act of renewal from God and punctuates his continued silence. The prayer of lament carries with it the opportunity both for a deepening of relationship and for its damage and abandonment. Lament brings the crisis of the particular and concrete to generalized statements of God's love, justice, power, and faithfulness. By exposing such statements to the test of contrary experience, the prayers of lament make possible both the revitalization of those statements and their negation. In the context of lament, beliefs about God can be either owned anew or abandoned.

The prayer of lament is resolutely and courageously hopeful. Suffering need never have the last word while speech to God continues.

Lament willingly risks speaking the truth about both the belief in God's presence and the experience of his absence. When only one of these truths is voiced, risk is dissolved and the outcome is all but assured. By voicing only the truth of the experience of God's hiddenness, we do away with the expectation of a presence that transforms, and as a result we must resolve ourselves to getting on with the task of suffering through our lives without the "false hope" that God can or will intervene to save. Should we voice only the truth of belief, we would substitute denial and a cowardly fatalism for God's presence, embracing any and every experience as evidence either of God's presence and goodness or of our own sinfulness and failure. God can never disappoint, never fail, never be called to account, and never lose face. Lament accepts neither the experience of abandonment nor the fatalism of unquestioned belief as final, but creates a communion between these disparate truths.

When the Bond Between Belief and Experience Is Broken

The bond that exists between belief and experience keeps both truths alive. To dissolve the tension created by crises in our relationship with God in favor of either belief or experience is to abandon lament, for it is precisely in this exchange between the two that lament realizes its potency. If we let go of belief in favor of our experience, we come to believe nothing outside of our own encounters with life. Unless we experience it for ourselves, it is not "real." The testimonies to experience that have formed and sustained communities of faith through the millennia and which form the basis for the doctrinal statements of those communities can only be validated, then, to the extent that each individual can share directly in those experiences. Truth becomes wholly immediate and existential. Experiences that are not tempered by beliefs that can challenge and transcend them are inevitably prone to the danger of self-delusion. The conviction that nothing lies beyond our immediate experiences results in a world that is shaped wholly by direct engagement.

If, on the other hand, we hold rigidly to belief statements at the expense of experience, we cultivate a practice of denial and seek to encapsulate the mysteries of God's nature into highly digestible, inevitably predictable formulas. We lay aside the journey into newness, settling instead for increasingly more refined articulations of what we already know. Like an old married couple whose relationship has grown too familiar and predictable, so that all need for conversation ceases as each already knows everything that the other will say, there can be little newness in our relationship with God. Indeed, certain experiences of God are not "allowed" because they run counter to doctrinal norms. Newness is simply not permitted a hearing because it does not fit with what we "already know to be true" about God. Belief is preferred to encounter. Indeed, inflexible belief is the staunchest form of deism, because we neither require God's help to undergird our beliefs, nor do we desire any fresh move on his part that might imperil them. The result of such unbending commitment is a growing irrelevance of the very beliefs that we seek to affirm and defend. Doctrine becomes unyielding dogma and that dogma grows less plausible and less pertinent as it increasingly insulates itself from fresh encounters with the divine. Dogma buys certainty at the cost of authenticity.

The practice of biblical lament sustains the dialectic between the truth claims of belief and experience, neither forsaking the former nor renouncing the latter. The truth of experience sharpens and personalizes the truth of belief. The truth of belief interprets and lends meaning to experience. Belief, which often arises initially from experience, is kept vibrant by proximity to it. Faith is found neither in the repudiation of experience nor in the relinquishing of belief, but in addressing both truths in a creative tension before God. Thus, the prayer of lament is an act of faith. To lament is to risk the move toward newness, a move that is certain to reshape both our beliefs about God and our most formative experiences of him.

The truth that experience offers us is characterized by movement and change. That change can be positive, energizing and releasing new directions in our lives. Education, travel, new friendships, and the discovery of a wider world can bring our potentials to full flower. But experience can also be debilitating, robbing us of our youthful optimism, so that we exchange life for mere subsistence. The loss of a loved one, the slow death of our dreams in the gristmill of daily existence, and the violation of trust in our relationships can leave us closed and embittered. Experience is more immediately transformative than belief. It offers us a truth that is both personal and easily accessible.

Ours is a world in which, increasingly, experience is preferred over doctrine. In the unfolding post-modern world, static, universal doctrines are being readily exchanged for highly contextualized beliefs that are overtly local, constantly shifting, and essentially experiential in orientation. A rigid dogmatism that filters every existential encounter through a static belief system, reshaping it so that it "fits" a doctrinal construct, is becoming rare in theological reflection (although the global community is seeing a sharp resurgence of dogmatism among fundamentalist religious movements).

In this contemporary environment, experiences of God's silence in the face of profound suffering have increasingly challenged and overturned traditional doctrinal beliefs. Some have seen in God's hiddenness a limiting of his power to enact justice in the world. God is not present to save because such presence would violate human freedom and absolve humans of their responsibility. Such an understanding shifts the focus of human suffering from God to persons. Experiences of hiddenness are interpreted as signs of the reduced presence or even the absence of God in the world.

If God's silence is indicative of reduced presence and restricted power, then God's relevance to our suffering becomes uncertain. Samuel Terrien, in his book *The Elusive Presence*, asserts that God progressively withdraws himself from active participation in human history as the Old Testament unfolds. The visual theophanies of God in the early events surrounding the Exodus evolve to less direct ecstatic visions of God for the prophets, to a sacramental awareness of God in the Psalms, and to God present in the personification of wisdom in the later wisdom writings. As a result, by the close of the first testament, history has become "a stage now empty of God."[9] Terrien understands God's presence today to be continual, but elusive and intangible, never breaking into human history in any discretely identifiable event.

Terrien's argument has a certain appeal. When we compare our own experiences of the divine with those found in scripture, it is not surprising that we find some records of encounter with God more familiar and comfortable than others. Many of us can identify much more readily with the Elijah's experience of "a sound of sheer silence" or "a still, small voice" on Mount Horeb than we can with the divine fire that consumed Elijah's sacrifice on Mount Carmel in the preceding chapter. Terrien's claim, though, that later encounters with God in the

9. *The Elusive Presence*, 380. Friedman also offers a careful outline of God's withdrawal from active participation in the biblical narrative in *The Hidden Face of God*.

Bible are less immediate than earlier ones is rather arbitrary. Why, for example, should we understand the theophany of God in the opening of Ezekiel to be less tangible than the burning bush or the pillars of fire and smoke recorded in Exodus? Most ironic in Terrien's model is the assumption that the appearance of Emmanuel, "God with us," is a less poignant expression of God's presence than are the theophanies of the Old Testament. The argument for a less involved God as the biblical record unfolds is decidedly forced.

But a more fundamental shortcoming with Terrien's elusive presence is that it is finally neither testable nor negatable. What, after all, would constitute evidence that God is not elusively present, but simply absent? A World War? The holocaust? A worldwide AIDS epidemic? The genocidal slaughter of whole tribes and nations in increasingly more numerous wars? None of these events can offer evidence either for or against an elusive God. Terrien has raised God above the fray of human interactions and removed any element of risk that experience creates for belief. He has assured presence, after a fashion, by sacrificing any tangible evidence of that presence. God becomes our cosmic "imaginary friend." And as with an imaginary friend, the relationship can have no content apart from that which we bring to it. The elusively present God is simply a blank screen upon which, as Freud has claimed, we project our own needs and neuroses. An elusively present God is little more than an illusion of our own making.

The gains of such an approach, however, cannot be easily dismissed. By removing God from any immediate involvement within history, we bring a solution of sorts to the problem of God's justice in the face of innocent suffering. The greatest challenge to faith in the goodness and presence of God in the twentieth century has been the Jewish holocaust. And to this defining event can be added a growing list of ethnic genocides around the world. Such vast human suffering, along with the triumph of such pervasive human evil, challenge our belief in God to its core. Eliezer Berkovits tells the story of a small boy who, as he is being led away to the gas chamber, cries to his mother, "But, Mama, I was a good boy!"[10] The crisis of the holocaust is not simply the vastness of human suffering and evil, but that God makes no division between the just and the unjust, nor does he offer any answer to their pleas for

10. Berkovits, *Faith after the Holocaust*, 126.

deliverance. As we multiply such suffering by the weak and innocent millions of times over, how can we continue to speak of Yahweh as the God who "defends the poor and fatherless," "watches over the stranger and upholds the orphan and widow," and is "a stronghold for the oppressed in times of trouble"?

Berkovits argues for the hiddenness of God and for his self-absencing from human history. For God to be both present and active in history would be to destroy the wicked without hope of repentance and to eliminate free will. For Berkovits, God could not be present to save children from the ovens of Auschwitz, but only less directly, by assuring the survival of Israel as a people. History is the arena for human rather than divine action and the failure of the holocaust was not God's but humanity's. "The question raised by the holocaust that concerns man most directly is not 'Where was God?', but 'Where was man?' . . . The Jewish experience in the ghettos and the death camps made manifest in our days the collapse of man as a moral being."[11]

Berkovits has distanced God from the holocaust, but he has done so at the cost of lament. If God is truly absent from history, then prayers arising from the holocaust can no longer legitimately protest that suffering or call upon God in the same way that the Israelites did in response to the destruction of the temple by the Babylonians:

> Rise up, O God, plead your cause;
>   remember how the impious scoff at you all day long.
> Do not forget the clamor of your foes,
>   the uproar of your adversaries that goes up continually.
> (Ps 74:22–23)

Neither can there be any place for the prayer "Pour out your anger on the nations that do not know you, and on the kingdoms that do not call on you name" (Ps 79:6). Berkovits has preserved a place for God in the post-holocaust world, but he has done so by making God largely extraneous to our lives.

The principal difficulty with Berkovits' approach is that he offers a quantitative solution as though it were a qualitative one. He has simply taken one step back from the problem and offered that as a resolution to it. Why should insuring the survival of the nation of Israel as a whole not be seen as impinging on or destroying human freedom, while de-

---

11. Ibid., 36.

livering Jews from the Nazi gas chambers is understood to constitute just such an interference? How can we speak of God guaranteeing the survival of a nation without any active intervention in history? Why would the miracle of the Six Day War not constitute divine interference (assuming that Berkovits would recognize divine activity in such an event), whereas granting victory to the Jews in the Warsaw ghetto uprising would have done? If God is in any sense involved in guaranteeing Israel's survival, then he is a God who intervenes in history to save and, presumably, a God who responds to prayer. If God is truly not involved, then prayers of lament can be safely set aside. If, however, God is involved, then he also bears responsibility for his silence. Berkovits' argument falters at the point of trying to maintain divine action in general (the preservation of Israel as a nation), while denying any and all individual experiences of that action.

Furthermore, Berkovits' God of the large brush strokes of history is no more discernable or testable than is Terrien's elusively present God. The presence of God is truly in the eye of the beholder. Berkovits' dilemma underscores the basic issue. Either God is completely removed from human history, in which case we can cease from our prayers, or he is involved selectively and we are left to struggle with the question of "Why here, but not there?"

Both Terrien and Berkovits settle the problem of suffering by making God irrelevant to it. For Terrien, God is present, but powerless to affect salvation. For Berkovits it would be morally wrong of God to respond to our suffering, lest in doing so he destroy the very think that he seeks to save, namely our independent selves. But if God is not a relevant consideration in the extreme moments of life, we might reasonably conclude that he is not particular significant in the more mundane moments either. Of what value is a God who may be experienced as present in some elusive, non-intrusive, and ill-defined sense only in times of stability and wellbeing? The crisis of the elusive God is a crisis of relevance.

Experience is compellingly powerful and seductively immediate. It collapses the distinction between the world as we perceive it to be and as it is apart from us. If unmodified by any force outside of ourselves, experience offers us our own perceptions as an expression of ultimate truth. When experience stands alone, being balanced neither by the wider experience of the community of faith nor by the beliefs of that community, it becomes little more than a mirror in which we see only our own reflections. Experiences of loss can only energize prayers of lament in the presence of that which transcends them, namely, the beliefs of the larger community of faith. The prayer of lament draws from the wellspring of belief. That belief may be shaken and tested by experiences of divine hiddenness, but it is also shakes and tests those experiences. Experience by itself loses its power to cry out for newness.

Belief, by comparison, is far more stable and safe than experience. It provides a degree of shelter from the unpredictable and highly changeable currents of experience. But it does so by suppressing much of experience's spontaneity, flexibility, and dynamic energy. Belief resists growth, change, and movement. It tends toward the permanent and archetypal, at the expense of the immediate and imminently recognizable. Belief is also constructive. It builds for us a world that "makes sense," and then defends that world against any and all challenges. It is better at describing what ought to be than what is. Belief offers security but can never quite match our perception of the reality around us.

One response to the questions that experience raises is to insist that they conform to and be interpreted by a system of doctrinal beliefs. When the tension between experience and belief is dissolved in favor of the latter, all fresh encounters are filtered through a belief system that reshapes and even removes conflicting experience. Established belief systems are extremely resilient and are strongly resistant to anything that might contest them. In a classic study that has implication for our discussion, Thomas Kuhn challenged a widely held understanding of the way that change occurs in scientific investigation.[12] In an ideal world, science gathers data through observation and experimentation and develops theories and models that organize and explain that data. As new data is collected, those theories and models are adapted to fit new discoveries. So, it was assumed, scientific models are always open to and shaped by the data harvested through scientific investigation and are, therefore, subject to constant development and change. Kuhn argues, though, that once a scientific model gains general acceptance, it becomes extremely resistant to challenge or change. Contradictory data is ignored, suppressed, or radically reinterpreted so that it does not oppose the established model. Only as cognitive dissonance from

12. Kuhn, *The Structure of Scientific Revolutions*.

the quantity and diversity of conflicting data builds up, so that pressure grows on an increasingly dubious model, is there the possibility of a major shift in thinking. When it comes, scientific change is not gradual but cataclysmic, like flood waters overwhelming and bursting a dam. Kuhn's understanding is equally applicable to the interaction between experiences of God and belief structures that describe him. Once a belief system is firmly established, there is great reluctance to entertain experiences that question it. Such factors as the length of time that a particular model has enjoyed hegemony, its usefulness for organizing and explaining the data of religious experience, and the degree to which it provides cohesiveness and stability in life all affect the extent to which that doctrinal model resists change. There is, then, a certain native animosity between belief and experience and it is in the process of lament that this antipathy is most effectively negotiated.

In speaking of our doctrines of God, the most potent "contrary data" is provided by what Walter Brueggemann has referred to as the "embrace of pain." "By *embrace of pain* is meant the full acknowledgment of and experience of pain and the capacity and willingness to make that pain a substantive part of Israel's faith-conversation with its God."[13] The data of pain relentlessly probes the accepted doctrines of the goodness and power of God. Not surprisingly, dogmatism insists on the repression of pain. After all, extremities of pain can drive us to the place where we might be willing to question any and all of our assumptions about our relationship with God. As Sigmund Freud has helped us to understand, though, repressed pain does not simply go away; it builds up, becomes distorted, and seeks alternate outlets. Finally, when the pressure has become sufficiently intense, unaddressed pain bursts forth, often in highly destructive ways, sweeping away all restraining structures. By engaging in the regular, programmatic expression of pain through the act of lament, Israel insures that doctrinal structures are re-formed, rather than obliterated, and that their relationship with Yahweh remains vibrant and healthy, rather than becoming cripplingly destructive. When lament is abandoned, though, the build up of unexpressed pain threatens the very fabric of that relationship.

As beliefs about God are organized and formalized into doctrinal systems, a basic shift in their function occurs. They move from

---

13. Brueggemann, "The Shape of Old Testament Theology, II: Embrace of Pain," 25.

being descriptive to prescriptive. Instead of merely describing what is, doctrinal systems begin to dictate what must be. Our beliefs become constructive, shaping the world that we perceive by filtering and restructuring our experiences. In his study *The Nature of Doctrine*, George Lindbeck argues that doctrine is, in fact, wholly prescriptive, determining completely the nature of experience. In what he has called a "cultural-linguistic" approach, Lindbeck maintains that religious tradition provides a "cultural and/or linguistic framework or medium that shapes the entirety of life and thought." [14] Without the proper language symbols to give them shape and expression, he argues, not only is it impossible for us to describe an experience, it is impossible for us to *have* it. "There are numberless thoughts we cannot think, sentiments we cannot have, and realities we cannot perceive unless we learn to use the appropriate symbol systems."[15] Furthermore, the richness of a person's experience is connected directly to her or his ability to give expression to that experience. "In short, it is necessary to have the means for expressing an experience in order to have it, and the richer our expressive or linguistic system, the more subtle, varied, and differentiated can be our experience."[16]

Lindbeck underscores the potential pitfalls that arise from relying uncritically on experience as a means of knowing by highlighting the subjective nature of experience. The act of experiencing is not simply a passive reception and recording of an objective event, but also involves an ongoing process of interpretation so that two persons witnessing the same event do not simply interpret it differently; they have two distinct experiences. Put another way, an "experience" results from the interaction of an event and the witnessing of that event. Experience is never simply raw data, but includes the interpretation of that data. To a certain extent, then, each individual creates the experience in which he or she participates.

Lindbeck does not, however, give adequate attention to either the intrusiveness or otherness of experience. Highly intrusive experiences, such as profound suffering, shatter existing structures of understanding. Dramatic loss punctuates the process by which experiences affect and

14. Lindbeck, *The Nature of Doctrine*, 33.
15. Ibid., 34.
16. Ibid., 37.

alter the shape of one's perception of the world. A period of extended unemployment for a middle aged man who has never known joblessness, the seeming betrayal by her own body as a woman confronts breast cancer, the violation of trust that infidelity brings to a relationship, or the death of a child are all experiences of loss that leave in their wake the sense that the world has changed and will never again be as it was. If it is in the nature of belief to be constructive, it is in the nature of suffering and loss to prevent those constructs from becoming monolithic. And it is through the practice of lament that the fluidity and flexibility of our beliefs is maintained.

There is also an "otherness" to experience, by which I mean that many of our experiences happen in the context of our relationships. We are not simply detached, objective observers but experience life both in harmony with and in conflict with other participants. Transforming experiences often happen as we impact and are impacted upon by the will, needs, desires, and worldview of those in a position to influence our lives. Marriage exemplifies this process at its most intimate level. When two people marry, two separate worlds come together. Each brings to the relationship their families' customs, practices, traditions, outlooks, religious beliefs, social perspective, etc. and the marriage, particularly in the early years, is largely a process of integrating and adjudicating these two worlds to create one new one. "Therefore a man leaves his father and mother and clings to his wife, and they become one flesh." The creating and perpetuating of one flesh calls for a boundless willingness to be open another and to adapt.

The film *Remember the Titans* tells the story of the forced racial de-segregation of a high school in Alexandria, Virginia in the early 1970s. The recently appointed black coach of the newly integrated football team forced black and white players to room together in training camp, to share with each other details of their personal lives, and to endure physical hardship together. As the result of the new experiences forced on them, the team was able radically to transform the racial prejudices of its members who, in turn, were able to impact the perspective of the community at large. For many (although not all), experience transformed a strongly entrenched doctrine of bigotry.

Martin Buber speaks of the "I-It" relationship, which is the relationship between a detached observer and the object of her study, and the "I-Thou" relationship, which recognizes that both participants in a relationship are active agents.[17] While Lindbeck's model in which language and culture create experience might hold true for an "I-It" relationship, his conclusions are at best qualified in an "I-Thou" relationship and the experiences that it produces. These two factors, the intrusion of pain and commitment of one's self to relationship, constantly press against the familiar and established, calling our visions of the world and our relationships with God in the world toward newness.

To the extent that our beliefs are insulated from the disruptions of pain and relationship, they become increasingly fanciful. Like playing a virtual reality game for too long, the player who insulates herself from external intrusions can eventually forget that she is playing a game, rather than engaging reality. And there is in such play the temptation to prefer virtual reality with its tidy, preprogrammed order, to the messiness and unpredictability of a reality that is ever in the process of becoming. Like a mother calling a game-player to dinner, it is worthwhile reminding ourselves periodically that our theological models are just that, models.

Bernard Maza, in his exploration of the holocaust, dramatically subjugates experience in a doctrinally driven interpretation of that defining event. In his book *God's Fury Poured Out*, Maza interprets the holocaust as a saving act of God.[18] He understands the holocaust first of all as a judgment from God for the secularization of Judaism in the first part of the twentieth century. Young Jews living in the Soviet Union became enamored of socialism, while those that had immigrated to the United States had been seduced by capitalism. As a result, younger Jews had increasingly abandoned a lifestyle centered on the study of the Torah. Through a national act of martyrdom as much as judgment, God's fury was poured out on European Jews, so that Torah loving Jews had the opportunity to offer their lives for the advancement of God's planned restoration of the Torah to the center of Jewish life and faith. The result of the holocaust, says Maza, has been a return to Torah-centered living in homogenously Jewish communities.

Maza's central model for the notion of God's fury being poured out for the purpose of strengthening Torah observance is taken from the prophecies of Ezekiel. "As I live, says the Lord GOD, surely with a

17. Buber, *I And Thou*.

18. Maza, *God's Fury Poured Out*; see also the critique offered by Cohn-Sherbok, *Holocaust Theology*.

mighty hand and an outstretched arm and with wrath poured out, I will be king over you" (20:33). He sees God as the direct cause of the holocaust, which he brought about in order to restore Torah-centered Judaism. Maza interprets Ecclesiastes 1:5, "the sun rises and the sun goes down," to refer to the place of Torah in Jewish faith. When the prominence of Torah "sets," then Yahweh acts in order that it might rise once more.

Of relevance to our study is not that Maza has appealed to scripture in order to interpret the horrors of the holocaust, but rather the way that he has idealized, distorted, and transformed experience in order to sustain his interpretation. Maza gazes through nostalgic lenses at the simpler, more pious life of the self-contained Jewish villages in Russia prior to the Communist revolution. He paints a utopian picture of constant devotion and study of Torah, from dawn until dusk, with every member of the community joyously and willing placing Torah at the center of their lives.

> There was no activity—social or communal—unrelated to the Torah. Jewish learning was sacred and any book unconnected with Torah study was considered unclean. All lectures focus on Jewish subjects. There were no political organisations, discussion groups, reading rooms or non-Torah classes. Jewish life in this *milieu* was completely Torah-centred, a self-contained world of Jewish worship and study dedicated to God's law.[19]

Maza portrays the victims of the holocaust as noble, fearless martyrs who understood themselves to be dying for God's good purposes, giving themselves so that others might be brought back to God. "As they waited for their salvation, they went on with their lives as Jews, finding courage, hope, and even joy in their Jewish heritage. They studied Torah and observed Jewish practices. Neither suffering, nor pain, nor the fear of death discouraged them."[20] Downplaying the trends in Judaism toward Zionism, secularization, or the abandonment altogether of the Jewish faith, he sees only the revival of Torah interest among conservative Jews as the primary result of the holocaust.

There is ample testimony to the unimaginable courage and faith of so many of the Jews who lost their lives in the holocaust, as well as

---

19. Cohn-Sherbok, *Holocaust Theology*, 20.

20. Maza, *Fury Poured Out*, 130.

among the survivors. It would be fair to ask the question, though, "How many of them would describe their experience in terms of martyrdom to advance God's purposes?" Maza is both highly selective and idealistic in his use of experience, generalizing the experience of pious Jews to the nation as a whole and forming his perceptions to fit his interpretive model. He envisions Eastern European Jewish life in pre-communist Russia as being idyllic, those who were thrust into the Nazi ovens as being fearless, and post-holocaust Jewish society as being once more Torah-centered. Experience is oversimplified and distorted in order to conform to a particular interpretive explanation of an event that threatens to destroy Jewish faith. The result is a stifling of outrage and a silencing of protest as the horrors of the death camps are relativized by the needs of God' s greater good. As with Job's friends, Maza has clouded the very issues that he seeks to clarify. By insisting that experience align itself with a particular vision of the Torah-centered life, Maza has also not "spoken of God what is right."

Lament as a Language of Newness

The language of lament does that which is impossible for ordinary language; it destroys one world while laying the groundwork for the birth of another. It exhausts the familiar religious speech of form and safety, straining to find new words for a new reality. Lament seeks to give expression to experiences of loss and newness, and of the emptiness that lies between them. Perhaps the most poignant expression of the experience of transforming newness in the prayers of lament is the language of silence.[21] For seven days following his being struck down by the Satan, Job sat mute, with no words to express his anguish over events that had so completely devastated and altered his world. Job had come to the end of language. The extremity of his sufferings had shattered Job's worldview and had dismantled all structures of response. Job met the flood of suffering with silence. But then, after the silence, Job found words again. He began to explore the world into which he had been thrust. By voicing his lament, he identified and dismantled those

21. André Neher in his exploration of the use of silence by both God and people in the Bible points out that silence is just as vital to genuine dialogue as is speech. Only when one dialogue partner is silent can another speak and only through genuine dialogue is newness possible. *The Exile of the Word*, 47–49.

elements of his old world that no longer functioned in the wake of the disasters that had overwhelmed him. Job investigates the landscape of his new life in which God the protector has become God the enemy, and challenges God to participate with him in rebuilding his world. The new world that results is one that is forever altered by the experiences of pain and loss.

When the language of silence is finally broken, active lament can begin. The speech of lament starts often with bewilderment, asking "Why?" "How long?" and "Will you forget us forever?" A fresh structure is being called forth, one that will frame the experience of profound loss. Ordinary language seems wholly inadequate to articulate such a horrific bereavement, so it is not surprising that such prayers resort to the language of poetry and metaphor. Poetry describes novelty through the free play of images. It allows for ambiguity and openness, both putting experiences into words and leaving space for those words to take on altered meanings in new situations. Metaphors, by combining familiar images in novel ways, reach toward an expression of that which is surprising, other, and to a certain extent, indescribable.

> Many bulls encircle me,
>   strong bulls of Bashan surround me;
> they open wide their mouths at me,
>   like a ravening and roaring lion.
> I am poured out like water,
>   and all my bones are out of joint;
> my heart is like wax;
>   it is melted within my breast;
> my mouth is dried up like a potsherd,
>   and my tongue sticks to my jaws;
> you lay me in the dust of death. (Ps 22:12–15)

The use of silence, questions, poetry, and metaphor in the prayers of lament all point to the intrusion of experiences that transcend the familiar and exhaust the speaker's established structures for coping.

Out of the process of lament, a fresh perspective and new language are generated. Characteristic of the prayers of lament is an abrupt shift from complaint to praise. In the midst of lament, the one praying experiences a breakthrough into newness. Job declares "I had heard of you by the hearing of the ear, but now my eye sees you." The psalmist proclaims "But when I thought how to understand this, it seemed to me a wearisome task, until I went into the sanctuary of God; then I perceived their end" and "Depart from me, all you workers of evil, for the LORD has heard the sound of my weeping." The one who lamented now speaks a unique language and sings a new song. "He put a new song in my mouth, a song of praise to our God." Walter Brueggemann has pointed out that the praise which follows lament is not the same language as the praise that precedes it. This new song is shaped by the memory of pain and the silence of God, and bears witness to that memory even in the midst of praise.[22] The language of lament is the language of transformation, of innovation. Such novelty is only possible, though, with the articulation of both pain and belief.

Should We Run the Risk of Keeping God in History?

As we consider the world around us, can we still afford to speak of a God who led his people out of Egypt and rose from the dead? Locating God in human history is endlessly problematic in light of the suffering of the innocent. Assertions of God's presence, goodness, and power are inevitably qualified by such realities. One way to resolve the problems posed by God's silence in the face of our suffering is simply to exchange silence for absence. A God who is absent cannot be expected to save or blamed for his failure to do so. He can, at most, be criticized for his absence. An absent (or elusive) God offers us a measure of resolution to the problem of human suffering, but at what cost? Can we exclude God from human history, thus transferring responsibility for suffering wholly to human beings, without completely transforming and even abandoning biblical faith? If the richness of biblical faith is founded on and draws from divine encounter, does the loss of divine presence mean eroding irrevocably that foundation?

Emil Fackenheim identifies the heart of Jewish faith as being historical in nature. The Jewish nation was created and defined by "root experiences," without which they would not exist as a people. Using as his example the song of triumph that the women sang when the Egyptian army was drowned by God in the Red Sea, Fackenheim specifies three conditions necessary in order for an event to become a root experience for Israel. First of all, it must be a clearer vision of God than is normally available. We must acknowledge that the maidservants and the rest of

---

22. Brueggemann, *The Message of the Psalms*, 124.

Israel saw what we did not and that, therefore, their vision is superior and defining. Put a different way, we cannot restrict their vision to include only those things that we ourselves can see. Not all experiences are created equal, so that we cannot define reality solely in terms of our own. Secondly, in order for it to constitute a defining root experience for Israel, the experience must be a public event in history, available for all to witness and not a private, internal, subjective experience. Finally, that past experience must be accessible to the present as a public, historical experience in order for it to speak with defining power for the nation. We must be able to experience in the present God's deliverance from those things that threaten to destroy us.[23]

For Fackenheim, to abandon a God that we encounter in history, as Berkovits has done, is to abandon the root experiences that preserve Jewishness. In the face of Auschwitz, though, how can we understand God to be present in history? The death of a million Jewish children in the Nazi camps is, says Fackenheim, sufficient proof that the holocaust cannot be interpreted as a punishment for Jewish sins. "Here is the rock on which the 'for our sins are we punished' suffers total shipwreck."[24] Nor can we excuse God by understanding him as powerless in this world, thus pinning all our hopes on a future response from him outside of history at the end of time.

> To stake all on divine powerlessness today, therefore, would be to take it both radically and literally. God suffers literal and radical powerlessness, i.e., actual death; and any resurrected divine power will be manifest, not so much within history as beyond it. A Jew, in short, would have to become a Christian.[25]

To turn loose of a God of power is to turn loose of those root experiences that identify what it means to be a Jew. Furthermore, I would argue, to be the kind of Christian that Fackenheim envisions would require a severing of the Old Testament from the New and would compel us to abandon the prayer of lament. Prayers of sorrow and complaint that expect no concrete answer have no point of contact with biblical lament.

Herein lies the quintessential scandal and extravagant risk of lament. Lament becomes nonsensical if it accepts as its starting point

23. Fackenheim, *God's Presence in History*, 9–11.

24. Ibid., 73.

25. Ibid., 77.

either that bad things only happen to us because of our sins or that God is no longer (or never has been) able to save. Indeed, biblical prayers of lament accept the former possibility only occasionally and utterly reject the latter. The act of lament both threatens the loss of faith and opens the door to its revitalization. Fackenheim recognizes clearly the risk that is run when we insist that God remain in history.

> In faithfulness to the victims we must refuse comfort; and in faithfulness to Judaism we must refuse to disconnect God from the holocaust. Thus, in our case, protest threatens to escalate into a totally destructive conflict between the faith of the past and faithfulness to the present.[26]

Certainly there are many scholars today who, recognizing the inherent threat of a God in history, have concluded that only by excusing God from history can a way forward be found. Founding faith in root experiences in the sense that Fackenheim describes them, though, makes it possible to take seriously the presence of God that is the object of faith and the challenge that God's silence poses for those root experiences and that faith. To insist on keeping God involved in history by clinging doggedly to root experiences of faith is to run the risk of losing that faith entirely. But to excuse God from history is to abandon all need for faith. Lament both gives shape to that fundamental crisis and abides in its presence.

Without Risk There Can Be No Lament

Prayers of lament assault the ears of those who are at ease. They explore the extreme places of our lives, raising difficult questions about our relationship with God and expressing a cavernous depth of suffering and need on the part of the person praying them. Because they are such intense expressions of pain, laments are uncomfortable for those standing by who cannot share directly in the experiences of the person praying. They open the listener to participation in the experience of the speaker. They speak too frankly and bear too much of the soul of the person praying, and they remind us that we can each find ourselves in a similar situation. So it is not surprising that we should seek to avoid prayers of lament at those times when our lives are in balance.

26. Ibid., 76.

So what do we do with these uncomfortable texts when we would rather not be reminded of our own mortality and the uncertainty of our lives? One response, as we have seen, is to simply remove lament from our religious vocabulary, avoiding it as much as possible. Another is to reduce lament to a mere prelude to thanksgiving for the presence and response of God that is already assured and always guaranteed. Gregory Polan exemplifies this tendency.

> The lament was actually considered an expression of praise for a moment of crisis, the person or community willingly turned to the only One who could help or effect a change—God! Such prayer acknowledged God to be the sole hope in a situation that seemed hopeless. The lament acknowledged God's power, compassion, forgiveness, mercy, and fidelity. Calling out to God in the form of a lament was truly an act of praise because it arose from the suffering person's belief that the Lord's goodness is without end.[27]

Polan confuses a faithful response with active praise, misunderstanding both lament's function and its relationship to praise. Faithful lament offered in trust to God is not the same as praise. Lament is the experience of loss that gives praise its power. It precedes praise and is a necessary forerunner of thanksgiving, but it does not guarantee that praise will follow and should not be collapsed into praise. Without the experience of genuine loss, abiding uncertainty, and unrelieved suffering, we cannot be overtaken by joy and newness.

While lament may result in praise, this can never finally be a certainty. Prayers of lament explore precisely that territory in which the compassion, forgiveness, mercy, and fidelity of God are being questioned by the circumstance of the one praying. This exploration, as we have seen, is frequently characterized by questions: "How long, O Lord?" "Why do you hide your face from me?" "Will God spurn for ever, and never again be favorable?" "Has he in anger shut up his compassion?" Polan's understanding fails to appreciate the risk involved in confronting God with experiences that call into question beliefs about him. If the answer to the lamenter's questions are known and assured prior to the prayer, then lament is reduced to pure rhetoric; a liturgical form that has been robbed of its transformative power.

27. Polan, "The Book of Lamentation," 17.

The psalms of lament, however, demonstrate both expectancy and uncertainty. There is a strong confidence in the Lord, in spite of his present silence. "I keep the LORD always before me; because he is at my right hand, I shall not be moved" (Ps 16:8). "O my God, in you I trust; do not let me be put to shame; do not let my enemies exult over me" (Ps 25:2). "The LORD is the strength of his people; he is the saving refuge of his anointed" (Ps 28:8). But there is also the recognition that God's deliverance is not assured and may come late. "How long, O God, is the foe to scoff? Is the enemy to revile your name for ever?" (Ps 74:10). "Consider and answer me, O LORD my God! Give light to my eyes, or I will sleep the sleep of death" (Ps 13:3). "Hear my prayer, O LORD, and give ear to my cry; do not hold your peace at my tears. For I am your passing guest, an alien, like all my forebears. Turn your gaze away from me, that I may smile again, before I depart and am no more" (Ps 39:12–13). This tension between trust and uncertainty defines lament. Experiences of loss have collided with belief, prompting the one praying to examine doubts and questions about the nature of their relationship with God. Only by risking truth is the move toward newness possible. There truly is no such thing as risk-free lament.

But where is God to be found as we lament? Is he safely ensconced above the fray as truths collide? Is the risk involved in exploring the covenant relationship to be owned exclusively by his human partners? Does God risk nothing himself by choosing silence and hiddenness in response to the suffering of his people? Traditionally it has seemed far safer and more appropriate to think of God in terms of belief rather than experience. We imagine God as stable, immovable, predictable, and unaffected by change. In short, we describe God in terms of static belief, rather than fluid experience. But a God committed to relationship is a God to be both experienced and believed, and he is found in the clash between the two. In the next chapter, we will consider what it means to speak of a God who is found in our laments. Yahweh is a God who also risks, suffers, and laments.

2

Risking an Imperfect God

One day when we came back from work, we saw three gallows rearing up in the assembly place, three black crows. Roll call. SS all round us, machine guns trained: the traditional ceremony. Three victims in chains—and one of them, the little servant, the sad-eyed angel . . .

The three victims mounted together onto the chairs. The three necks were placed at the same moment within the nooses . . .

"Where is God? Where is He?" someone behind me asked. At a sign from the head of the camp, three chairs tipped over . . .

Behind me, I heard the same man asking: "Where is God now?"

And I heard a voice within me answer him: "Where is He? Here He is—He is hanging here on this gallows . . ."[1]

The Death of Perfection

THE TWENTIETH CENTURY HAS WITNESSED NOT THE DEATH OF GOD, but the death of an image of God that has dominated Christian thought for most of its history; an image of God as one who stands apart from and above his creation, watching a suffering that he can neither directly experience nor fully comprehend. The death of such an image has been hastened by the vast scope of human anguish in our technological age. Though suffering is not new, advances in technology have enabled it to take place on a scale heretofore unimagined and have provided the communications networks that bring human misery into our homes on a daily basis. The suffering and death of literally millions of innocent persons, both at the hands of their fellow human beings and as the result of a seemingly endless parade of natural disasters, has forced God

---

1. Wiesel, "Night," 71–72.

as we know him off of the fencepost of a detached and untouchable perfection. The pain of humanity has demanded that God be either completely cast aside or that he be drawn closer, into the midst of our hurt. Either God has abandoned his creation to its fate, so that he is no longer relevant to our lives, or he bleeds and dies along with us as one of us. The very first casualty whenever the innocent are slaughtered must be our image of God as unmoved and unmovable, unlimited, untouched by passion, and unchanged by his relationship with us. Such a classic view of God's perfection cannot long survive the determined onslaught of pain and loss.

The placing of the cross at the center of our discussions of God's nature, so that suffering is not simply an isolated experience of the Son but is something in which the entire godhead participates, makes suffering integral to the divine nature. Coming to a fuller understanding of the death of God on the cross has been the single most significant advance in our understanding of God in the twentieth century. Until the beginning of the twentieth century, the notion that God could and did suffer was thought to contradict fundamentally the framework within which Christian theology was formulated.[2] As with every theological enterprise, those early theologians who struggled in the first centuries of the church's existence to articulate a right understanding of God as he is presented in the Bible were greatly influenced by the worldview in which they found themselves. For the early church this meant that theology was expressed out of a worldview that had been dramatically shaped by Greek philosophical thought and that initial influence can still be found in our theologies today.[3]

Among the more important ideas flowing from Greek philosophy into Christian thinking was the concept of perfection espoused most

2. Mozley's study of divine impassibility in the first part of the twentieth century provides an excellent look at the transition away from this doctrine that began in the nineteenth century. *The Impassibility of God.*

3. Although many have been critical of this Hellenizing influence, Wolfhart Pannenberg defends the formulation of Christian theology utilizing Greek categories. Even if we could de-Hellenize Christian theology, it would not necessarily follow that the result would be a more clear understanding of God. Pannenberg is not unsympathetic to Hellenistic shaping of our reading of scripture, opting for the position that Greek contributions need to be adequately processed and critiqued, rather than simply removed. "The Appropriation of the Philosophical Concept of God as a Dogmatic Problem of Early Christian Theology."

influentially by Plato. For Plato, the closer to perfection something is, the less it can be affected or changed. So, for example, the soul is more perfect and less affected by external influences than is the body. While the body can be easily shaped by exercise, hunger, or illness, the soul is more durable and less easily shifted. God, by nature of his perfection, cannot be affected or changed in any way, particularly not by anything of lesser perfection.[4] To be perfect, for Plato, was to be both unchanging and self-sufficient. For God to be in any way dependent on another is to be incomplete, and therefore imperfect, in himself. Perfection is like standing on the highest point of a mountaintop. To move by taking a step in any direction is to descend into imperfection.

A related concept that also helped shape Christian thinking about God was the Greek notion of *apatheia* or apathy. For the Stoics, emotions were inferior to reason and had a negative influence on it. The goal of the Stoic was to detach him- or herself from emotion and to respond to life apathetically, that is, without pathos or passion. The assent toward perfection required the subjugation and casting aside of every passion. For Stoics, divine perfection was characterized by a perfection of reason, devoid of feeling and emotion.

For the Greek philosopher Aristotle, God is the unmoved Mover who is completely separate from all that he creates; perfect, eternal, unchangeable, and wholly unaffected by his interaction with humanity. Following Plato, Aristotle saw a dualistic relationship between perfection and that which is imperfect. Reason, being seen as purer and more objective, was considered to be superior to emotion. Thus, perfection could best be envisioned and expressed through reason, unclouded by emotion. [5] Drawing on these understandings of perfection, classic Christian theologies of God portray a deity who neither feels emotions nor is in any way affected, touched, or changed by his relations with his creation.

The impact of the acceptance of a Greek perspective can be seen in the way that Christian theologians struggle to understand the incarnation of Christ and the way that his incarnation affects the godhead as a whole. Classic incarnational models have a persistent tendency to subordinate Jesus' humanity in favor of his divinity, while classic

4. Hallman, *The Descent of God*, 2–8.
5. McGrath, *Christian Theology*, 215.

trinitarian models lean toward the distinction, rather than the unity of the three persons of the godhead, thus limiting the impact of the incarnation on the nature of God. The early church father Clement of Alexandria maintained divine immutability and impassibility, denying that God felt emotions. Tertullian, early in the third century, was the first Christian theologian to articulate clearly a doctrine of divine impassibility by both the Father and Son. "The Father did not suffer with the Son . . . If the Father is impassible, then he cannot suffer with another; if He can suffer with another, then He is passible . . . But the Father is as unable to suffer with another as the Son is unable to suffer in virtue of His divinity."[6] Gregory of Nazianzus, while affirming the unity of the divine Logos and the human body in Christ's nature, nevertheless maintained that he was "passible in His flesh, (and) impassible in His Godhead."[7] By making the physical body and emotions the antitheses of divine perfection, Christian theologians, while wanting to hold onto the humanity of Christ, were nevertheless forced to find ways to limit the impact of that humanity on the divine nature.

Thomas Aquinas recognized that love implies vulnerability and openness to being hurt, so that he denied the feeling of emotions to God. Speaking of mercy Aquinas reasoned that "Mercy is especially to be attributed to God, provided that it is considered as an effect, not as a feeling of suffering . . . It does not belong to God to sorrow over the misery of others."[8] Jewish philosopher Benedict Spinoza argued that any passion experienced by God would inevitably change him, so that God does not experience passions. Thus, while it is the duty of humanity to love God, God is wholly separate and cannot experience or reciprocate love in any sense that is like the human experience.[9]

While Christian theology has on the whole been more accepting of the idea that God loves, nevertheless there has often been a residual reluctance to speak of God as feeling and being influenced by strong emotions such as grief, jealousy, hurt, or anger. Certainly the idea of God being carried away by his jealousy or anger, so that he says and does things as a result of what he feels, is completely foreign to classical

6. From *Against Praxeas*, chapter 29, as quoted by Ngien, *The Suffering of God according to Martin Luther's 'Theologia Crucis*,' 9–10.

7. Ngien, *Suffering of God*, 12.

8. McGrath, *Christian Theology*, 215.

9. Ibid., 207–15.

theism. When the Bible attributes such passions to God, therefore, they are disclaimed as mere anthropomorphisms and it is denied that the wrath, repentance, or jealousy of God can be equated with the human experiences of those emotions.

The seeds of change, however, were planted amidst the upheaval of the Protestant Reformation. Martin Luther, picking up on the dialectical nature of God revealed in the incarnation of Jesus Christ, proposed that we speak of God in terms of both a "theology of glory" and a "theology of the cross." Though we might seek to know God in his glory directly, because of our sinfulness we are unable to do so. It is in the "hidden" form of weakness and suffering that God is able to reveal somewhat of his glory to us. "The theology of glory seeks to know God directly in his majesty and power, whereas the theology of the cross paradoxically recognizes him precisely where he has hidden himself: in his suffering and in all that which men and women consider to be weakness and foolishness."[10] Luther recognized that, while sin is incompatible with God's perfection, human frailty is not. But the essential optimism that accompanied the rise of the age of reason meant that Luther's theology of the cross was largely ignored, while his theology of glory received far more attention. This began to change, however, in the first half of the twentieth century. Two World Wars and the tremendous poverty and suffering that resulted for many from the shift from an agrarian to an industrial economy sparked a re-examination of the idea that God suffers along with his creatures.

Beginning in 1930, Abraham Heschel challenged the notion that God does not experience suffering. He argued that God possessed not simply intelligence and will, but that he is also characterized by *pathos*. Heschel makes a distinction between pathos and passion. Whereas passion implies a loss of control and being dominated by one's emotions, pathos is "an act formed with intention, depending on free will, the result of decision and determination."[11] He understood divine pathos not as an attribute that God possesses, but as resulting from his decision to relate to his creation, so that the pathos of God manifests itself through expression.

10. Kärkkäinen, "Theology of the Cross," 157.

11. Heschel, *The Prophets*, 2:4.

> Pathos denotes, not an idea of goodness, but a living care; not an immutable example, but an outgoing challenge, a dynamic relation between God and man; not mere feeling or passive affection, but an act or attitude composed of various spiritual elements; no mere contemplative survey of the world, but a passionate summons.[12]

In choosing to express his love, God opens himself to being affected by the object of that love. Though Heschel makes it clear that we cannot cause God's pathos, we are nevertheless the occasion for it. Pathos describes the pivot point in the tension between the transcendence and immanence of God.

> In sum, the divine pathos is the unity of the eternal and the temporal, of meaning and mystery, of the metaphysical and the historical. It is the real basis of the relation between God and man, of the correlation of Creator and creation, of the dialogue between the Holy One of Israel and His people.[13]

Apart from God's interaction with his creation, there would be no occasion for divine pathos. Likewise, there can be no true relatedness devoid of pathos.

Writing immediately after the carnage of the Second World War, Japanese theologian Kazoh Kitamori explored the essential conflict in God's nature that arises from his expression of love and wrath. Kitamori identifies three orders of love that exist simultaneously in God: the love of God, the pain of God, and the love that is rooted in God's pain. Pain is not simply a byproduct of God's love, says Kitamori, but is fundamental to his nature. "The pain of God is part of his essence . . . The Bible reveals that the pain of God belongs to his *eternal being*."[14]

God's experience of pathos reaches its zenith in the incarnation and crucifixion of Christ. Eberhard Jüngel argued that, through the death of Jesus, God entered into the *Vergänglichkeit*, the "transitoriness," "instability," "passing away-ness," and "perishability" of human existence. Through the death of God on the cross, God was able to experience directly the human suffering that results from living in a

---

12. Ibid.

13. Ibid., 11.

14. Kitamori, *Theology of the Pain of God*, 45; cited from McWilliams, *The Passion of God*, 103.

temporary and perishing creation.[15] The incarnation is, then, the full embrace of humanity. Frailty, limitation, and transitoriness become integral to the divine nature, so that they can no longer be understood as contradicting his perfection.

Jürgen Moltmann has argued persuasively that the cross is both the foundation and critical measure of true Christianity theology. He directly challenges the Aristotelian notion that perfection means that God does not suffer. "A God who cannot suffer is poorer than any human. For a God who is incapable of suffering is a being who cannot be involved."[16] Aristotle's "unmoved Mover," says Moltmann, is also a "loveless Beloved." The experience of Jesus' suffering on the cross is not peripheral to the nature of God, but essentially defines it. The inability to suffer and die protects God's perfection, in the classic platonic sense, but at the price of keeping God from full relatedness to humanity.

> Finally, a God who is only omnipotent is in himself an incomplete being, for he cannot experience helplessness and powerlessness . . . A man who experiences helplessness, a man who suffers because he loves, a man who can die, is therefore a richer being than an omnipotent God who cannot suffer, cannot love, and cannot die.[17]

The suffering and death of Christ on the cross is the key point of contact between the divine and human. God's ability and decision to love people opened him to the experience of suffering that comes with choosing a faithless lover. But it is precisely God's willingness to love and to suffer that gives his presence meaning in the face of profound human suffering. Amidst the horrors of the Holocaust, God's presence can be found not in spite of innocent suffering, but in the midst of it. "To speak here [in the suffering at Auschwitz] of a God who could not suffer would make God a demon. To speak here of an absolute God would make God an annihilating nothingness. To speak here of an indifferent God would condemn men to indifference."[18] A God who cannot suffer has

---

15. "Denn wenn Gott sich im Tode Jesu *als* Gott definiert hat, dan hat der Tod *ontologische* Relevanz für das Sein Gottes und also für das Leben Jesu Christi." Eberhard Jüngel, "Von Tod des lebendigen Gottes: Ein Plakat," 18.

16. Moltmann, *The Crucified God*, 222.

17. Ibid., 223.

18. Ibid., 274.

no place among the victims of the Holocaust, but can only be the God of its judges and executioners.

The full humanity of Christ as part of his divinity, the full unity of the Godhead alongside of its distinct personages, and the full relatedness implied by the covenants of both Testaments all point to a fundament insight, that the categories of impassibility and apathy are inadequate for understanding God as he is portrayed in the biblical writings. The experience of suffering is not peculiarly human or a diminishment of the divine nature, but is integral to our understandings of biblical covenant and of the incarnation of Christ. Profound suffering, both divine and human, has at last claimed the life of an ideal of God that was always foreign to his nature. The death of the impassible and passionless God has made room for a God who raises others from the dead, but only after he himself has laid down and died.

The Risk of Relationship

> Indeed, to this very day whenever Moses is read, a veil lies over their minds; but when one turns to the Lord, the veil is removed. (2 Cor 3:15–16)

Once the veil of platonic perfection is taken away, or more accurately, once we become conscious of its presence so that we can see both over and through it, the portrait of God that we find in the Old Testament is transformed. We can attend anew to oft-neglected references to God and are reminded once more that our reading of the biblical text has been, and must always be, shaped by the presuppositions that we bring to it. We can let go of the need to dismiss automatically as anthropomorphic references to God experiencing emotion, feeling pain, or being in any way affected by his relationship with his creation, simply for the sake of preserving his perfection. God becomes less the passionless chess master, moving his pieces around the board to a script that was written before time was time, and more the husband, the mother, the jilted lover, and the covenant partner struggling to relate to his creation. When we lift the platonic veil, we find a God who willingly risks relationship, with all its awkwardness and uncertainty.

The pristine perfection that Plato envisioned is quickly marred in the messy give and take of relationships. The God that we meet in the Bible is not endlessly free, but is, from the very first chapter in Genesis, a God *in relationship*. We might speculate on a time when God was free to choose the shape of creation as he willed, but such speculations have no bearing on present reality. From the start he elected to love his creatures and to enter into a loving relationship with them. Within the context of biblical revelation it makes no sense to speak of God as ultimately free. God is revealed to us as the involved one already in Genesis 1:2 with his spirit brooding over the face of the waters.

Our first suspicions that the platonic God of perfection is little more than an illusion are kindled in the opening chapters of Genesis. Humanity is condemned, all of nature is cursed, and a guard is placed on the Garden of Life, all because of the sin of two people. We may suspect, but cannot know for certain at this point, that all has not gone according to plan for the creator. He has formed that which is good, only to have it marred by those in whom he has invested his own image. How could the perfect God have been so shortsighted? But suspicion turns to certainty as we read in Genesis 6:5–6 of God's repentance: "The LORD saw that the wickedness of humankind was great in the earth, and that every inclination of the thoughts of their hearts was only evil continually. And the LORD was sorry that he had made humankind on the earth, and it grieved him to his heart." Here is the first indication that, having created humanity in his image, God can now neither control nor adequately shield himself from his creation. It falls within the scope of human power both to make God sorry and to cause him to reverse his acts of creation. God is affected and his heart is changed as a result of what he sees and experiences in his dealings with humanity.

That the repentance of God springs from an active involvement with people, and is not simply the disappointment of a detached observer watching an experiment go wrong, becomes clear in the context of covenant. God's commitment to that relationship is often expressed in the Old Testament in terms of covenants. By entering into a covenant, God chooses a closer relationship with his people, while at the same time surrendering somewhat of his freedom and opening himself to constraint and hurt. This self-limitation is expressed almost immediately in both the Abrahamic and Sinai covenants. Immediately after establishing a covenant with Abraham, God says of his intent to destroy Sodom "Shall I hide from Abraham what I am about to do, seeing that Abraham shall become a great and mighty nation, and all the nations of the earth shall be blessed in him?" Abraham then proceeds to question the justice of God's plans for judgment, asking pointedly "Shall not the Judge of all the earth do what is just?" (Gen 18:17, 25). The relational God must suffer cross-examination by his new partner as together they discuss what it means for God to be God.

The covenant at Sinai brings another monumental step in God's movement toward relatedness. Not since the Garden of Eden have we been told that God moved in the midst of people, even going so far as to dwell with them. God was in the habit of walking with Adam and Eve from time to time, but the new covenant allows for the continual presence of God in the camp. No sooner is the covenant struck, though, than God is impinged upon. With the sin of the Golden Calf in Exodus 32, Moses and God must renegotiate the covenant, even before the lettering on the tablets has ceased to smoke. With stunning abruptness, God says to Moses in v. 10, "Now let me alone, so that my wrath may burn hot against them and I may consume them; and of you I will make a great nation." God, who was free to act prior to making the covenant, must now seek Moses' consent in order to carry out his proposed plan. Moses appeals to God's ability to control his emotions ("why does your wrath burn hot?"), to his reputation ("why should the Egyptians say?"), and to his integrity ("Remember your promise!"). As a result of this three-fold argument, we read that, "the LORD changed his mind about the disaster that he planned to bring on his people." The repentance of God is brought about this time not by God's own observation, as in the flood story, but by the active intervention of a covenant partner.

Covenant invites a relatedness that constrains God's actions and limits his options. For the prophet Ezekiel, such participation in the plans of God by someone who would intercede with him on Israel's behalf was more than simply a confirmation of God's intents and desires, but was essential to shaping the future of the divine/human relationship. Speaking of his reluctance to execute judgment on the nation of Israel, God says,

> And I sought for anyone among them who would repair the wall and stand in the breach before me on behalf of the land, so that I would not destroy it; but I found no one. Therefore I have poured out my indignation upon them; I have consumed them with the fire of my wrath; I have returned their conduct upon their heads, says the Lord God. (Ezek 22:30–31)

God is constrained by his relationships, both when his covenant partners respond to that relationship and when they do not.

But the restraint of God's freedom brought about by his decision to be in relationship with Israel goes beyond simply inviting intercession and participation in his decisions. God, having given his heart to this people, finds that his own emotions, his pathos, acts to restrain him. The book of Judges records an oft-repeated cycle of idolatry on the part of Israel, the removal of God's protection so that the people are afflicted by an enemy, the repentance and crying out of the people, God's raising up of a judge to deliver them from their oppressors, and the people's renewed apostasy. In Judges 10, God finally loses patience with Israel's refusal to make any substantive change in their dealings with him and refuses to hear any further cries for deliverance.

> Did I not deliver you from the Egyptians and from the Amorites, from the Ammonites and from the Philistines? The Sidonians also, and the Amalekites, and the Maonites oppressed you; and you cried to me, and I delivered you out of their hand. Yet you have abandoned me and worshipped other gods; *therefore I will deliver you no more.* (Judg 10:11–13)

But in spite of God's resolve to withhold his aide from this rebellious people, he finds himself unable to stick with his decision. We are told in v. 16 that "he could no longer bear to see Israel suffer," so that he is constrained to respond to their cries for deliverance.

Biblical descriptions of a relational God not only include language of God's repentance, but they also use that language with apparent inconsistency. In 1 Samuel 15, God says to Samuel "I regret (*naham*) that I made Saul king," but concerning God's rejection, Samuel says to Saul later in the same chapter, "Moreover, the Glory of Israel will not recant or change his mind (*naham*); for he is not a mortal, that he should change his mind." Terence Fretheim locates the source of this seeming inconsistency in the limits of conceptual language when speaking of God. He argues that all language that seeks to describe God must, of necessity, be metaphorical.[19] Thus, says Fretheim, we must think in

19. Fretheim notes the historical discomfort in Jewish and Christian thought with those metaphors that are perceived to be anthropomorphic. "The tendency in OT scholarship has been to forfeit many such metaphors, primarily by collecting a large number of them and drawing a few general conclusions (e.g., God is personal, living), rather than examining each in turn for the insight it might generate." Fretheim, *The Suffering of God*, 9.

terms of a God who, by his nature, both does and does not repent. That which drives God's repentance, leading him to change his mind, is his unerring prejudice for mercy and salvation over against judgment and destruction.

> God's constant availability for repentance stands in the service of this unchanging divine intention [to save rather than destroy], not simply for Israel (so Joel) but also for the world (so Jonah). To speak in other terms, it would appear that it is essential to speak of both immutability and mutability as essential divine attributes, each in its own sphere.[20]

A platonic understanding of the perfection of God fails to describe adequately and fully his willingness to change direction in the service of his larger goal, the salvation of his creation. He has made himself responsive to and, therefore, is affected by his creation. God opts consistently for the uncertainty of relationships over the kind of perfection that is only possible in isolation and through manipulation.

The prophets speak of a God who is compelled by his own compassion. Isaiah describes God as a new mother who cannot help but respond to the cries of her baby as her milk-engorged breasts ache and leak milk in response to her baby's cries (Isa 49:15). Having punished Judah for her sins, the prophet Jeremiah declares that God is moved within himself.

> Is Ephraim my dear son?
>   Is he the child I delight in?
> As often as I speak against him,
>   I still remember him.
> Therefore I am deeply moved for him;
>   I will surely have mercy on him, says the LORD. (Jer 31:20)

The phrase translated by the NRSV "I am deeply moved" is literally the expression "my bowels roar" or "are in an uproar," the bowels rather than the heart being the seat of emotion in Hebrew thinking. Kazoh Kitamori has pointed out that when the verb *hamah* (to murmur, growl, groan, roar) is used elsewhere in the Bible to speak of an emotional condition, it carries not so much the sense of compassion or mercy, but rather of anguish and pain. Kitamori argues that here we have an example of God's pain that results from the rejection of his love by

20. Fretheim, "The Repentance of God," 61.

sinful humanity. Thus, he speaks of "love rooted in the pain of God," to describe God's continuing love in the face of rejection.[21] In spite of, or rather because of Ephraim's repeated rejection of God, his heart is tormented.

The most profound glimpse of the divine pathos, though, is afforded us by the prophet Hosea. The failed marriage of the prophet mirrors the failed marriage of God. Confronted with an incessantly adulterous wife, God is both justified and compelled to divorce her. In chapter 11 he rehearses her long history of infidelity and reaches the inescapable decision to divorce and destroy her. But in the end, God finds himself unable to do so. His heart constrains him.

> How can I give you up, Ephraim?
>> How can I hand you over, O Israel?
> How can I make you like Admah?
>> How can I treat you like Zeboaiim?
> My heart recoils within me;
>> my compassion grows warm and tender.
> I will not execute my fierce anger;
>> I will not again destroy Ephraim;
> for I am God and no mortal,
>> the Holy One in your midst,
> and I will not come in wrath. (Hos 11:8–9)

Having gone through marriage counseling, initiated divorce proceeding, and finally sat down with the lawyers to sign the divorce papers that will put an end to his union with Israel, God finds himself unable to sign the papers. The passionate God is ultimately trapped in a bad marriage with Israel.

The decision of God for relationship does a number of things to God. He elects in grace. He pours out love, mercy, and compassion. He commits himself. As a result, he becomes vulnerable, experiencing grief, hurt, and anger. Though the suffering of God is poured out in judgment, it is also restrained and given a redemptive direction by God's experience of love and the loss of that love. Experientially the God who has passed through the Exile with his people is not the same God who said "let us make man in our image!" God has gotten involved and there really is no turning back. As with anyone who experiences marriage,

---

21. Kitamori, *Theology of the Pain of God*, 151–67.

separation, and the threat of divorce, things can never be as they were before. Relationships may be severed, but they cannot be unmade.

Terence Fretheim understands God to suffer as a result of his decision to "get his hands dirty" by entering into a relationship with humanity. As that relationship begins to break down, the prophets portray God's anguish over its demise. Because the prophet speaks to the people out of the heart of God, says Fretheim, "a prophetic work begins, not with hellfire and damnation, but with a picture of the pain and anguish of God."[22] The prophet stands between God and Israel to deliver God's word. The form of the prophetic message is found not only in what he or she speaks, but in the prophet's direct participation in the pain of God. "The prophet's life was reflective of the divine life . . . God is seen to be present not only in what the prophet has to say, but in the word as embodied in the prophet's life."[23] The prophetic ministry is one of shared pathos.

Walter Brueggemann sees the articulation of pathos as the necessary first step of prophetic ministry. Prophecy must begin with an open expression of grief in order to cut through every attempt to cover up or to deny the reality of a crisis in the divine/human relationship. Until pain is exposed and grief expressed, there can be no move toward renewal. "Newness comes precisely from expressed pain. Suffering made audible and visible produces hope, articulated grief is the gate of newness, and the history of Jesus is the history of entering into the pain and giving it voice."[24] Thus, Brueggemann maintains that grief, pain, and lament are essentially constructive in nature. The expression of prophetic pain produces hope rather than despair. Jesus too spoke in this prophetic tradition. "So the speech of Jesus, like the speech of the entire prophetic tradition, moves from woe to blessing, from judgment to hope, from criticism to energy."[25] If the embodiment of the divine message in prophetic suffering can be seen as a move toward newness, this suggests that the suffering of God always carries with it the seed of hope and is creative in nature. The laments of God, though often accompanied with acts of judgment, bring with them too an invitation to newness. The

22. Fretheim, *The Suffering of God*, 115.

23. Ibid., 149.

24. Brueggemann, *The Prophetic Imagination*, 91.

25. Ibid., 109.

lament of God, "And the LORD was sorry that he had made humankind on the earth, and it grieved him to his heart," carries with it the hope of new life, "And God said to Noah, . . . 'Make yourself an ark.'" By extension biblical prayers of lament offered to God, far from being acts of doubt or faithlessness, invite an act of new creation from God.

To summarize, the assertion that God invites a love relationship with humanity carries with it the necessity for divine pathos. The covenant relationships that God initiated in the Old Testament placed constraints on God and opened him to being wounded. Through the experience of the cross, God entered directly not simply into the knowledge of our suffering as finite, limited creatures, but into a shared experience of that finitude. This experience of suffering is potentially destructive, threatening to dissolve relatedness, but the response that God both initiates in himself and calls for in his people brings with it the hope of newness. The frank expression of grief and the recognition of the threat that suffering brings to the divine/human relationship is the first step toward renewal. After the betrayal of adultery, Israel's marriage can only be salvaged and rebuilt by the tears of God.

When God Laments

God does not suffer in silence, but like his human partners, he gives voice to what he is experiencing in the relationship. Certainly we are accustomed to expressions of his wrath and judgment, particularly in the Old Testament. But, as Kitamori has pointed out, the wrath of God springs from his pain, pain that results from rejected love. It is pain, rather than offended honor or the violation of some arbitrary cosmic standard, that reveals the nature of God's wrath. Thus, it should not surprise us that the God who suffers and responds in wrath also expresses his pain in other ways, including cries of lament. Where God's wrath is devoid of pain, its expression would be little more than a desire for vengeance and an act of hopelessness that merely seeks to put an end to relationship. But wrath that is born of pain carries with it the hope that the relationship can be repaired and can continue. The cry of lament on the lips of God is a creative word, just as surely as is his command, "Let there be light!" Or perhaps it is more accurate to say that lament brings a "re-creative" word, a word of resurrection, because it clings to that which is dying in the belief that it can live again. By taking up a lament,

God refuses simply to abandon his relationship with Israel, but lingers on in the place of pain, humiliation, and abandonment, believing that it is still possible to rediscover his first love.

As we look for signs of God's pain and expressions of his lament, we begin with divine language that looks and sounds like human prayers of lament. Terence Fretheim has pointed out that God's use of questions to express pain and consternation mirrors the form of human prayers of lament.[26] Questions are a common feature of lament prayers. "How long, O LORD? Will you forget me forever? How long will you hide your face from me?" (Ps 13:1). "Why did I not die at birth, come forth from the womb and expire?" (Job 3:11). "How could we sing the LORD's song in a foreign land?" (Ps 137:4). "Is your steadfast love declared in the grave, or your faithfulness in Abaddon? Are your wonders known in the darkness, or your saving help in the land of forgetfulness?" (Ps 88:11–12). God also expresses his pathos with similar questions. "I have seen your abominations, your adulteries and neighings, your shameless prostitutions on the hills of the countryside. Woe to you, O Jerusalem! How long will it be before you are made clean?" (Jer 13:27). "Why do you seek further beatings? Why do you continue to rebel?" (Jer 9:7). "Therefore, thus says the LORD of hosts: I will now refine and test them, for what else can I do with my sinful people?" (Isa 1:5). "What shall I do with you, O Ephraim? What shall I do with you, O Judah? Your love is like a morning cloud, like the dew that goes away early" (Hos 6:4). Such questions point to consternation, anger, and hurt.

God's pain, anger, and sorrow are also revealed to us most particularly by the latter prophets whose task it was to reveal the heart of God, even as the covenant relationship with Israel came unraveled. The prophets themselves lament as they experience directly the pain of Israel's rejection of their message. But part of the prophetic ministry includes sharing in the divine suffering. Claus Westermann calls our attention to the frequency with which the expressions of God's lament are interwoven with those of the prophet. Amidst the laments of Jeremiah in chapters 12, 15, and 18, God breaks in to express his own resentment and grief over the sins of the people. Jeremiah 12:7–13; 15:5–9; and 18:13–17 contained the laments of God embedded in the laments of the

---

26. *The Suffering of God,* 121–23.

prophet.[27] So, for example, in Jeremiah 12:7–8 we read: "I have forsaken my house, I have abandoned my heritage; I have given the beloved of my heart into the hands of her enemies. My heritage has become to me like a lion in the forest; she has lifted up her voice against me—therefore I hate her." The cries of God are characterized by rage and indignation, but there is alongside of these an undercurrent of grief and loss.

The failure of Israel to keep covenant is the principal context for the laments of God. Psalm 81 recalls God's graciousness in heeding the cry of Israel while they were still slaves serving Pharaoh. Almost from the first moment, though, Israel responded to Yahweh with a self-willed rejection of God's calling and a determined deafness to his voice. In frustration God calls to the people "Hear, O my people, while I admonish you; O Israel, if you would but listen to me!" God's plea, however, goes unheeded and his frustration turns to anguish. "O that my people would listen to me, that Israel would walk in my ways!" God longs for expressions of repentance and obedience that will never come.

The most expressive laments of God are found in the prophecies of Jeremiah. The prophet personifies the suffering of God, so that it is not always clear when the prophetic laments have as their subject Jeremiah and when it is the voice of Yahweh that we hear.[28] The most poignant lament shared by the prophet and God is found in Jeremiah 8:18–9:11. In some places, the voice of lament could just as easily be that of the prophet.

> My joy is gone, grief is upon me, my heart is sick . . .
> For the hurt of my poor people I am hurt,
>   I mourn, and dismay has taken hold of me . . .
> O that my head were a spring of water,
>   and my eyes a fountain of tears,
> so that I might weep day and night
>   for the slain of my poor people!

But in 8:19b it is clearly Yahweh who speaks demanding, "'Why have they provoked me to anger with their images, with their foreign idols?'" God determines to punish the people for their wickedness in 9:7, but seems reluctant to do so. "Therefore, thus says the LORD of hosts: I will now refine and test them, for what else can I do with my sinful people?

---

27. Westermann, *Praise and Lament in the Psalms*, 279–80.
28. Mark S. Smith, "Jer. 9:9—A Divine Lament."

. . . Shall I not punish them for these things? says the LORD; and shall I not bring retribution on a nation such as this?" Finally, in 9:10, God's laments actively for the desolation of the Jerusalem and Judah that will result from the pouring out of his wrath. The NRSV translates God's response as an instruction to others (possibly the prophet), "Take up weeping and wailing for the mountains, and a lamentation for the pastures of the wilderness." The Greek, Syriac, and Hebrew texts, however, attest uniformly to the first person, imperfect: "*I* will take up weeping and wailing . . ." The lament of the prophet is an echo of God's lament at the judgment and destruction of Israel, even though such treatment is both expedient and justified.

One of the more striking features of God's laments in the prophetic writings is its unrestricted scope. God does not grieve for his people alone, but he saves some of his most poignant laments for those who stand outside of the covenant. In Jeremiah 48 the prophet announces God's coming judgment on the Moabites, a judgment so severe that her neighbors are called upon to lament her fate. In vv. 31–32a, God himself takes up the lament for Moab. "Therefore I wail for Moab; I cry out for all Moab; for the people of Kir-heres I mourn. More than for Jazer I weep for you, O vine of Sibmah!" Isaiah uses similar language in his oracle against the Moabites. Amidst the wailing and tears of the people of Moab God says "My heart cries out for Moab" (Isa 15:5).

One way to interpret the wrath and judgment of God has been to see him as an offended monarch who, having been denied his due, executes the law without compassion and pours out judgment with a sense of satisfaction. This is not, though, the picture of divine wrath with which the Old Testament presents us. As Herschel and Kitamori have suggested, we can only understand divine wrath in terms of divine pathos and love. Kathleen O'Connor affirms that the laments of God situate expressions of his judgment in the context of relatedness: "Language of divine tears offsets language of the divine punisher and wrathful judge, for it posits God's vulnerability to the conditions of others."[29] The basic context of divine lament is the same as its human counterpart. God cries out over a relationship in crisis.

The fact that God laments suggests a number of important points. First of all it underscores the relational nature of lament. The suffering

---

29. O'Connor, "The Tears of God and Divine Character in Jeremiah 2–9," 185.

of God always results from his initial decision to enter into relationship with his creation. From his grief over the decision to create humanity in Genesis to his hurt and anger as the exodus generation consistently rebels against him to the profound pathos expressed by the prophets as the covenant comes unglued and the people of God are taken from the land of the promise, the suffering of God is responsive. Relatedness creates pathos in God and is the catalyst for his lament.

Secondly, the lament of God qualifies and gives shape to expressions of his wrath. The fact that God should weep aloud, even as Jerusalem is destroyed, illumines for us the nature of divine wrath. God's wrath is an expression of his justice, but it is not a dispassionate, detached, objective justice. God's love for his humanity has created in him a tension between what he should do and what he wants to do. The wrath of God is tempered, and at times even extinguished, by the tears of God. Indeed, we can even speak at times of the "injustice" of God as he fails to execute judgment not because to do so is unjust, but because he is constrained by his compassion. In Hosea's prophecy, the rational sentence of God, "They shall return to the land of Egypt, and Assyria shall be their king," is overturned by his pathos; "How can I hand you over, O Israel? . . . My heart recoils within me; my compassion grows warm and tender" (Hos 11:5, 8). God is a judge who weeps as he passes sentence and executes judgment, and he is a judge in whom justice is, at times, overcome by compassion.

Thirdly, if lament is God's response to choices and actions that threaten his relationship with humanity, this validates the prayer of lament as a god-like response to circumstances that threaten or damage our relationship with God. This relational grounding of lament suggests that it is a valid, indeed an essential part of prayer in the new covenant. Christ's lament on the cross, "My God, my God, why have you forsaken me," expresses his experience of broken relationship, of God-forsakenness. The cry of lament is not disloyal to God, nor is it a denial of Christ's finished work on the cross. It arises from the suffering of a relationship not yet perfected and from life lived in a fallen world. Lament does not deny relatedness, but presses toward it. Christ did not remove the lament from our language of prayer, but has invited his disciples to share both in his suffering and in his cries over a lost and dying world.[30]

Finally, if, as our discussion of God's suffering suggests, divine pathos should be seen as essentially creative in nature, then the aim of lament should be the restoration and strengthening of our relationship with God. Yahweh seeks to preserve that which by any reasonable measure of justice ought not to be preserved, his relationship with Israel. God's lament presses inexorably toward forgiveness, restoration, and the preservation of a remnant. This is highly suggestive for our wider understanding of biblical lament. As we have seen, lament is occasioned not simply by an external crisis, but by the silence of God. Prayers of lament do not stop short at simply describing the immediate problem and seeking relief. Lament pushes more deeply into the relationship that is in crisis.

In summary, Yahweh is a God who limits himself by choosing relatedness. In the context of that relationship, he both executes fierce judgment and suffers the pain of rejection. In that relationship the grief and repentance of God precedes our own. God gives voice to the cry of lament that becomes our model for reaching toward God when he is silent. The prayer of lament is, for God and people alike, the language that seeks after and allows for the renewal of broken community.

Is God My Enemy?

Our exploration of God's pain leads us to speak of God as one who suffers with us, or more accurately because of us, so that we might be tempted to cast God solely as the *victim of relationship*. Because of our sin, our failure in relationship, God's wrath is both provoked and reluctantly poured out. We might also reasonably suppose that all human lament has its ground in our own failures. Certainly there are those laments that identify the cause of ruptured relationship with human sin. In the prophetic writings where the bulk of divine lament is to be found, the unfaithfulness of God's covenant partners elicits from both God and prophet alike cries of lament. Similarly, some lament psalms identify sin as the cause of God's silence and seek, through repentance, to repair the damaged union.

30. Patrick Miller suggests that for the Christian lament is in part intercessory. "So finally Christ teaches us a new mode of crying out, a crying out in behalf of others." "Heaven's Prisoners: The Lament as Christian Prayer," 23.

Have mercy on me, O God,
  according to your steadfast love;
according to your abundant mercy
  blot out my transgressions.
Wash me thoroughly from my iniquity,
  and cleanse me from my sin. (Ps 51:1–2)

There is no soundness is my flesh
  because of your indignation;
there is not health in my bones
  because of my sin.
For my iniquities have gone over my head;
  they weigh like a burden too heavy for me. (Ps 38:3–4)

Do not remember the sins of my youth or my transgressions;
  according to your steadfast love remember me,
  for your goodness sake, O LORD! (Ps 25:7)

Such suffering is self-inflicted and the divine silence that results is far from mysterious. The psalm writer's punishment is just and his or her lament appeals to God's name, his mercy, and his steadfast love over against his justice.

Such, however, is not uniformly the case in the Psalter. There are times when God's silence persists in the face of suffering, even though the one praying maintains his or her innocence. "If you try my heart, if you visit me by night, if your test me, you will find no wickedness in me" (Ps 17:3). "Vindicate me, O LORD, for I have walked in my integrity, and I have trusted in the LORD without wavering" (Ps 26:1). There are even those laments that see God as the active agent, punishing the innocent without cause.

All this has come upon us,
  yet we have not forgotten you,
  or been false to your covenant.
Our heart has not turned back,
  nor have our steps departed from your way,
yet you have broken us in the haunt of jackals,
  and covered us with deep darkness. (Ps 44:17–19)

In short, there are those laments that identify God as the source of the broken relationship.

Fredrik Lindström's study of the Psalms of lament has underscored a fundamental distinction between prophetic laments and those found in the Psalter. Whereas for the prophets human sin is the root cause of lament, frequently in the Psalms there is no reliable correlation between suffering and sin.[31] God's hiddenness in times of need cannot be consistently attributed to failure on the part of the one praying. While this is clear in many of the Psalms of lament, it becomes programmatic for Job. Job is the quintessential innocent sufferer, with God as the direct cause of both his loss and the divine silence that follows it. It is God and not Job who has failed to uphold the covenant relationship as Deuteronomy defines it. Job has acted righteously, but has been rewarded as one who is faithless. God has become Job's enemy without cause and it is the charge of divine faithlessness that energizes Job's lament.

Stepping away from a platonic view of God and attending anew to the various ways in which he is portrayed in the Old Testament is, at times, highly problematic. This has, perhaps, been one of the reasons for Plato's staying power. By divorcing his model from the messiness, the ambiguity, and the uncertainty that is part of life lived in relationship, Plato can offer us a God that "works" and that is explainable, even predictable. There is something tremendously attractive about a being that successfully avoids all that is potentially negative about the human experience. While everything else in life is uncertain, God is a fixed, unmovable, predictable anchor in our world. But when we attend to the texts that do not "work" within this model, we meet a God who is not above the chaos, but in it with us. Certainly, as we have seen, this implies that God himself suffers the effects of that chaos. More challenging and frightening, though, are those texts that offer God as the one who brings chaos into our lives. Here we meet not a God who suffers, but one who causes suffering in others. A minority voice, yet one that speaks consistently throughout the Old Testament, presents God as the enemy of the innocent, bringing suffering to those who do not merit it, while leaving unscathed those who do. At times laments are offered to a God who stands against his people without cause.

We begin the move toward speaking of God as the enemy of the innocent when we consider his genocides. In Genesis 6:5 God discovers that which we heretofore have yet to witness, the loss of any spark of goodness in humanity. "The LORD saw that the wickedness of humankind was great in the earth, and that every inclination of the thoughts

31. Lindström, *Suffering and Sin*.

of their heart was only evil continually." Are we to understand this statement as pure hyperbole or should we imagine that in those days no
thirsty stranger was ever offered a cup of cold water, no mother ever
gave her life for her child, and no one was ever moved with compassion for the suffering of another? Should we envision the imagination of
every small child as only evil continually? Indeed, what a relief it would
be if such were the case, for who could identify with such an alien race?
God would simply be ordaining the death of those who had ceased to
be human. He would merely be slaughtering animals, rather than human beings. But such, we may suspect, is not the case.

The genocides of God do not cease with the flood, nor do they
confine themselves to the "pre-history" of Genesis 1–11. With the advent of the Abrahamic covenant, Yahweh immediately engages his new
partner in adjudicating the slaughter of Sodom and its neighbors. Thus,
from almost the first moment of his covenant involvement, Abraham is
implicated in the rough and all-embracing exercise of divine judgment.
The central salvation event in Israel's story, the Exodus from Egypt, is
marked by two genocides. The first, carried out by Pharaoh, seeks the
destruction of Israel's children by a tyrannical and autonomous dictator. The second, perpetrated by God against Egypt's first-born, brings
judgment to every family and household of the Egyptians, regardless
of the fact that the common people have no say in the decisions and
policies of their leaders. As Israel moves into the land of promise, God
commands the destruction of whole peoples, men and women, babies
and the elderly, even dumb animals, because of the depravity of their
religion and culture. Yahweh is one who calls for the destruction of a
community, without regard for the degree to which a particular individual may or may not be involved in the sins for which the group as a
whole is being called to account.

Such actions on God's part, though regrettable, can seem necessary, even justifiable, as long as we depersonalize and stereotype whole
groups of persons, buying into the myth that "every inclination of the
thoughts of their hearts was only evil continually." But when we put a
human face to the destruction of whole peoples, the picture changes.
When we imagine not a nation whose inhabitants are all "little pha-
raohs," but an average man and woman, with average kids and average
debts, with hopes and aspirations for their kids that keep them plug-
ging away at dead end jobs, with their share of sickness and bad luck,

who feel mistreated by their leaders and powerless to change the course of their lives, and who both love and lose those that they love to death, then we can be filled with wonder because our own family is spared, while theirs is not. God's decision to slaughter multiplied thousands of such families can never be easily explained. Nor is it sufficient to say that God suffers with those innocent ones who are swept up alongside the guilty. The suffering of God cannot and should not be understood apart from his judgment. Also the suffering of God is mitigated by the reality that he is, at times, the bringer of suffering on those with whom he suffers.

In destroying peoples and nations, corporate sin is said to provoke God's judgment, even if those devastated are not uniformly guilty. The book of Job, though, makes explicit the affliction by God of the innocent. The opening two chapters of the book stress that Job has done nothing to merit the suffering with which he will be struck down and that God directs his servant, the Accuser, to bring about Job's downfall. In a similar way, the prophet Jeremiah complains that he has been forced by God into a position of suffering. "O LORD, you have enticed me, and I was enticed, you have overpowered me, and you have prevailed. I have become a laughing-stock all day long; everyone mocks me" (Jer 20:7). Hosea is commanded to marry a harlot and Ezekiel's wife is taken from him in order to punctuate their prophetic messages.

At times the psalmist will affirm that it is God himself and not human enemies that is at the heart of his or her affliction.

> You have put me in the depths of the Pit,
>   in the regions dark and deep.
> Your wrath lies heavy upon me,
>   and you overwhelm me with all your waves.
> You have caused my companions to shun me;
>   you have made me a thing of horror to them.
> I am shut in so that I cannot escape;
>   my eye grows dim through sorrow.
> Every day I call on you, O LORD;
>   I spread out my hands to you. (Ps 88:6–9)

The God who has protected Israel so often in the past can also lift that protection, so that his people cry out, "Because of you we are being killed all day long, and accounted as sheep for the slaughter" (Ps 44:22). How, then, are we to understand the God who strikes down and afflicts in relation to the God who stretches out his arm to deliver or the God who suffers alongside of us?

The biblical writers struggle with this question in their prayers of lament. It is significant that the question is both raised and wrestled with in the context of Israel's relationship with Yahweh. Even when such prayers rage against God, skirting dangerously close to blasphemy as in the case of Job, nevertheless lament is offered invariably from the posture of an insider, that is, from one in a covenant with God. A covenant implies expectations and obligations, restrictions and rights of access, and presumes on the availability, even the obligation of God to hear and respond. Though God may adopt the role of an enemy, nevertheless Israel will invariably address him from within the bonds of relatedness.

Finally, though, the question "Why does God, at times, present himself as my enemy?" is an unanswerable one. True, the writer will have some partial insights into God's actions. The narrator of Job (though not Job himself) attributes God's actions to a divine test of Job's faithfulness. Such an "answer," though, is finally unsatisfying and raises more questions than it answers. Why did God need to test Job in the first place? Didn't he know whether Job would be faithful or not? Why would God give the Satan permission to smite Job and then complain to him "you incited me against him, to destroy him for no reason?" Did the Satan manipulate God? What does it mean to say that God would destroy any innocent person "for no reason"? In laments, though, the "Why?" question is seldom asked and even less frequently answered. The questions on the table when God strikes down the innocent is not "Why?" but "Can God still be trusted?"

The anguish of lament is that of violated trust. Without a history of relatedness and of love, there is no trust to be violated. This is clear not only in human laments, but also in the laments of God as he expresses hurt, betrayal, and outrage, often in terms of a husband whose wife has been unfaithful. The prayer of lament does not find injustice in the fact of death, nor does it approach God as a stranger, but lament protests the death of the innocent and the betrayal of trust by a covenant partner. The cry of lament, "My God, my God, why have you forsaken me?" suggests both a history of trust and a relationship that continues, even in the midst of abandonment.

It is precisely in the context of lament that the analogy of God as enemy finally breaks down. The appeals and protests of the prayer of lament are not offered to an enemy, but to one with whom a relationship of commitment and trust has been enjoyed. One does not appeal to the trust or fidelity or commitment or faithfulness of an enemy. To speak of God as our enemy is only usable as a metaphor to the extent that we can place it in tension with God's justice and covenant faithfulness. This provides no explanation for and only tentative insight into those occasions when God acts as an enemy, but it does provide shape for and make relative our use of the term "enemy" to describe those dark experiences of God as one who inflicts suffering and brings death. In and through the prayer of lament we find Israel seeking to adjudicate between God as enemy, God as rejected lover, God as abandoning parent, God as just judge, and God as powerful deliverer. Lament provides the space for all of these expressions of who God is.

The God Who Hears Our Laments

Only by risking the death of the perfect God can we take Israel's lament on our lips and make their prayers our own. The prayer of lament does not find in God's distance, silence, and hiddenness marks of his perfection. Nor does it contend that faithfulness to God is expressed through the passive acceptance of suffering. Lament is unseemly in its haste to draw close to God and impertinent in the way that it presumes to know what can be begged from and demanded of the sovereign of the universe. The prayer of lament violates the sovereign distance of God. It rages against a God who pretends to be impassive and immutable, knowing intuitively that these are the qualities of idols, and therefore wholly alien to the God of Israel. Israel's prayer of lament must die stillborn before the platonic god, for such a god has no heart to be broken, no passions to be stirred, and no love to demand of it change. Casting all such impotent idols aside, Israel takes up her lament and reaches toward the God who delivers, protects, rages, destroys, and suffers. At the heart of such prayers is the cry for intimacy with the God of covenant.

Lament, though, is finally not a human invention, but one that has its origin in the laments of God. It was God who initiated relationship, opening himself to be both loved and rejected. It was God's cry of pain that gave shape to the cries of the prophets. This means that we cannot suffer alone, for God always suffers with us. God himself cast aside perfection in his desire to draw near to his creation.

There is in God, though, that which is alien, strange, and frightening. Like Job before the whirlwind, we cannot fully know the God with whom we share covenant. The God who cries out with us is also the God who can reach out to afflict and destroy us. One way to articulate this *otherness* of God is to speak of him as an enemy, set on the destruction of the weak and careless of justice for the innocent. But as we have seen, the image of God as the enemy is only sustainable when held aloof from his suffering. Brueggemann speaks of the tension that exists in our images of God. God is both committed to relationship and sovereign, both held captive by his love for us and free from its constraints. "Thus the theological dialectic of *accessibility* and *freedom* for Yahweh is matched by Israel's experience of *assurance* and *precariousness*. It is no small matter to speak of this issue so that these two agendas are kept in responsible tension with each other."[32] And it is precisely in the context of lament that the tension between the God who both suffers and afflicts is most effectively sustained in Israel's push toward closeness. The greatest strength of lament is its ability to live in the tension between God's accessibility and his freedom.

Finally it is relationship that makes lament possible. Outsiders cannot lament, nor can those who have no story and no history with God. Lament is born from an experience of God that tells against the story of who God is and how he has been experienced in Israel's past. Yahweh is the God who delivers slaves from their captivity. With a long arm and an outstretched hand, he brings plagues, works miracles, overthrows kings, brings food from the heavens and water from the rocks, destroys armies, and makes a great nation from a weak and feeble people. Yahweh is the God of covenant, of presence, and of land. The silence of God in the face of suffering and death places this story of who God has become for Israel at risk. One of the primary tasks of lament is to seek from the silent God a renewal of Israel's story.

32. Brueggemann, "The Crisis and Promise of Presence in Israel," 151.

3

Is the Story Still True?

The Use of Lament in the Psalms

You have to begin to lose your memory, if only in bits and pieces, to realize that memory is what makes our lives. Life without memory is no life at all . . . Our memory is our coherence, our reason, our feeling, even our action. Without it, we are nothing . . .

—Luis Buñuel

WITH THESE WORDS OLIVER SACKS SETS THE STAGE FOR HIS DESCRIP-tion of Jimmy G, a patient who had lost the ability to form new memo-ries. His memories of the distant past were clear and detailed, but he had no memory of the previous twenty-five years of his life. Nor was Jimmy able to remember any new information or experience for more than a few seconds, or to modify in any way what he did remember. He could meet the same person over and over again each day for the "first time." Although in his forties, he thought of himself as a teenager and was deeply shocked and highly agitated when presented with the image of a gray-haired man in the mirror, at least for the few seconds the it took for him to forget what he had just seen. Jimmy had only a distant past, but one that was wholly segregated, so that it could have no meaningful or lasting interaction with new experience. "He was, as it were, . . . isolated in a single moment of being, with a moat or lacuna of forgetting all around him . . . He is man without a past (or future), stuck in a constantly changing, meaningless moment."[1]

---

1. Sacks, *The Man Who Mistook his Wife for a Hat and Other Clinical Tales*, 29.

Our memories bring context and significance to the "meaningless moments" of suffering, isolation, and loss that we encounter in our lives. Lament is both anchored and energized by the memory of wholeness and belonging. The reliance on memory in the context of lament is a particular feature of the Psalms. Because these are prayers offered in the midst of the community and in a setting of worship, they are predisposed to draw on the community's memories in moments of crisis. In this chapter I want to focus on the singular role that memory plays in Israel's lament psalms.

Journeying through the Psalms

Moving through Life

The Psalms are words offered to God from every season of life. In almost any circumstance or experience, we can open the Psalter and find a prayer that expresses the deepest longings of our heart; our fears, our joys, our doubts, our triumphs, and our most profound faith. Psalms give us the words to pray in every part of life's journey, and in doing so they connect us to the faith community that has shared, in one form or another, experiences similar to our own.

When we think of the book of Psalms, we can be forgiven for associating them principally with praise, adoration, confidence, and triumphant faith. These are the Psalms that we hear most often in public worship; as with our choice of worship songs and prayers, we gravitate toward those psalms that uplift and instill confidence. God is in control, we are in the palm of his hand, and all doubts and fears are little more than fodder for our praise. In the western church at least, the book of Psalms is characterized as a liturgy of confident praise. This is, however, not the dominant voice in the book. The single largest category of Psalms is not psalms of praise or worship or adoration, but rather psalms of lament. Approximately one third of the Psalter consists in laments of the individual and the community.

The dominance of lament psalms in the Psalter is far from accidental. The Psalter as a whole both reflects the spiritual life of the people that prayed it and mirrors in that people a life journey taken with God and the community. Claus Westermann has provided a useful key to understanding the preponderance of lament psalms in Israel's prayers by calling our attention to the sense of movement, of journey in the Psalms.[2] He attests to the prevailing move within the book of Psalms from lament toward praise. This movement can be seen in the Psalter as a whole, with the majority of the lament psalms being found in the first half of the book of Psalms, and in individual psalms of lament, as approximately half of these psalms transition from lament to active praise during the course of the prayer. Lament shares a connection with praise, leading Westermann to affirm that,

> There is no petition, no pleading from the depths, that did not move at least one step . . . on the road to praise. But there is also no praise that was fully separated from the experience of God's wonderful intervention in time of need, none that had become a mere stereotyped liturgy.[3]

Often lament precedes praise, energizing it and giving it content. Westermann does not, however, understand this as a purely linear relationship, with lament moving inexorably and finally toward praise, but as a continuum, with an individual prayer being located between the poles of lament and praise, having a degree of relatedness to both.

While the dominant current in the Psalms is from lament toward praise, in true active tension there is a persistent back eddy in which praise also moves toward lament. Such is the case, for example, in Psalm 89 where the praise and remembrance of God's eternal covenant with the house of David becomes the occasion for a cry of lament because God appears to have abandoned that covenant.[4] Lament flows into and out of praise, but to collapse the dialectic, so that lament becomes simply an introduction to praise, is to miss its dynamic function and to misunderstand its relationship with praise. Just as it is true that almost all lament psalms take at least one step in the direction of praise, it is also true that praise psalms carry with them memories of lament. The birth of Israel as a nation is founded on a cry for deliverance; "Then the LORD said, 'I have observed the misery of my people who are in Egypt; I have heard their cry on account of their taskmasters'" (Exod 3:7), and it is that cry that gives shape and meaning to the song of victory at the crossing of the Red Sea; "I will sing to the LORD, for he has triumphed

2. Westermann, *Praise and Lament in the Psalms*, 74–75.

3. Ibid., 154.

4. Other examples include Pss 9; 27; 40; 44; 85; and 126.

gloriously; horse and rider he has thrown into the sea" (Exod 15:1). Lament does not serve simply to affirm praise, but it works over against praise, endlessly qualifying and placing at risk claims of God's presence to save. To collapse lament into praise not only nullifies lament, but changes the character of praise.

Worship in the Psalms is dynamic rather than static, being characterized by both movement and development. While the dominant movement is from lament to praise, that praise is never fixed and cannot be adequately sketched when isolated from lament. Walter Brueggemann provides a helpful model for understanding both the process of dynamic movement in the Psalms and the sense of interdependence between the individual prayers. He identifies three basic psalm types: psalms of orientation, psalms of disorientation, and psalms of new orientation.[5] Psalms of orientation present praise from a position of stability and security when God seems very much in control of life's vagaries and when everything in our relationship with God functions as it should.

> The LORD brings the counsel of the nations to nothing;
>   he frustrates the plans of the peoples.
> The counsel of the LORD stands forever,
>   the thoughts of his heart to all generations.
> Happy is the nation whose God is the LORD,
>   the people whom he has chosen as his heritage. (Ps 33:10–12)

Such praise is more general in nature, often separated by some distance from the specifics of experience that would qualify God's perfect control. Psalms of orientation tend toward reductionism, seeming at times to oversimplify and overstate the particulars of divine/human interaction. They make overboard claims about God's relationship with his people that are insulated from the slippage and vagaries of everyday life. When the psalm writer affirms "I have been young, and now am old, yet I have not seen the righteous forsaken or their children begging bread" (Ps 37:25), he or she makes an unguarded affirmation about the provision of God, undergirded no doubt by numerous examples of that provision. The word "never," though, flies in the face of some of our experiences of God. Such an affirmation begs the question, "Where does such a person live that they *never* see the suffering of the righteous and

---

5. Brueggemann, "Psalms and the Life of Faith"; see also idem, *The Message of the Psalms*, *The Spirituality of the Psalms*, and *Praying the Psalms*.

the pain of the innocent?" These kinds of statements may be true about God in the "bigger picture," but only after all the bumps, traffic jams, grinding gears, missed turns, and flat tires of life have been factored into the journey.

Psalms of disorientation are those psalms of lament and complaint that result from the loss of order and control. An experience of crisis drives the psalmist back to a God who is now inexplicably silent as the emergency unfolds. Such psalms are characterized by questions, cries, complaints, pleas, bargainings, and protests.

> O God, the nations have come into your inheritance;
>   they have defiled your holy temple;
>   they have laid Jerusalem in ruins.
> They have given the bodies of your servants
>   to the birds of the air for food,
>   the flesh of your faithful to the wild animals of the earth.
> They have poured out their blood like water
>   all around Jerusalem,
>   and there was no one to bury them.
> We have become a taunt to our neighbors,
>   mocked and derided by those around us. (Ps 79:1–4)

The calm assurance of orientation is overturned and basic questions assail the psalm writer's relationship with God as that relationship is suddenly uncertain and very much at risk.

Psalms of new orientation are initiated when God breaks his silence, answering the call of lament, reasserting order, and reintroducing his presence into the situation. New orientation, though, is not the same as the old orientation. It carries in itself the near memory of the silence and hiddenness of God. It gives thanks and praises God for a fresh act of deliverance following a time of struggling to be heard by God.

> When the LORD restored the fortunes of Zion,
>   we were like those who dream.
> Then our mouth was filled with laughter,
>   and our tongue with shouts of joy;
> then it was said among the nations,
>   "The LORD has done great things for them."
> The LORD has done great things for us,
>   and we rejoiced. (Ps 126:1–3)

A strange thing happens to new orientation, though, with the passage of time. The memory of the crisis and the silence of God fades and new orientation, like freshly poured cement, gradually sets and hardens to become plain, ordinary orientation once again, setting the stage for the move toward disorientation to begin again. These three types of prayer reflect the different places that we stand in our relationship with God.

Brueggemann's model suggests a cyclic, rather than a linear pattern to our life lived in community with God and neighbor that fits more closely our experience of life. But Brueggemann's proposal should not suggest to us the endless cycle of a Tibetan prayer wheel where we inevitably end up back where we started. Nuancing Brueggemann's proposal, John Goldingay describes our movement through life as not simply circular, but as an upper spiral. As the community of faith moves from orientation to disorientation and into new orientation, they do not simply return to their starting place, but grow through their experiences of God's presence, hiddenness, and fresh appearing. Thus Israel's prayers track an upward movement, a development in their relationship with Yahweh.[6] We may find ourselves once more dragged unwillingly into disorientation, but, thanks to our past experiences of the journey, we need not return to the place we began, but grow in our ability to remember and to trust God in deeper, longer silences.

The dynamic tension that exists between lament and praise is fundamental to growth and forward movement in our relationship with God. Experiences of suffering are a crucial part of our maturation both as human beings and as covenant partners with God. To remove lament from our prayer vocabulary is to silence us during precisely those times in life when we most need to be able to offer our prayers to God. Lament is not a denial of our faith in God, but is simply honest and faithful speech that keeps the conversation going as we journey with him through desert places. Such speech is crucial to the health of our relationship with God.

Lament and the Move from Isolation back into Community

The move from orientation to disorientation is a move away from community and into isolation. First of all, the psalm writer often finds him- or herself cut off physically and emotionally from the community's

6. Goldingay, "The Dynamic Cycle of Praise and Prayer in the Psalms."

worship and is rejected both by the community at large and even by his or her closest friends. "These things I remember, as I pour out my soul: how I went with the throng, and led them in procession to the house of God, with glad shouts and songs of thanksgiving, a multitude keeping festival" (Ps 42:4). "Even my bosom friend in whom I trusted, who ate of my bread, has lifted the heel against me" (Ps 41:9). "You have caused friend and neighbor to shun me; my companions are in darkness" (Ps 88:18). The suffering of the psalmist is intensified by the removal of his or her support network and sense of access to God.

But there is a second sense in which the psalmist is disconnected, not simply from his or her immediate community, but from the larger community of Israel in whose heritage the songwriter shares. The person in crisis is confronted by the prospect that he or she is cut off from the birthright of Israel and is not counted among those for whom Yahweh acts to save.

> LORD, you were favorable to your land;
>   you restored the fortunes of Jacob.
> You forgave the iniquity of your people;
>   you pardoned all their sin . . .
> Restore us again, O God of our salvation,
>   and put away your indignation towards us. (Ps 85:1–2, 4)

> In you our ancestors trusted;
>   they trusted, and you delivered them.
> To you they cried, and were saved;
>   in you they trusted and were not put to shame . . .
> All who see me mock at me;
>   they make mouths at me, they shake their heads;
> "Commit your cause to the LORD; let him deliver—
>   let him rescue the one in whom he delights!" (Ps 22:4–5, 7–8)

> We have heard with our ears, O God,
>   our ancestors have told us,
> what deeds you performed in their day,
>   in the days of old:
> you with your own hand drove out the nations,
>   but them you planted,
> you afflicted the peoples,
>   but them you set free . . .
> Yet you have rejected us and abased us,
>   and have not gone out with our armies. (Ps 44:1–2, 9)

Integral to the threat raised by the silence of God in the face of crisis is the very real possibility that Yahweh no longer counts the petitioner as being part of the community for whom he acts to save. This is certainly the accusation of the psalmist's enemies. And as long as God remains silent, their allegation that "there is no help for you in God" is upheld. Much of the prayer of lament is grounded in the threat of a loss of place in the community, so that the psalmist seeks of God restoration to that fellowship, with the covenant protection that that return implies.

One of the premier features of the Psalms is the central place that it gives the community of faith. We run the risk of misunderstanding and misapplying these prayers if we read them from a strictly individualistic perspective. The writers of lament psalms are continually aware of and reaching out to that which transcends the self. This is visible first of all in the laments of the individual that confront and struggle with isolation. But the writers of the lament psalms do not seek simply to rejoin the congregation of the Lord in the present. There is a sense of time that transcends the present moment and the immediate location. The community of faith to which the songwriter belongs is larger than a single generation. Israel is in a relationship with an eternal God and that relation stretches from their creation on into the future. Psalm 102 gives us a sense of the scope of that relationship. It can, at first glance, seem somewhat disjoined, as though the writer cannot hold onto his or her train of thought. The petitioner starts off with a typical cry of lament; "hear my prayer," "let my cry come to you," "do not hide your face," "incline your ear," and "answer me speedily." The most remarkable feature of Psalm 102, though, is the disappearance of this lament. The suffering of the individual and the crisis of the moment are swallowed up in the contemplation of that which transcends both—Israel's relationship with the eternal God, a relationship that will outlast even creation itself. By the close of the psalm, the problems that occasioned it have disappeared from view and the psalmist ponders the security not of his or her own place with God, but rather of the community's relationship with their creator.

> Long ago you laid the foundation of the earth,
>   and the heavens are the work of your hands.
> They will perish, but you endure;
>   they will all wear out like a garment.

> You change them like clothing, and they pass away;
>> but you are the same, and your years have no end.
> The children of your servants shall live secure;
>> their offspring shall be established in your presence.
> (Ps 102:25–28)

That to which the psalmist appeals is far greater than the crisis of the moment or even the community that is physically present. The community of Israel shares in an enduring relationship with an eternal God. Through the prayer of lament, the individual seeks to reconnect with both God and the community that is in an ongoing relationship with him.

As the psalm writer seeks his or her place in the heritage of Israel, we frequently find in the psalms of lament an outward movement from isolation toward community and from the local toward the universal. This movement is temporal and takes place in three parts: from present, into the past, and on toward the future. The supplicant begins with the present reality of God-forsakenness, of divine silence in a time of crisis. The complaint portion of the psalm is an expression of the hard reality faced by those who are outside of God's favor. A frequent response to the silence of God is the recollection of a time when he was experienced as present to save. Numerous psalms move from the present experience of abandonment to a remembered past when God acted to save.[7] The psalmist longs to be reconnected with that past so that the present may be transformed and tries to persuade God that he or she is still a part of the community for whom he acts to save. The third movement often accompanies the frequent shift in the psalms of lament from lament to praise. Having begun in the present and looked to the past, the one praying now moves toward a restored future. This can either take the form of an anticipated future, so that the psalmist offers a vow of praise[8] to be fulfilled when God responds to his or her prayer, or can be expressed in an act of public testimony for an accomplished deliverance.[9]

---

7. There are frequent references in the lament psalms to God's power and saving acts in the past, including references to his power in creation, to the Exodus, and to personal experiences of the psalm writer; Pss 3:4–5; 9; 22:4–5, 9–10; 25:6; 31:5–8; 40:1–5; 42:4–5; 44:1–3, 4–8; 71:5–6, 20; 74:12–17; 77:5–6, 11–20; 80:8–13; 83:9–12; 85:1–3; 86:12–13; 89:9–12, 19–37; 94:16–19; 102:18–20, 25–26; 106; 126:1–3; and 143:5–6.

8. Pss 7:17; 9:1–2; 22:25; 26:7, 12; 35:18, 28; 43:4; 51:13–15; 54:6; 56:12; 61:5, 8; 71:15–18; 79:13; 80:17–18; and 102:21.

9. Pss 9:11, 14; 22:22–26; 31:21–24; 40:9–10; 55:22–23; 56:12–13; 57:5–11; 59:16–17;

The praise that arises from answered prayer frequently takes the form of public testimony in which the person who has experienced God's deliverance proclaims before the great assembly that God has acted once more to deliver and to heal. "Awake, my soul! Awake, O harp and lyre! I will awake the dawn, I will given thanks to you, O Lord, among the peoples; I will sing praises to you among the nations" (Ps 57:8–9). "Then I will thank you in the great congregation; in the mighty throng I will praise you" (Ps 35:18). "All day long my tongue will talk of your righteous help, for those who tried to do me harm have been put to shame, and disgraced" (Ps 71:24). As in the case with remembering the past, there is a distinct move from the local to the universal as testimony to God's salvation is offered in the assembly, before the nations, and even to generations and peoples yet unborn. This three-part movement from present to past to future serves to reverse the isolation of the psalmist, reconnecting him or her to the community of faith. Nearly one third of the lament psalms contain both a memory of God's power and presence in the past and some element of testimony for God's fresh act of deliverance.[10] "When the LORD restored the fortunes of Zion, we were like those who dream . . . Restore our fortunes, O LORD . . . Those who go out weeping bearing the seed for sowing, shall come home with shouts of joy, carrying their sheaves" (Ps 126:1, 4, 6). "You brought a vine out of Egypt; you drove out the nations and planted it . . . Then we will never turn back from you; give us life, and we will call on your name" (Ps 80:8, 18).

> These things I remember, as I pour out my soul;
>> how I went with the throng, and led them in procession to
>> the house of God,
> with glad shouts and songs of thanksgiving,
>> a multitude keeping festival . . .
> Hope in God; for I shall again praise him,
>> my help and my God.
> My soul is cast down within me; therefore I remember you
>> from the land of Jordon and of Hermon, from Mount Mizar
>>
>> . . .
> Hope in God; for I shall again praise him,
>> my help and my God. (Ps 42:4–5, 11)

69:30–36; 71:22–24; 79:13; 102:18; and 109:30–31.

10. Pss 9; 22; 25; 40; 42; 44; 71; 74; 77; 80; 85; 86; 89; 94; 106; 126; and 143.

The lament writer sets up a tension between what is and what was in order to provoke God to change what will be.

The Distance between What Is, What Was, and What Will Be

Reality—Our Experience of the Present

The prayer of lament starts with an uncensored expression of the experience of the moment. One of the most poignant features of lament is its unwillingness to engage in denial. We find in these prayers few attempts to qualify or tone down cries of pain or anger or desperation with safer, more theologically acceptable language.[11] It is precisely at this point that lament clashes with so much of contemporary belief and practice. The psalmist does not try to excuse God by providing easy explanations for his silence. There is no suggestion that God only "seems" absent or that he is merely "perceived" as the enemy of the songwriter. Such prayers are not intended to offer an objective, detached, ontological assessment of the nature of God, but rather are descriptive of the way that relationship is experienced. The distress of the petitioner is reported as it is experienced, without embarrassment and without the felt need to blunt its hard edges. "My God, my God, why have you forsaken me" (Ps 22:1). "Your wrath has swept over me; your dread assaults destroy me. They surround me like a flood all day long; from all sides they close in on me" (Ps 88:16–17). "And I say, 'It is my grief that the right hand of the Most High has changed" (Ps 77:10). The writer does not devote much thought to analyzing her or his feelings in order to censor them theologically.

Also, the sufferer does not shrink from identifying God as her or his principal oppressor. Such prayers are rich with second person pronouns.

> Yet you have rejected us and abased us,
>   and have not gone out with our armies.
> You made us turn back from the foe,
>   and our enemies have taken spoil for themselves.

---

11. Occasionally affirmations of orthodoxy such as that found in Ps 73:1 act as a theological safety harness that allows the psalmist to explore the extremes of experience, voicing fears that shake the moral world of the one praying to its foundations.

You have made us like sheep for slaughter,
  and have scattered us among the nations.
You have sold your people for a trifle,
  demanding no high price for them.
You have made us the taunt of our neighbors,
  the derision and scorn of those around us.
You have made us a byword among the nations,
  a laughingstock among the peoples. (Ps 44:9–14)

You have put me in the depths of the Pit,
  in the regions dark and deep.
Your wrath lies heavy upon me,
  and *you* overwhelm me with all *your* waves.
You have caused my companions to shun me;
  you have made me a thing of horror to them. (Ps 88:6–8)

While the "presenting problem" may be advancing armies, physical disease, or political enemies, these are merely symptoms of a much deeper concern. God stands in opposition to the one praying. As long as the psalmist avoids the actual problem there is no possibility for healing. Careful prayers that avoid placing God's silence at their center leave the root pain unaddressed. Lament requires of the psalm writer a candid assessment of the relationship as she experiences it and not as she would like it to be.

Remembrance—The God that We Have Come to Know

God reveals himself in the Bible through his words and actions. For Israel images of God as deliverer, protector, provider, and judge are dominant. Yahweh is the God who speaks a word and light comes into existence, a God who rebukes the waters and the Red Sea parts, a God who feeds his people with heavenly bread, and a warrior God who goes out to battle at the head of Israel's armies. Such "root experiences," as Emil Fackenheim calls them, stand out as formative for Israel's faith, not simply because of what happened, but because in and through these experiences God was understood to be present with his people. Thus, at the parting of the Red Sea and the overthrowing of the Egyptian armies, the maidens of Israel celebrate not simply the destruction of their enemies, but the understanding that it was the warrior Yahweh, present in the midst of his people, who threw horse and rider into the sea.[12]

Psalms of lament are characterized by a core tension between the image of God as present to save and an experience that casts doubt on that perception as the God with whom Israel shares covenant is now hidden and unresponsive to the people's prayers. The core memories of Israel are placed at risk in the act of lament. The circumstances that occasion lament threaten to qualify, change, and even negate Israel's stories of Yahweh, the God who delivers them. Rather than covering over or denying the tension between experienced present and remembered past, the psalms of lament make this tension their central focus.

One of the more prominent features of the lament psalms is their sense of continuity with the past. Israel's past is fundamental to their identity and the writers of the Psalms draw frequently upon memories of that relationship. Three basic categories of memory are drawn upon by the Psalm writers. The most commonly appealed to memories for Israel are those events surrounding their formation as a nation. The Exodus, the wilderness wanderings, and the conquest of the land chronicle the transition for Israel from being a group of slaves serving one of the great superpowers of their day to being a powerful nation in their own right, a nation both created and actively led by their God. In times of trouble it is not surprising, therefore, that the prayers of lament hearken back to a time when God was remembered as powerfully present to lead and to save.

> We have heard with our ears, O God,
>   our ancestors have told us,
> what deeds you performed in their days,
>   in the days of old:
> you with your own hand drove out the nations,
>   but them you planted;
> you afflicted the peoples,
>   but them you set free. (Ps 44:1–2)

> Your way was through the sea,
>   your path, through the mighty waters;
>   yet your footprints were unseen.
> You led your people like a flock
>   by the hand of Moses and Aaron. (Ps 77:19–20)

12. Fackenheim, *God's Presence in History*, 10–11.

Psalm 106 contains the most extensive recitation of these events. For thirty-eight verses the psalm writer describes the ceaseless rebelliousness of the people through the events of the Exodus and the conquest of the land in order to underline God's faithfulness to forgive Israel's iniquity and to plead for his forgiveness in the present. The assumption is that God will continue to be the God of the Exodus in the present.

A second type of core memory to which the psalms make frequent reference is the creation of the world by Yahweh. Such appeals to the creation story are made most often in order to describe Yahweh's power in dealing with Israel's enemies.

> O LORD God of hosts,
>> who is as mighty as you, O LORD? . . .
> The heavens are yours, the earth also is yours;
>> the world and all that is in it—you have founded them.
> The north and the south—you created them; . . .
> You have a mighty arm;
>> strong is your hand, high your right hand. (Ps 89:8, 11–13)

> Long ago you laid the foundations of the earth,
>> and the heavens are the work of your hands.
> They will perish, but you endure;
>> they will all wear out like a garment.
> You change them like clothing, and they pass away;
>> but you are the same, and your years have no end.
> (Ps 102:25–27)

Whereas the modern reader might be tempted to think of the creation accounts as taking place "outside" of recorded history and as therefore distinct from Exodus memories, there is no such sharp segregation in the way that both types of recollection are appealed to in the praying community. So, for example, Psalm 136 praises God both as creator of the universe and as deliverer from Egypt. While a number of translations insert a break between vv. 9 and 10, there is no break in the flow of the description as the narrator moves from creation to Exodus memories.

> who made the great lights,
>> for his steadfast love endures forever;
> the sun to rule over the day,
>> for his steadfast love endures forever;

the moon and stars to rule over the night,
    for his steadfast love endures forever;
who struck Egypt through their firstborn,
    for his steadfast love endures forever;
and brought Israel out from among them,
    for his steadfast love endures forever;
with a strong hand and an outstretched arm,
    for his steadfast love endures forever. (Ps 136:7–12)

Both Exodus and creation memories appeal to Israel's fundamental understanding of who Yahweh is and how he should act in his relationship with his people. Together these memories make up Israel's "story," a narrative that often centers of Yahweh's power to save in the face of Israel's need.

References to God's creation are surprisingly rare in the Old Testament. The two creation narratives in Genesis 1 and 2 make formative observations about God's relationship to his creation. In chapter one he is the God who has merely to speak the word and chaos is transformed into beautiful harmony and perfect order. It is a narrative about limits, order, and creation's unhesitating conformity to the divine design. This first account stresses God's absolute mastery of that which he has created. In Genesis two the accent falls more heavily on God's involvement with his creation. Rather than speak human beings into existence, God rolls up his sleeves, takes a nice mucky double handful of mud, and shapes the first man. He then takes a rib and forms the first woman. Genesis one asserts that God and God alone creates by his word, so that he is unrivaled in his lordship over creation. Genesis two rejects the notion that humanity is an afterthought or that we are simply mass-produced in some divine assembly line. Rather, men and women are presented as being handcrafted by a master craftsman who is neither hidden away in heaven nor afraid to get his hands dirty in the act of creation.

Having set up the order of God's universe, though, the Bible makes use only sparingly of this theological well-spring. Apart from Genesis, the most significant concentrations of creation references are found in the prophecies of Isaiah and the prayers of the Psalms. Yahweh's role as a creator is particularly important to the theology of Second Isaiah (Isaiah 40–55) where the literary setting is the preparation of the exiles for their return from captivity in Babylon. Yahweh who created the cosmos is compared repeatedly to idols built by human hands. The gods of the Babylonians described in Isaiah 46:1–7 seem to cause more problems than they solve. They are heavy and are a burden for those who must carry them about. Though they purport to be gods, they cannot even walk and must be carried into battle in order to deliver those who serve them. But Yahweh, on the other hand, takes upon himself the burden of carrying his people (cf. Isa 40:12–20; and 45:5–21).

Yahweh is extolled not only as the creator of the cosmos, but also as he who created the nation of Israel. Isaiah 43 affirms both that Yahweh created Israel in the Exodus and that he is preparing a "new Exodus" for his people.

> But now thus says the LORD,
>   he who created you, O Jacob, he who formed you, O Israel:
> Do not fear for I have redeemed you;
>   I have called you by name, you are mine.
> When you pass through the waters, I will be with you;
>   and through the rivers, they shall not overwhelm you;
> when you walk through the fire you shall not be burned,
>   and the flame shall not consume you . . .
> Do not fear for I am with you;
>   I will bring your offspring from the east,
>   and from the west I will gather you;
> I will say to the north "Give them up,"
>   and to the south, "Do not withhold;
> bring my sons from far away
>   and my daughters from the end of the earth—
> everyone who is called by my name,
>   whom I created for my glory,
>   whom I formed and made." (Isa 43:1–2, 5–7; see 43:14–21)

Yahweh lays claim to being the only true creator both of the Babylonians and Israel. It is Yahweh and not the Babylonians with their gods who will determine Israel's future. Neither, though, is Israel free to determine their own future, for they were created by God as a "covenant to the people, a light to the nations" (Isa 42:6).

The psalm writers draw on these creation traditions in order to emphasize Yahweh's power over all enemies that threaten their survival. We have already seen the example of an appeal to God's creation in Psalm 102 as the writer contemplates the permanence of the covenant relationship. Appeals to creation memories in Psalms 74:12–17; 77:16–

19; and 89:9–12 all adopt elements found in the creation stories of the Babylonian conquerors that carried Israel away in captivity. In each case the emphasis is on Yahweh's dominion over all other gods and powers.[13] The purpose of such remembering is by no means disinterested. It is Yahweh's power and dominion that are being called to mind specifically in circumstances where that power is not being exercised.

A third source of community memories is those occasions in the past when foundational narrative and personal experience have come together. On various previous occasions the songwriter has experienced directly the in-breaking presence of God to save and now, in the context of lament, draws upon those memories. A time is recalled when God was not hidden and silent, but very much part of the life of the one now struggling.

> When my enemies turned back
>   they stumbled and perished before you.
> For you have maintained my just cause;
>   you have sat on the throne giving righteous judgment.
> (Ps 9:3–4)

> If the LORD had not been my help,
>   my soul would have lived in the land of silence.
> When I thought, 'My foot is slipping',
>   your steadfast love O LORD, held me up. (Ps 94:17–18)

The psalm writer is not simply reciting a story that he or she has received from others, but is also remembering his or her own part in that story in the past.

By appealing to memories of the Exodus, God's creation, and personal experiences of presence, Israel places the current reality of God's hiddenness in the broader context of his history of relating to his people. Israel both remembers and calls upon Yahweh to remember those occasions when he acted to deliver his people. In doing so, the hiddenness of God is placed in the larger context of memories of his presence. Such memories do not negate or overcome the present silence, but rather they serve to punctuate it. The absence of God tells against his story as the God with "a might hand and an outstretched arm."

---

13. For a discussion of Israel's borrowing and adaptation of elements from the creation stories of their neighbors, see Levenson, *Creation and the Persistence of Evil*; Anderson, *Creation versus Chaos*; and Lee, *Creation and Redemption in Isaiah 40–55*.

Response—The Call to Testify in the Great Assembly

There is a dynamic interaction between prayers of lament and prayers of thanksgiving, between disorientation and new orientation. Thanksgiving is born out of lament, so that apart from the temporary experience of God's hiddenness, there can be no testimony to the breaking of his silence and to fresh acts of salvation. "Lament," says Rickie Moore, "is not, as is commonly assumed, a negation of praise, but it is ultimately the deep well from which the highest manifestation of praise springs forth."[14] Proclamations like "Depart from me, all you workers of evil, for the LORD has heard the sound of my weeping" (Ps 6:8); "For he has delivered me from every trouble, and my eye has looked in triumph on my enemies" (Ps 54:7); and "Out of my distress I called on the LORD; the LORD answered me and set me in a broad place" (Ps 118:5) draw their joy and power from experiences of prolonged pain, so that lament gives shape to thanksgiving.

The sense of connectedness in the Psalter is not limited to looking back at Israel's formative memories. Remembering the larger story is a resource appropriate in the prayer of lament. When, however, the lament turns to praise a different type of reaching out is called for. Just as the songwriter drew from the tradition in the midst of the crisis, he or she must now add to that tradition as the crisis is resolved. Public testimony is a frequent response to a lament that has received God's answer. The lament psalmist both looks ahead to the offer of testimony at some future point, vowing to testify to God's salvation when he answers prayer, and actively offers testimony once that salvation is manifest.

When God responds, the psalmist speaks to the congregation, sharing with them this new experience of God—this journey through the shadows of doubt and this breaking through into the renewed light of God's presence. "Love the LORD, all you his saints. The LORD preserves the faithful, but abundantly repays the one who acts haughtily" (Ps 31:23); "I will tell of your name to my brothers and sisters; in the midst of the congregation I will praise you" (Ps 22:22); and "With a freewill offering I will sacrifice to you; I will give thanks to your name, O LORD, for it is good. For he has delivered me from every trouble, and my eye has looked in triumph on my enemies" (54:6–7).

---

14. Moore, "The Prophetic Path from Lament to Praise," 26.

Claus Westermann argues against thinking of Israel's history in terms of a series of isolated events. Each event in Israel's history occurs within the flow of a continuous relationship and when a past event is "re-presented" in a lament in the present, past and present are joined as God responds to that prayer. "The idea of a continuous event, and therewith historical time, is perceived when, in the context of God's relationship to humanity, two points in time are united in the reciprocal relation of word and deed (that is, in the sense of word and response)."[15] The psalmist does not reach back across a gulf of centuries to a past event, but re-enters the stream of relatedness that extends from past to present.

Offering testimonies is an act of *traditioning*. They are both drawn from and poured back into the stream that is Israel's ongoing story of their relationship with Yahweh. Westermann sees in the vow of praise that is offered in the lament prayer a move to connect the present with the future.

> Just as in the section "looking back at God's earlier saving deeds" there is a binding together of the present moment of national lament with a moment in the past when divine deliverance occurred, so in the vow of praise a moment in the future is tied into the present moment of national lament.[16]

The twin acts of remembering and testifying connect the present moment both with Israel's past and with her future. The isolation experienced by the psalmist as she or he is cut off from the community of faith is also a separation from the stream that is Israel's story of relatedness to Yahweh.

Testimonies to God's saving acts in the present are, therefore, more than just an acknowledgment of having "re-entered" the stream of Israel's story. They become resources for the future when Israel will again face new crises. Today's thanksgiving is recycled and becomes a memory resource for encountering tomorrow's lament. This process can be witnessed in the Psalter as "old" testimonies are brought to God's attention in the context of renewed lament.

> I waited patiently for the LORD;
> he inclined to me and heard my cry.

15. Westermann, *Praise and Lament in the Psalms*, 222.
16. Ibid., 221.

He drew me up from the desolate pit,
  out of the miry bog,
and set my feet upon a rock,
  making my steps secure. (Ps 40:1–2)

LORD, you were favorable to your land;
  you restored the fortunes of Jacob.
You forgave the iniquity of your people;
  you pardoned all their sin. (Ps 85:1–2)[17]

The act of testifying to a fresh move of God revitalizes such old memories. Through testimony, the past becomes present again. The story is re-experienced as it is added to. Israel's worship is not a retreat into past memories, but a re-entering into a "continuous event" as testimony is given to fresh acts of creation and exodus in the lives of the praying community. The past is only successfully "remembered" with a fresh experiencing of the presence of God and such remembrance calls forth a new act of traditioning.

The Move from Reality to Remembrance to Response

Today's thanksgiving for deliverance becomes tomorrow's memory that is offered before God in the face of his silence. Testimonies of God's deliverance are plowed back into the prayer of lament as a means of calling on God to respond again. Thus a dynamic, generative relationship exists between lament and thanksgiving. Psalm 22 illustrates this process of moving from an experience of abandonment, to memories of God's presence to save, to public testimony as the experiences of God's presence and salvation are renewed for the psalm writer. The psalm opens with a cry of abandonment; "My God, my God, why have you forsaken me? Why are you so far from helping me, from the words of my groaning?" The psalm writer then begins to remind God of his faithfulness in the past to help those who put their trusted in him.

In you our ancestors trusted;
  they trusted, and you delivered them.
To you they cried, and were saved;
  in you they trusted, and were not put to shame. (Ps 22:4–5)

---

17. Other psalms of lament which make use of memories of past deliverance as a resource for prayer include Pss 9; 22; 42; 44; 71; 74; 77; 80; 89; 94; 106; 126; and 143.

The thrice-repeated use of "they trusted" sets up the expectation. If one places his or her trust in Yahweh, he will not fail to deliver. The psalmist then adds to these memories his or her personal experiences of God's favor and protection.

> Yet it was you who took me from the womb;
>   you kept me safe on my mother's breast.
> On you I was cast from my birth,
>   and since my mother bore me you have been my God.
> (Ps 22:9–10)

These memories of God's faithfulness to protect and save are a primary motivation in the prayer for God to act again in the present as he has in the past. The enemies of the songwriter, however, do not believe that God will act to save him or her. They mock with words of counter-testimony, "Commit your cause to the LORD; let him deliver—let him rescue the one in whom he delights!", not believing that God truly "delights" in this person, seeing as he or she has been so obviously abandoned by him. That which remains open and in doubt, then, is whether or not the songwriter truly trusts Yahweh. As long as God remains silent, the accusation of the enemies is upheld.

Verse 21 marks a sharp reversal in the psalm. Beginning with v. 22 the psalmist has done a complete about face and begins praising God for his or her deliverance. As a result of God's salvation, the psalm writer goes to the temple and begins to testify. The remainder of the psalm is crowded with verbs of speaking as the songwriter promises to "tell," "praise," "praise," and "pay vows." As a result of the psalmist's testimony others will "praise," "glorify," "stand in awe," "praise," "bow down," "serve," "tell," "proclaim," and "say." This testimony to God's deliverance begins to spread, first socio-economically, then geographically, and finally temporally. "The poor shall eat and be satisfied . . . All the ends of the earth shall remember and turn to the LORD; and all the families of the nations shall worship before him . . . Posterity will serve him; future generations will be told about the Lord." Psalm 22, then, models the process both of drawing on memories of past salvations as a resource in the face of a fresh crisis and of *memory building* as fresh testimony of God's deliverance is adds to the communities' memories.

This relationship sheds further light on another feature of the lament psalm, the vow of praise.[18] Often following the petition for help, vows are made by the songwriter in order to motivate God to respond. When he does "remember" the psalmist and "hear" his or her prayer, those vows must be paid. The vow of praise can take place alongside of, and perhaps as part of, animal sacrifices.[19]

> I will come into your house with burnt offerings;
>> I will pay you my vows,
> those that my lips uttered
>> and my mouth promised when I was in trouble.
> I will offer to you burnt offerings of fatlings,
>> with the smoke of the sacrifice of rams;
> I will make an offering of bulls and goats. Selah (Ps 66:13–15)

More often, though, the vow of praise takes the place of animal sacrifices.

> Not for your sacrifices do I rebuke you;
>> your burnt offerings are continually before me.
> I will not accept a bull from your house,
>> or goats from your folds.
> For every wild animal of the forest is mine,
>> the cattle on a thousand hills.
> I know all the birds of the air,
>> and all that moves in the field is mine.
> If I were hungry, I would not tell you,
>> for the world and all that is in it is mine.
> Do I eat the flesh of bulls,
>> or drink the blood of goats?
> Offer to God a sacrifice of thanksgiving,
>> and pay your vows to the Most High.
> Call on me in the day of trouble;
>> I will deliver you, and you shall glorify me.[20] (Ps 50:8–13)

The proper response to God's salvation is not animal sacrifice alone, but also publicly offered praise for his deliverance.

---

18. For a helpful discussion of the vow of praise, see Patrick D. Miller, *They Cried to the Lord*, 130–33.

19. See Westermann, *Praise and Lament in the Psalms*, 221.

20. The vow of praise is also associated with giving praise, rather than offering sacrifices, in Pss 56:12; 61:5, 8; 65:1; and 116:14, 18.

> Deliver me from bloodshed, O God,
>> O God of my salvation,
>> and my tongue will sing aloud of your deliverance.
> O Lord, open my lips,
>> and my mouth will declare your praise.
> For you have no delight in sacrifice;
>> if I were to give a burnt offering, you would not be pleased.
> The sacrifice acceptable to God is a broken spirit;
>> a broken and contrite heart, O God, you will not despise.
> (Ps 51:14–17)

The one whom God saves from distress is under an obligation to testify publicly to what God has done. To withhold such news from the great assembly would be to hold in contempt God's gift of deliverance.

Psalm 71 is a lament in which the psalm writer's past faithfulness to testify of Yahweh before the great assembly becomes his or her basis for approaching and appealing to God in the present distress. The song-writer has lived a life of faithful telling.

> My praise is continually of you . . .
> My mouth is filled with your praise . . .
> But I will hope continually,
>> and will *praise* you yet more and more.
> My mouth will *tell* of your righteous acts,
>> of your deeds of salvation all day long,
>> though their number is past my knowledge.
> I will come *praising* the mighty deeds of the Lord GOD,
>> I will *praise* your righteousness, yours alone.
> O God, from my youth you have taught me,
>> and I still *proclaim* your wondrous deeds.
> So even to old age and gray hairs,
>> O God, do not forsake me,
> until I *proclaim* your might
>> to all the generations to come. (Ps 71:6c, 8a, 14–18a)

God should respond to save his servant, so the argument goes, because that servant has been faithful to testify of his deliverance in the past and he or she wishes to live long enough to pass on that testimony to future generations.

Just as the prayer of complaint is not a private matter to be brought before the Lord secretly in one's prayer closet, so too the testimony of God's deliverance is community property. Testimony is too valuable a resource to keep hidden away and to remain silent is to betray the community of faith, both today and in the future. Everyone needs to be reminded again that Yahweh is a God who saves, because tomorrow is another day and fresh disasters await those who today are in comfort. The stories and memories of God's saving belong to the community as a whole and that is why those individuals who experience afresh and anew the healing, saving, and vindicating of God must go before the great assembly and "tell of his marvelous works." In this way the particular testimony of what God has done both draws on and is added to the growing story of Israel's relationship with this God who saves. In standing amidst the great assembly and offering public testimony, the individual story becomes part of the community's story, even as that larger story is being reaffirmed.

Lament and the Appeal to Israel's Story

Remembering Israel's Story

The psalm writers ground the prayer of lament in the telling of Israel's story. The narratives of God's creation of the world, of his calling of Abram, of the Exodus from Egypt, of the conquest of the land, and of the establishment of the Davidic monarchy provide a baseline for evaluating all subsequent experiences of God and it is against that standard that the lament presses as it journeys into the silence of God. These stories have created a core identity for Israel as the people of God and it is the presence of Yahweh with Israel that defines who they are. "For what other great nation has a god so near to it as the LORD our God is whenever we call to him? And what other great nation has statutes and ordinances as just as this entire law that I am setting before you today?" (Deut 4:7–8).

The stories that Israel tells are formative. They set the interpretive parameters within which the people of Israel understand themselves, their world, and their relationship with God. As individual Israelites remember and retell these stories, they engage in the process of defining reality. Brynolf Lyon suggests that the act of remembering is neither haphazard nor disinterested, but is governed by the need to formulate one's identity.

> . . . the activity of remembering says something important not only about the past, but also about the present. More exactly, it

says something not only about how our past was constituted, but also about how we are presently constituting ourselves. In remembering, therefore, we are not recalling events that are severed from the present. Rather, we are bringing to awareness, in the manner in which we are presently constituting ourselves, the influence of the past on our present identity.[21]

There is inherent in the remembering and telling of Israel's story by each new generation a seeking for continuity between the present generation and the larger narrative. In remembering the story, each community, indeed each individual, seeks to find a place in that story. Recollection involves integrating present and past, local and universal. Each new context both draws its shape from and lends its own shaping to that which is remembered.

The story that Israel remembers and recites is not static. The remembering is selective as the story is retold and reinterpreted in light of changing contexts and new needs. Ernest Schachtel has described the act of remembering as the "capacity for the organization and reconstruction of past experiences and impressions in the service of present needs, fears, and interests."[22] This flexibility in remembering Israel's core story can be seen in three recitals of the story of Yahweh's deliverance of the people from captivity in Egypt found in the psalms 105, 106, and 78. Psalm 105 is a song of praise that testifies to God's power and greatness in the events surrounding the Exodus deliverance. The psalm writer calls on his or her hearers to "give thanks," "call," "make known," "sing," "sing," "tell," "glory," "rejoice," "seek," "seek," and "remember." Yahweh is to be praised for "the wonderful works he has done, his miracles, and the judgments he uttered." The purpose of the psalm is to exhort and encourage the people to keep Torah.

> For he remembered his holy promise,
>   and Abraham, his servant.
> So he brought his people out with joy,
>   his chosen ones with singing.
> He gave them the lands of the nations,
>   and they took possession of the wealth of the peoples,
> that they might keep his statutes and observe his laws.
> Praise the LORD! (Ps 105:42–45)

21. Lyon, "The Unwelcome Presence," 142.

22. Schachtel, *Metamorphosis*, 284.

The emphasis is placed on Yahweh's power and dominance over the power of the Egyptian empire.

Psalm 106 covers the same territory, but with a very different emphasis and function. The writer contrasts the continual rebellion of the people with God's grace and patience to forgive and restore, regardless of how frequent and how heinous their sins. After all of Israel's rebellions, the outcome was Yahweh's continued grace.

> Nevertheless he regarded their distress
>   when he heard their cry.
> For their sake he remembered his covenant,
>   and showed compassion according
>   to the abundance of his steadfast love.
> He caused them to be pitied
>   by all who held them captive. (Ps 106:44–46)

The reason for the writer's emphasis on God's long-suffering graciousness becomes clear only in the last two verses. The people are again in need of God's forgiveness in the face of their sin. The function of this historical recital, then, was to motivate God to forgive in the present based on his long track record as a forgiving God throughout his dealings with Israel.

Psalm 78 also tells Israel's story, once again focusing on the constant rebelliousness of the people. This time, however, the reason for the recital is very different. Judah is faced with the destruction of the Northern Kingdom and seeks to interpret this event in light of the larger story. Thus in this telling it is Ephraim who turned back rather than enter the promised land, and Jacob and Israel who felt the weight of his wrath. Over and over again "they tested the Most High God, and rebelled against him." As a result of these constant rebellions,

> He rejected the tent of Joseph,
>   he did not choose the tribe of Ephraim;
> but he chose the tribe of Judah,
>   Mount Zion, which he loves.
> He built his sanctuary like the high heavens,
>   like the earth, which he has founded forever.
> He chose his servant David,
>   and took him from the sheepfolds. (Ps 78:67–70)

Now only part of the nation is responsible for being continually stiffnecked and rebellious. It was the Northern Kingdom that persisted in this heritage of disobedience, so that God rejects the North and chooses the South. He prefers Jerusalem to Samaria and chooses the line of David over the rebellious kings who follow in the footsteps of Jeroboam. The story of God's deliverance is offered as an interpretive strategy and the demise of the Northern Kingdom becomes an extension of God's judgment of sin in the wilderness wanderings.

In all three instances the salvation narrative of the nation is drawn upon selectively and is set to serve three different functions in three varied contexts; firstly as a call to keep Torah and walk faithfully in Yahweh's covenant, secondly as a motivation for Yahweh to forgive and restore his scattered people, and lastly as a rational for legitimating the Southern Kingdom centered around the Davidic line and temple worship in Jerusalem. Remembering serves a purpose in the prayers of Israel and that purpose guides the selection process. "Not only is Israel under no obligation whatever to remember the entire past," says Yosef Yerushalmi, "but its principle of selection is unique unto itself. It is above all God's acts of intervention in history, and man's responses to them, be they positive or negative, that must be recalled."[23] As the memories of the past are reapplied in new contexts in order to provide continuity between the past and the present, the core story is at times reinterpreted and its emphasis redirected. Samuel Balentine has suggested that the act of prayer itself is a constructive one that "recharacterizes" and creates a potential for newness in both God and humanity.[24]

This is not to say, however, that the memories of Israel are endlessly malleable. If the story could be reshaped at will, the need for lament would be greatly reduced, even eliminated altogether as the story is simply recast to fit with new experiences. In the context of lament, though, the songwriter and the community cling to the telling of the community's story, often in the face of overwhelming evidence that their recollection of the story is no longer a true construction of reality. It is precisely the fact that the story no longer mirrors experience that gives the lament prayer its power. Israel's story is held up against experiences that threaten to negate it and the praying community will neither deny the reality of those experiences, nor will they distort or abandon the core story in order to reduce the dissonance between past

23. Yerushalmi, *Zakhor*, 11.
24. Ballentine, *Prayer in the Hebrew Bible*, 268–69.

and present. A primary function of lament is to place in sharp relief the tension between experienced present and remembered past, creating the possibility for present and past to be integrated. But in setting up this tension, lament also introduces the possibility that the story may be contradicted or even negated entirely. By insisting that experiences in the present be integrated with their salvation story, Israel places their core story endlessly at risk, while at the same time making possible a fresh owning of that story by each new generation.

Finding a Place in Israel's Story

The immediate threat to the supplicant in the psalms of lament is that he or she is no longer eligible to receive Yahweh's protection, provision, and deliverance. The petitioner has "fallen out of" the story of those for whom God acts to save, so that, while the story remains true, it no longer applies to the one praying. As the result of sin or sickness or some other reason that the sufferer cannot identify, he or she appears to be God-forsaken. With the loss of access to Israel's story comes the loss of the psalmist's primary approach to God in the silence.

The conclusion that the psalmist has fallen outside of Israel's story is supported not just by the circumstances of God's failure to respond and save, but by the counter-testimony of the enemies who question the psalmist's relationship with Yahweh. Such counter-testimony takes the form both of accusation ("There is no help for you in God" Ps 3:2; "Pursue and seize that person whom God has forsaken, for there is no one to deliver" Ps 71:11) and of mockery ("Commit your cause to the LORD; let him deliver—let him rescue the one in whom he delights!" Ps 22:9; "Where is your God?" Ps 42:4, 11). It is important to note that it is not just the psalmist who is at risk in such accusations, but also Yahweh. Should he continue to be silent with no sin in the life of the psalm writer that is able to account for that silence, then the accusation of the wicked and the fool that "there is no God" might be proven correct. Thus Yahweh is also asked to save the psalmist for the sake of his own name.[25] In such cases, the act of prayer is an act of lobbying for one's place in the community for which Yahweh acts to save, and memory recital is frequently accompanied by arguments intended to demonstrate that the psalmist does, in fact, still belong to that com-

25. Ps 25:11; 31:4; 79:9; 106:8; 109:21; and 143:11.

munity. Principal among the arguments used to answer the counter-testimony of the enemies are the constant hope and trust of the psalmist in Yahweh to save and vindicate.

> And my enemy will say, 'I have prevailed';
>   my foes will rejoice because I am shaken.
> But I trusted in your steadfast love;
>   my heart shall rejoice in your salvation. (Ps 13:4–5)[26]

The threat in many psalms of lament is not to the story's ultimate integrity, but rather to the supplicant's place in that story. In at least one psalm, though, the continued validity of the story itself is threatened by God's continued silence. Psalm 77 is heavily laden with remembrance. The sufferer will "consider the days of old, and remember the years of long ago." Verbs of remembering run thick in the psalm. The writer will "seek," "think," "consider," "remember," "commune," "meditate," "call to mind," "remember," "mediate," and "muse" on God's mighty saving acts. The content of the songwriter's remembrance is Yahweh's deliverance of his people from Egypt and vv. 13–20 are taken up with a recital of that core memory. Sandwiched in the midst of this stream of recollection, though, is a series of questions that raise doubts about the continued veracity of Israel's story.

> Will the Lord spurn for ever,
>   and never again be favorable:
> Has his steadfast love ceased for ever?
>   Are his promises at an end for all time?
> Has God forgotten to be gracious?
>   Has he in anger shut up his compassion? (Ps 77:7–9)

The psalmist's questioning reaches its climax in v. 10 with the conclusion, "And I say, 'It is my grief that the right hand of the Most High has changed.'"[27] Psalm 77 places in sharp relief two basic truths. First of

---

26. Cf. Pss 22:10–12; 31:14; 42:6, 12; and 71:5–6, 14.

27. The correct translation of v. 10 has been widely debated. The problem turns on the meaning of the Hebrew word *shinot*, which may be translated either as a construct plural of the noun "year" ("the years of . . ."), resulting in the somewhat softer translation "the years of the right hand" (KJV, RV), or as an infinitive construct of the verb "to change" (NRSV, JB, REB, NEB, TEV, TANAKH). The translation in the King James Version, "[but I will remember] the years of the right hand of the Most High," would require that a verb be supplied and seems motivated by a desire to take from the psalmist's mouth the devastating accusation that God has changed. The net result,

all, Yahweh cannot remain silent forever, for if he does Israel's memories will finally fade and be abandoned. The potency and relevance of memories that are trapped in the past cannot endure forever. Secondly, it is the remembered story that grants Israel the resources needed to ask such questions of Yahweh. Psalm 77 is the most dangerous of psalms. Here more clearly than anywhere else in the Psalter the writer stares into the abyss and asks the most perilous of questions, "Has the right hand [strength] of the Most High changed?" Here more boldly than in any other lament psalm, Israel's story is placed at risk. Here too, under the threat of the story's undoing, the psalm writer responds with relentless remembrance. In excruciating tension, the psalmist both asks the fearsome question, "Is it finally over?" while returning doggedly to Israel's story and challenging the conclusion to which the evidence of God's extended hiddenness has inexorably led. The approach taken by the psalmist brackets out all but two possible responses; either God will remain silent, in which case the story will finally come to an end, or he will respond anew, revitalizing and personalizing the story of his wondrous works through a fresh act of deliverance. The psalm writer consistently resists the temptation to tweak the story, leaving its more provocative elements in the past. Nor will he or she rationalize God's rejection, suggesting that it is merely apparent or offering some imagined sin that might account for it. He or she would rather risk the story's loss than its growing irrelevance. Either Yahweh is still the God who leads his people out of slavery or else his hand has truly changed.

The Importance of Risking the Story

There has been a great deal of debate among Old Testament scholars as to the extent to which Israel's core stories can be considered to be historical.[28] To a certain extent, though, the historicity question imports a series of concerns and constraints peculiar to modernity and attempts to impose them on the biblical worldview. Certainly the writers of the Bible were not engaging in writing a history in the modern sense of that

---

however, is that the questioning of vv. 8-10 does not reach its obvious conclusion and the suspicion that "God has changed" continues to be present implicitly rather than being explicitly stated. Regardless of how the word is translated, then, the question of Yahweh's continued salvation remains very much open.

28. For a discussion of the limits of modern historical approaches in addressing Old Testament issues see Perdue, *The Collapse of History*.

term. It is unlikely, for example, that an ancient writer felt that objective detachment was in and of itself a virtue in writing an historical account. Having said that, though, the psalm writers were intensely interested in what happened in the past to the extent that those events inform what may happen in the present. George Stroup has argued that it is this interest in the impact of the past on the present that helps to define the writer's understanding of these stories as history. "Christian narrative . . . is 'history' in that it attempts to interpret the past and to explain what is done in the present and expected in the future in light of the claims made about the past."[29] Israel's recollections of the past take on historical dimensions to the extent that they are seen to make historical claims on the present.

Such historical claims on the present can be seen in the way that the lament psalms appeal to Israel's story. Psalm 44 opens with praise, testifying to God's granting of military victories both to those ancestors who first took possession of the land and to the current community offering the prayer in its earlier military campaigns (vv. 1–8). Psalm 44 is, however, a lament rather than a praise psalm and those testimonies are placed in sharp contrast with the experience of the moment. On this day when Israel went out to battle they were defeated and Yahweh is the cause of that defeat. "Yet you have rejected us and abased us, and have not gone out with our armies" (Ps 44:9). Furthermore, the community affirms in vv. 17–22 their innocence and faithfulness in keeping covenant. Even if they are being dishonest or are self-deceived about their spiritual state before the Lord, "would not God discover this? For he knows the secrets of the heart." Clearly the expectation of the praying community is that God both granted victory in battles in the past and that he is able and indeed should intervene and grant victory in the present conflict. Israel's victories over the inhabitants of the land that became their own are neither spiritualized nor seen as metaphor, but are understood in an historical sense. Thus, while the stories told may not be history in the modern sense of that term, nevertheless, the whole basis of the appeal to past salvations in battle is the belief that they did happen, that God was their cause, and that he is able and should act similarly today. Put another way, while Israel's stories may not be history in the modern sense, they are nevertheless appealed to as historically true, rather than

29. Stroup, *Promise of Narrative Theology*, 92.

as myth or literary fiction. Israel's appeals to the nation's story in the context of lament require a historical referent that can, in some concrete sense, be related to the present circumstance of need.

Israel's story is not above the fray of lived experience, but can be contradicted and even rendered "untrue" by the experience of the community that tells the story. This vulnerability of Israel's story is related directly to the use to which it is put. As long as it refers only to the distant past or to an eschatological future, the tensions and apparent contradictions between the story and present experience can be negotiated with relative ease. But Israel's expectation that the story will impact on and transform the present circumstance makes attempts to rationalize any dissonance between story and experience vastly more problematic. Present experiences of dissonance bring with them the expectation that the story both can and should be re-experiencable in the present in some quantifiable way. As a result, Israel both testify to the truth of their story and tell their story in the arena of lived experience, so that the story is available for confirmation, adaptation, qualification, and even negation. This "reality testing" is essential for understanding the way in which Israel view their story, because it is only by testing the story against lived experience that the story may be affirmed to be true in an "historical" sense for each new generation that tells it.[30] Conversely, precisely because the story's truth can be tested using present experiences of God, it is also open to negation and the claim of untruth in ways that a purely fictional, metaphorical, mythical, or non-historical story would not be. By placing their story at risk historically, the people of Israel make possible both the loss and the fresh owning of their story.

While this places the story of Israel perpetually at risk from contradiction by lived experience, it also allows the story to be declared a historically "true" story. In the Psalter the truth of Israel's story is never declared to be ultimate, that is, it is never removed from the fray and placed above the possibility of contradiction and negation.[31] It never

30. John McKay has suggested that the one testifying cannot engage in the academic task of evaluating their own testimony for ". . . if this happens there is the implicit admission that witness may not be true. And there also lies a dilemma." "When the Veil is Taken Away," 38. While the task of testing belief against experience is not an objectively detached venture, and is therefore not a scholarly study in the traditional sense, nevertheless, it would be incorrect to say that the witness neither doubts nor seeks any external "proof" outside of his or her own subjective belief in the story being told.

31. Brueggemann speaks of God as being "in the fray" rather than above it and

becomes an absolute truth or a dogmatic statement. When, however, God responds to the prayer of lament in a specific situation and moment in time, so that the psalmist declares "You have answered me," he or she is able to affirm before the great assembly that "the story is true." Israel cannot and does not attempt to make a final pronouncement about the truth of their story, for in order to do that it would be necessary to remove it from the arena of life experience and to cloister it within a form of the cult that denies any concrete connection with the world outside of the temple. It is precisely because Israel insist that their story is historical and test that story against lived experience that the truth claim of that story is forever at risk and, at the same time, capable of being declared true with each new encounter with God. The prayer of lament requires that we risk abandoning a monolithic national history that is purely past and wholly unchallengeable, and invites us instead to engage in a dynamic, interactive, and growing history that is forever seeking to integrate past and present.

Walter Brueggemann locates the risk element of the story in the character of God himself. There is, he argues, a fundamental tension between God's sovereign self-regard and his covenantal regard for Israel.

> *These resolutions appear to me to be characteristically provisional and tenuous, likely to be unsettled in the next crisis, undone by the next text.* The reason for this unsettlement is not finally—speaking theologically—that Israel speaks with many voices (which it does), or that Israel cannot make up its mind (which it cannot); the unsettling quality belongs definitionally to the character of Yahweh. In my judgment, the texts permit no overall solution, because self-regard [by Yahweh] and regard for Israel are not, in the end, the same.[32]

In the midst of lament the risk remains that God, for reasons of his own, may remain silent, hidden, and unresponsive, thus allowing the story of his relationship with Israel to be negated. Without such a risk, the language of lament becomes pure rhetoric and acts as merely an introduction to praise. The testimony of the psalmist is that God will not remain silent and that his relatedness with Israel and with the one praying will

---

argues that "*the Old Testament in its theological articulation is characteristically dialectical and dialogical, and not transcendentalist.*" *Theology of the Old Testament*, 83.

32. Brueggemann, *Theology of the Old Testament*, 303.

have the last word. But testimony is not certainty and the element of risk and doubt can never be laid fully aside while God remains silent.

Establishing the historicity of Israel's stories in a modern sense of that term will always be problematic and is ultimately a misplaced goal. For the psalmist the only "resolution" which can salvage the story placed radically at risk by circumstance is a response from God. Indeed, even if it could be proven that the ancient stories are "historically" true, that would be of little interest to the psalm writer unless God acts again in the present. The songwriter is dealing with two historical contexts, that of the story and that of present experience. The latter challenges and places at risk the former. Because the story is cast as an historical one, the lament places the veracity of the story, the identity that Israel draws from it, and the understanding of reality that they construct out of it profoundly at risk. But it is also true that as the story is risked, the community's connection with the story is kept dynamic and immediate, and the story is granted the prospect of a future impact. Only as Israel remembers their past, holding both themselves and God accountable to it, can a present with God be realized and a future with him imagined.

While the psalms of lament explore and place at risk Israel's founding story, in the wisdom tradition it is principally the moral order of the covenant world as it is constructed by the Mosaic law that is placed at risk through the offering of prayers of lament. Job is staunchly committed to a moral order in which Yahweh blesses the righteous and punishes the wicked, to the point where it becomes the defining feature of his life. But Yahweh abruptly and decisively dismantles that moral world, leaving Job with a basic choice. He can cling doggedly to a moral order that no longer fits his experience of God or he can risk the permanent loss of that order as he confronts God with his lament. In the chapter that follows we will consider the laments of Job that both call for the abandonment of any and all mechanical formulas that explain God's moral dealings with his creation and risk a far more dynamic and uncertain foundation for moral order, namely an encounter with the one who "destroys with no reason," calls the innocent sufferer to account for himself, and restores the fortunes of the one who has lost everything. As with the lament psalms, lament in Job risks a move from the monolithic and static certainty of dogma to the dynamic and flexible uncertainty of fresh encounter.

4

Risking the World in Job

On August 29, 2005, Hurricane Katrina slammed into the gulf coast of the United States. The sixth strongest Atlantic hurricane to date, it breeched the levees protecting New Orleans, flooding 80% of the city. By the time it dissipated, Katrina had caused $75 billion dollars worth of damage and had killed some 1,600 people. New Orleans mayor Ray Nagin echoed the sentiments of some, while outraging others, when he declared that the destruction of the city demonstrated that "God is mad at America."[1]

When God Refuses to Play by the Rules

FOR SOME PERSONS OF FAITH, ATTRIBUTING WHAT WOULD OTHERWISE be meaningless suffering and loss to God serves to preserve a sense of order and security in what can otherwise be a chaotic and frightening world. For others, though, connecting disasters, both natural and manmade, with the hand of God seems silly, blasphemous, and even dangerous. That God would torment and kill the innocent in order to punish the wicked or to deliver some message to the rest of us who have escaped that suffering assumes both a cruelty on God's part and an inability to communicate more directly and less destructively. Such assumptions tempt us to divination, so that we examine history in the same way that pagan priests gaze at the stars, read color patterns on the surface of pools of oil, and study the entrails of sacrificed animals in order to discern the minds of the gods. God becomes the immedi-

---

1. In his speech on January 16, 2006 marking Martin Luther King Jr. Day, Nagin went on to tie the expression of God's judgment in the destruction caused by hurricane Katrina to his displeasure with the U.S. war in Iraq and with the political disunity and violence rampant within black communities.

ate cause of every effect, while remaining unable or unwilling to speak directly and plainly to his creation.

Many of the same persons of faith who would deny God's involvement in the suffering of the innocent would nevertheless acknowledge that God interacts with his creation and that he involves himself in their lives. God sees and hears, speaks and acts, saves and judges. How, though, are we to understand the form and scope of his involvement? Is God the direct cause of every event in history? Can he ever be said to be directly involved in any event in history? If God can and does act to save one person or to bring judgment on another, why does he not act similarly for everyone? Is the God who can and does save one innocent person in some way responsible for letting others die, or worse yet, for causing their death with a saturation bombing approach to judgment? Is God's judgment in history little more than a cosmic drive-by shooting where the innocent are as likely to die as are the intended targets of his wrath. To maintain that God acts or speaks directly even one time within the confines of our world and experience is to open the floodgate. If God has ever caused one earthquake, brought rain to one drought stricken land, protected one person in an automobile accident, engineered the downfall of one dictator, fed one starving widow, then it becomes reasonable, even expedient to ask, "Why here but not there?" "Why some but not all?" "Who has sinned that God should remain silent as these little ones die?"

The belief that God is in some way involved in the catastrophes of life rests on two basic assumptions. The first of these is that God takes an active hand in the day-to-day running of the universe, so that both blessings and curses can be traced to his intervention. Rejected is the deist argument that God has set up the world to function like a giant machine, according to divine laws and eternal principles, so that he is no longer involved in the running of the cosmos and any "malfunction" of the machine can be traced unfailingly to the human operators' error. Secondly, such a belief assumes that God's actions follow some logical, discernable, predictable pattern. If the good creator is still actively involved with his creation, then life is not, as Elbert Hubbard has suggested, just one damn thing after another, but reflects a divine will and purpose. Apart from the assumptions that God has established and maintains some form of moral order in his creation, the prayer of lament is invalidated.

> Trust that the world is orderly, then, divides believer from skeptic. Lament is the province only of the believer, because it shatters that trust. Without hope, one cannot lament, for there is no meaningful pattern to life to be disrupted. Lament is the outraged cry of the believer when anticipated order collapses.[2]

Lament becomes irrelevant in a world bereft of God and unnecessary in a world where God's moral order functions predictably and reliably.

In the Mosaic covenant God's actions to bless and to curse are tied to the keeping of the covenant. Faithfulness toward God and the practice of justice and mercy toward neighbor will result in God's blessing, while abandoning the true God to follow after idols and withholding compassion from the widow, the orphan, and the foreigner will result in God's curse.

> If you will only obey the LORD your God, by diligently observing all his commandments that I am commanding you today . . . Blessed shall you be in the city, and blessed shall you be in the field. Blessed shall be the fruit of your womb, the fruit of your ground, and the fruit of your livestock, both the increase of your cattle and the issue of your flock. Blessed shall be your basket and your kneading-bowl. Blessed shall you be when you come in, and blessed shall you be when you go out . . . But if you will not obey the LORD your God by diligently observing all his commandments and decrees, which I am commanding you today . . . Cursed shall you be in the city, and cursed shall you be in the field . . . (Deut 28:1, 3–6, 15–16)

Such things as storms may be a natural part of the order and balance of the cosmos, but at least on some occasions their severity and effect are overseen by a sovereign God, so that Jonah's ill advised attempt to evade the divine commission by fleeing on a ship was thwarted when Yahweh "hurled a great wind upon the sea, and such a mighty storm came upon the sea that the ship threatened to break up" (Jonah 1:4). If God manipulates the weather to suit his purposes then the devastation wrought by hurricane Katrina prompts such questions as, "Why would a God who could intervene to save choose not to?" "What have we done to merit such harsh treatment from an otherwise merciful and generous

---

2. Charry, "May We Trust God and (Still) Lament? Can We Lament and (Still) Trust God?" 96.

God?" and "Is New Orleans more wicked and more deserving of God's judgment than other cities?"

The wisdom teaching of the book of Proverbs expands and builds upon the deuteronomic principle of God's retributive justice and places even greater emphasis on human choices and actions. According to proverbial wisdom, there are things that we can do and things that we can avoid which both promote blessings in our lives and help us to avoid curses. This emphasis adds a third assumption to our understanding of the working of God's justice, namely that it is essentially responsive in nature. Walter Brueggemann points to the wisdom tradition's tendency to place responsibility for life's outcomes firmly in human hands. "The clear affirmation of wisdom is that human choices fix human destiny."[3] Far from being the unwitting victims of a mysterious and maliciously capricious God, we find in the biblical tradition a strong current that moves us toward personal accountability and empowerment. The administration of God's justice in Proverbs is essentially reactive in nature, so that while he may be the judge, we determine through our choices the sentence that we receive. These, then, are the assumptions with which we arrive at Job's doorstep, that God's interaction with his creatures extends beyond that first act of creation and into our daily lives, that God's actions and choices are neither haphazard nor cruel, but conform to his righteousness and wisdom, and that, at least in the broader landscape of our lives, we receive from him what we have earned.

This understanding of the world and the way that God works within it are, however, placed fundamentally at risk by Job's experiences. The book of Job overturns the conviction that the justice of Yahweh is invariably responsive, being tied unfailingly to our own moral choices and actions. The book of Job does not relinquish the conviction that God is directly involved in the experiences that impact our lives for good or for ill, but does question whether God will allow himself to be held to the conditions of the covenant that he himself imposes on his human partners and that describe the terms of his relationship with them. The writer of Job insists that Yahweh both visits calamity on his creatures and that his choices need have little to do with whether they deserve such affliction.

---

3. Brueggemann, *In Man We Trust*, 20.

Of particular relevance to our study is the observation that Job responds to the shaking of his world with a cry of lament. His laments repeatedly assert his innocence and call for justice. Through the practice of lament, Job seeks to make sense of his experiences of loss, to call God to give an account of his actions, and to rebuild his lost world. While Job's friends busy themselves with a defense of orthodox doctrine and a stable world, insisting that Job's experience conform to their belief, Job is forced by the extremity of his loss to turn loose of the world as he has always known it to be. He is compelled to discard a moral world in which God's justice can ever operate as a principle that is independent from his relatedness. He risks the loss of a moral order that is abstracted and generalized into "moral laws," and thereby is predictable and "guaranteed," and he risks gaining a moral order that is forever open and dynamic because God, the moral agent, has not withdrawn himself from active participation in its construction.

The Book that Refuses to Fit

The principal teachings of the biblical canon would look dramatically different where the book of Job to be excluded from its pages. The writer provides an invasive and enduring "Yes, but . . ." to the biblical story, casting doubt on our ability to formulate a coherent and consistent picture of God from the Bible. Statements about God's goodness, his power, his sovereignty, his wisdom, his trustworthiness, and his justice are all qualified by Job's experience. Notions of faithful speech about God are turned on their head. The orthodox defense of God's justice offered by Job's friends is decidedly overturned, while Job's near blasphemous assaults on the goodness and justice of God are first overwhelmed by the vast scale of God's sovereign power as creator, only to be resurrected and exalted as "right speech" by God at the close of the book. Almost single handedly this one story transforms the shape of biblical theology, standing as it does over against both the dominant portrayal of God's righteousness and the Sinai covenant that guides the faith community in righteous living. It is amazing that so disruptive a book should have found an enduring place in the Hebrew canon.

The problems inherent in formulating a coherent interpretation of Job and integrating it into the larger teachings of the Hebrew canon are both numerous and complex. To begin with, the book staunchly resists every attempt to discern a single, consistent, and lucid message. Some sections appear to be very much at odds with the larger whole, undermining and even threatening to contradict the writer's dominant themes. Most attempts to articulate a central message for the book require that some portions of it being de-emphasized or excluded altogether.[4] Beginning already with the writer of James, the Job tradition has been mined selectively, with some valued nuggets of insight being brought to the surface while others have been left buried and forgotten. "You have heard," says James, "of the endurance of Job, and you have seen the purpose of the Lord, how the Lord is compassionate and merciful" (Jas 5:11). In the body of the book of Job, though, we learn that his endurance was not in the acceptance of his suffering, as James implies, but rather in his efforts to win from God an accounting. "See, he will kill me; I have no hope;" says Job, "but I will defend my ways to his face" (Job 13:15).[5] A Job who patiently endures suffering cannot be found beyond the close of the second chapter. Similarly, as an example of the compassion and mercy of God, the book of Job is a conspicuous failure. Such attributes can be found only in the final chapter of the book as Yahweh restores Job's fortunes, and only there as long as the reader forgets both that it was God who robbed Job in the first place and that, short of resurrecting Job's dead children, true restoration is still lacking. The patient, long suffering Job who serves a merciful and compassionate God are images that can be found only through a highly selective reading of the book.

The exegetical pendulum, though, has swung decidedly in the opposite direction as more recently biblical scholars have focused attention and found value in the defiant and outspoken Job at the books center, while tending to devalue the more traditional portrait found in the introduction and conclusion to the book. David Clines exemplifies this latter trend.

4. Terrence W. Tilley provides a careful discussion of the vexing inconsistencies in the theology found in Job and of the choices made by many commentators explicitly or implicitly to focus on a canon within the canon of Job, sacrificing comprehensiveness for consistency. "God and the Silence of Job."

5. The King James Version offers a softer reading of this verse; "Though he slay me, yet will I trust him: but I will maintain mine own ways before him." But this in no way alters Job's defensive tone throughout the chapter. For a concise discussion of the issues relevant to translating 13:15, see Francis I. Andersen, *Job*, 166–67.

> We may distinguish between the *framework* of the book and its
> *core* or *center*, using the image of a painting surrounded by a
> frame . . . The *framework* of the book is *prose*, the *core* is *poetry*;
> and since the framework is naive (or so it seems) and the core is
> sophisticated, the distinction between the relatively cheap and
> unimportant frame of a painting and the painting itself sounds
> a convincing analogy.[6]

Regardless of whether we see Job as a rebel or a patient saint, then, a consistent, fluid reading of the characters of both Job and God seems possible only when the material is approached selectively.

As the above examples suggest, the most jarringly obvious contrast can be seen between the prose frame of the book (chapters 1–2; 42:7–17) and its poetic core (chapters 3–41). "The chief dissonantal feature of Job," says David Penchansky, "is the shocking disparity between the frame . . . and the center."[7] In a similar vein, Bruce Zuckerman suggests that "Like oil and water, the Prose Frame Story and the Poem naturally tend to disengage from one another despite all efforts to homogenize them."[8] The Job that we meet in the frame is radically different from the Job of the main body of the work, resulting in the belief among a number of biblical scholars that the prose frame represents a much older tradition that was adopted and adapted by the narrator to supply a counterpoint to the main body of his argument.[9] In the prose narrative that now provides the frame for the book, Job is presented as a pious man of seemingly endless patience in the face horrific tragedy and testing. When, with a fourfold stroke, he is bereft by the satan of wealth and family, he responds stoically; "Naked I came from my mother's womb, and naked shall I return there; the LORD gave, and the LORD has taken away; blessed be the name of the LORD." When he is robbed of his

6. Clines, "The Shape and Argument of the Book of Job," 126.

7. Penchansky, *The Betrayal of God*, 27.

8. Zuckerman, *Job the Silent*, 14.

9. Hartley, *The Book of Job*, 64. Perdue, "Wisdom in the Book of Job," 81. Not all scholars, however, agree that the disjunction between the prose and poetic portions of the book is complete. Robert W. E. Forrest, for example, has pointed to the shared themes of "skin," "wholeness/integrity," and "cursing" in order to argue for a theological unity between chapter three and the prose prologue. "The Two Faces of Job: Imagery and Integrity in the Prologue." Gordis argues on literary and linguistic grounds that the origin of the prose frame was post-exilic and, therefore, contemporary with the writing of the poetic center. *The Book of Job*, 25–26.

health, prodded by persistent pain, and tempted by his wife to curse God and die, he responds simply "Shall we receive the good at the hand of God, and not receive the bad?" Chapter 3, though, marks a dramatic shift in both the form and the content of Job's speech. Changing to poetry, he begins with an extended curse of the day of his birth, followed by a string of increasingly bitter complaints that challenge the justice of God's acts. He accuses God of ignoring justice and seeks to bring the Lord of the universe to trial for his actions.

Carol Newsom argues that the contrast between prose frame and poetic body is intentional and that the prose frame colors our reading of the book's core.

> More likely, what we have is no more or no less than what the author of the whole book of Job wrote. But the prose tale has been crafted in order to create something analogous to an optical illusion. Just as there are some drawings in which the eye can "see" a line that is not drawn on the page but that is necessary to complete the figure, so readers can perceive the outlines of the missing middle of the prose tale. The illusion created, that what has been displaced is the mirror image of the extant dialogue between Job and his friends, is a part of the overall strategy of the book.[10]

The presence of the Job of the prologue can be felt throughout the book over against the probing, questioning Job of the book's core. Whether penned by a single author, as Newsom suggests, or later selected and joined by an editor, the two most distinct portions of Job are characterized by contrast, even contradiction.

Claus Westermann points out that traces of the pious Job of faith can be found even amidst his laments and protests. He calls attention to confessions of trust offered by Job in 16:19–21 and 19:25–27, arguing that Job's expressions of faith and doubt do not exist in separate sections of the book, but characterize a tension that is sustained throughout. "This is the solution to the two faces of Job. The pious, humble man, submissive to God's will, and the desperate man who resists God—these are one and the same person, in touch with both possibilities."[11]

There is also a sense of disjointedness within the extended poetic dialogue. The characters seem at times to talk past one another. Job's

---

10. Newsom, *The Book of Job*, 37.

11. Westermann, "The Two Faces of Job," 21–22.

friends continually insist that his external state is a mirror of his spiritual condition, while Job concerns himself with access to Yahweh who is denying him justice. What is more, God's "answer" to Job, when it comes, is no answer at all. Job is never let in on the narrator's secret, that his sufferings are a test resulting from a wager between God and the satan. In his speeches in chapters 38–41, God pointedly ignores Job's questions, instead cross-examining him to determine his fitness even to understand the questions that should be asked, much less any answers that God might be prepared to offer. Instead of addressing the reason for Job's suffering or his doubts about God's justice, Job is overwhelmed by a barrage of declarations about the mystery of God as creator and his unquestioned dominance and power. The God who slew dozens of innocent people simply to settle a bet with an underling now comes across as a cosmic bully, hammering a dazed and demoralized Job with volley after volley of unanswerable questions.

Along with these inconsistencies in structure and character, the book of Job also introduces a baffling array of seemingly unanswerable questions. The relationship between Yahweh and the satan which opens the narrative, for example, is extremely puzzling. The satan is not the leader of angelic forces in open rebellion against God that we meet in the New Testament, but is one of God's servants. God provokes him to focus unfriendly attention on Job by asking "Have you considered by servant Job?" The satan then seems to manipulate God into a wager that will destroy lives and happiness. God himself admits both that he was goaded by the satan to destroy Job and that he does so "for no reason" (Job 2:3). Who is this satan who can so easily provoke God and who is this God who would destroy people for no reason? Equally odd is the satan's disappearance from the narrative after he has initiated the conditions of Job's test. There is no heavenly court scene in the epilogue to balance that in the book's prologue. The satan does not reappear and there is no mention of God having won his bet. Having served his purpose in setting the stage, the satan seems no longer to be of interest to the narrator. How are we to understand the role of the satan? Does he in any way shield Yahweh from responsibility for striking down the innocent without cause or does God, in fact, come off looking worse as a result of his dealings with the satan?

Among the most impenetrable statements in the book is the condemnation by Yahweh of Job's friends. They have consistently offered an explanation for Job's sufferings that reflects the covenant theology of the book of Deuteronomy and the wisdom perspective of the book of Proverbs. The content of their theology of God is orthodox and can appeal widely to both scripture and tradition for support. Nevertheless, Yahweh says to Eliphaz, "My wrath is kindled against you and against your two friends; for you have not spoken of me what is right, as my servant Job has" (Job 42:7). The orthodox theology of the friends has somehow missed the mark, while the near blasphemous attacks by Job on God are seen by him as "right speech." How can teachings with such a solid biblical basis be condemned by God as wrong speech and how can God first condemn Job for "darkening counsel by words without knowledge" and then commend him for "speaking of me what is right"?

There is also something deeply unsatisfying about the ending of the book. We are told that "the LORD restored the fortunes of Job when he had prayed for his friends; and the LORD gave Job twice as much as he had before." This "reward" for Job's faithfulness undermines the principal message of the book in two ways. First of all, having demonstrated by his faithfulness through the most extreme sufferings that he does not serve the Lord for what he can get out of it, Job is now given a material reward. Also this "happy ending" to the book rings somewhat hollow in its presumption that Yahweh can somehow replace what he has taken. No amount of material blessing and additional offspring, though, can restore even one of Job's dead children. Job surely bore to his grave the scares of his encounter with the God who tests and destroys "for no reason." How can we understand the goodness and justice of a God who first robs and then tries to pay back this "blameless and upright man who fears God and turns away from evil"?

This treacherous array of cross-currents and eddies makes any straightforward answer to the problems that Job places before us come across as simplistic and forced. The book of Job is characterized by an enduring tension. Westermann is critical of any approach that seeks to dissolve this tension through creative editing or an appeal to earlier sources. While acknowledging that the prose portion may well have an earlier origin, he points out that the tension in Job results from the joining of frame and body.

> Distinguishing two authors does nothing, however, to solve the problem: it merely postpones a solution. Supposing that this

theory of two originals is correct, who then is responsible for joining the narrative to the drama? If it is the work of an editor, he must have considered this conjunction to be theologically feasible. It is probable that the author of the Job drama himself set it in this narrative framework, as the end of the book, in particular, suggests. In that case the author of the drama both recognised and intended the opposition between drama and narrative.[12]

Similarly, in speaking of the inconsistencies and seeming contradictions in Job's views about the fate of the wick in his third speech, Carol Newsom points out that "to attribute it [the inconsistency] to scribal error is to evade rather than to acknowledge the issues."[13] Speculating about the pre-history of the resulting story does nothing to address the tension that has resulted from the joining of diverse elements that, by themselves, are far more coherent. Westermann both argues that the dissonance inherent in the book of Job is the result of an intentional decision on the part of either the author or the final editor and that it reflects a dissonance often encountered in life. "This is why the author of the Book of Job was not faced with an irreconcilable contradiction. Certainly he was aware of the opposition, but he saw it as one often met with in human life."[14] The messiness of the book of Job, then, does not result from a confused author or inept editor, but from lived experience's inherent resistance to theological codification. Job would not alter his experience of suffering to make it conform to any theological construct, not even one to which he remained deeply committed.

More recent scholarship has sought to honor the complexities and native tension so central to Job. David Penchansky argues that the discordant elements within the book provide the best key for understanding it. He suggests a dissonantal reading that seeks to bring the primary meaning of the text to the surface by focusing interpretive attention on points of literary conflict. "The act of focusing literature around the dissonant structural features is the reconstruction of the text."[15] Central to Penchansky's understanding is the notion of Job's integrity. It is integ-

---

12. Ibid., 15. Karl Kautzsch first makes this point in his book *Das sogenannte Volksbuch von Hiob*. See also Brenner, "Job the Pious?"

13. Newsom, *The Book of Job*, 88.

14. Westermann, "Two Faces of Job," 17.

15. Penchansky, *The Betrayal of God*, 19.

rity and not piety that drives Job to reject the version of religious belief
offered by his friends and to challenge God's justice.

> Integrity in Job concerns honest speech . . . But what if it is not
> honest to restrain one's curses of God? . . . Now integrity is held
> *against* God; integrity means asserting one's innocence, not
> God's innocence. In the frame Job is on trial, and to maintain
> his integrity he must not curse God. In the center God is on
> trial, and for Job to maintain his integrity, he must continue to
> assert his innocence, and God's guilt.[16]

Job refuses to compromise his integrity by flattening his experience
so that it conforms with pious belief. For Penchansky, the book was
produced by a number of authors over time. He identifies the source of
dissonance in Job with the changing social realities of the various interpretive communities that contributed to the formation of the book.
Thus, the dissonances within the book reflect the divergent experiences
and contexts of successive contributing communities.

Bruce Zuckerman also understands the complexity of the book to
result from its multilayered composition. A core story is overlaid with
successive traditions that challenge and refine that original tale, rather
than simply superceding it. Zuckerman adopts the metaphor of a musi-
cal fugue to describe the resulting interplay of themes, each one distinct,
even discordant, and yet woven together into an harmonious whole.

> It may be appropriate to see (or hear) the book of Job—built,
> as it is, over time—as not unlike a fugue. The tradition begins
> with one theme; then, as time goes on, another theme is scored
> on top of it, thereby forcing the original theme to take on a new
> harmonic role; then further themes are added in succession,
> again requiring the themes that precede to give way and take
> a different role from what their authors might have originally
> intended. In this respect, the Joban fugue is less predictable and
> more adversarial than its musical counterpart.[17]

Writers such as James, then, are free to pick up and emphasize those
strands of the music that best fit their context and need. The result
is a piece that is far more flexible and applicable in a multiplicity of
circumstances. Zuckerman's metaphor is, however, somewhat limited.

16. Ibid., 47.
17. Zuckerman, *Job the Silent*, 178.

A fugue weaves together a number of distinct themes. In order to do so successfully, the resulting composition must find a common thread that will bind the various themes together with a degree of coherence. Zuckerman's suggestion gives insufficient weight to the more sharply dissonant elements of the book, such as God both condemning (38:2) and commending (42:7) Job's speech. Also his suggestion that the fugue may be dismembered at will and applied piecemeal to new circumstances suggests that the story of Job, with all its complexity and dissonance, is really nothing more than the sum of its parts; a convenient container that can be disposed of at will.

Carol Newsom concludes that it is simply not possible to reconstruct the history of the formation of the book of Job, so that any attempt at reconstruction is little more than the advocacy of one reading strategy over another.

> We will never know in fact how the book of Job came to be. The various accounts of its composition are valuable not so much as historical reconstructions as suggestions for different ways of reading the book. These accounts are heuristic fictions, invitations to read the book "as if" it had come into being in this or that fashion, with the intents and purposes characteristic of such an origin.[18]

She suggests that Job be understood as a dialogue in which the author plays host to a variety of perspectives, each offering a distinctive "moral imagination." In the resulting "polyphonic" conversation, the author of Job regularly shifts genre in order to signal the introduction of a fresh moral imagination. The object of such a reading is not to provide a fixed answer or final closure, but to offer a platform for expressing a diversity of experiences and perspectives in an open and ongoing dialogue. Newsom identifies her own approach with the post-modern, reader-response interpretations offered by Edwin Good and David Clines.[19] Unlike Good and Clines, though, rather than deconstructing the text in search of minority voices that have been suppressed by the dominant ideology of the author, she uses an analysis of genre to bring those voices into the conversation as full participants.

---

18. Newsom, *The Book of Job*, 16.

19. Good, *In Turns of Tempest*; and Clines, "Deconstructing the Book of Job."

Without doubt reading strategies that account for the full range of ideas and make room for the sustained tensions within the book are preferable. As we shall see in the next section, key to Job's ability to maintain such tensions is his use of lament. Within the context of lament Job is able to balance his belief in an ordered world and his experience of chaos.

The Laments of Job

Traditionally the book of Job has been classified as wisdom literature. A piece of writing is identified with the wisdom tradition by its use of typical wisdom forms and/or by addressing common wisdom themes. In the case of Job, its designation as wisdom writing has more to do with the themes[20] addressed in the book than with the use of specific wisdom forms.[21] As in the book of Proverbs, Job is concerned with the choices that a person makes and the way that those choices effect their life. The pursuit of wisdom in Proverbs has as its goal a full, prosperous, and happy life. The key to contentment is found in a person's handling of relationships with family, friends, and the community at large. Job's friends assume that his sufferings result from some failure in these core relationships. Job also subscribes to proverbial wisdom and bases his defense almost entirely on his righteous actions in the horizontal relationships with his neighbors and most particularly with the weak and vulnerable. As is characteristic of wisdom writing, he has less to say about his faithfulness in his vertical relationship with God. In chapter 31, for example, Job makes a vow of innocence before God which consists entirely of a cataloguing of his relationships. Of the forty verses, thirty-four speak directly to his relationships with people. Only vv. 26–28 make mention of his faithfulness in his relationship to God by avoiding idolatry, while in vv. 38–40 he asserts that he has been a faithful steward of the land that has been entrusted to him. Job's primary argument is that he has acted righteously toward his own family, his neighbors, and most particularly toward the widow, orphan, slave, and

20. Such themes as divine rewards and punishments for our actions, fidelity to family, honesty in business practices, creation, the fear of the Lord, and care for the poor are all frequent wisdom themes. For a discussion of the wisdom themes found in Job, see Perdue, "Wisdom in the Book of Job."

21. A useful overview of wisdom forms can be found in Murphy, *The Tree of Life*, 7–13.

foreigner. The Book of Job sits at the center of wisdom's concern for managing relationships in ways that promote fullness and contentment, both for the individual and for the community as a whole. The problem, of course, is that Job's experience threatens to overturn the moral order of the community. Job is willing to evaluate his beliefs in light of this experience, whereas his friends continually insist that experience be reinterpreted, even denied, so that it not conflict with sound doctrine.

The author of Job uses a wide variety of literary forms, including some that are common to wisdom literature and many that are not. Norman Habel suggests that the complex mixture of forms reflects and helps to articulate the tension and ambiguity that are inherit in the story.

> Traditional forms are incorporated, adapted, and transcended through the integration of curses, disputation, lament, trial speeches, wisdom poems, and hymnic materials into an underlying narrative plot. Plot and dialogue interact in a complex structure. Their interaction highlights counterpoint and controversy, ambiguity and audacity in the account of a mortal struggling to discover the meaning of life in the face of tradition, experience, and faith.[22]

The writer's use of diverse forms mirrors and even adds to the conflict at the heart of the story.

By focusing on an analysis of form, Claus Westermann has concluded that the dominant form adopted by Job is not one of those typically associated with wisdom literature, but rather the lament. He identifies laments in all but the last of Job's six speeches, as well as in his introductory and concluding remarks in chapters 3 and 29–31.[23] Westermann's observation illustrates the way that our assumptions about form can shape and even pre-determine our understanding of meaning. The book of Job has traditionally been thought of as wisdom literature and has frequently been understood as wrestling with the problems of evil and innocent suffering. As a result, biblical commentators have focused on the derivative and more abstract questions raised

---

22. Habel, *The Book of Job*, 45. The central argument of Carol Newsom's commentary on Job is that the book's author utilizes distinct genre's to signal the bringing together of divergent viewpoints in the ongoing dialogue developed by the book; Newsom, *The Book of Job*, 16–17.

23. Westermann, *The Structure of the Book of Job*, 31.

as a result of Job's experience, rather than on the crisis with which Job himself is struggling, namely, a crisis of relationship. This has led to the tendency to cast the central message of the book in abstract, theological terms. "This book deals with the theoretical problem of pain and disaster in the life of the godly."[24] "The book of Job is concerned with the problem of the suffering of righteous people, which is part of what we today should call the 'problem of evil.'"[25] "Human suffering is the age-old problem discussed in the Book of Job."[26] "The book raises one of the most perplexing questions facing men and women: Are God's ways just? This is the question of theodicy."[27] "As for the book's purpose, it clearly wishes to discover a solution to the age-long problem of unmerited suffering."[28] "The quest of the wise to interpret reality, suffering, and the order of things is integrated with a struggle to understand the quest itself and the God who launched them on that quest."[29] This approach to understanding the central thrust of the book suggests that the basic problem is a lack of understanding, so that principal enterprise of the writer is to find an answer to a question or the solution to a problem. While this is certainly an interest of the author, Westermann's observation suggests that the search for intellectual satisfaction is secondary. Lament speaks to a relationship gone wrong and seeks restoration ahead of information. And indeed, while the narrator provides the reader with at least a partial answer, Job is left with only the voice from the whirlwind, a voice that offers no clear explanation for his suffering.

For Job the center of the book is not a theological question, but an experiential and relational crisis. According to Gerhard von Rad, "what concerned Job above all else was the credibility of God."[30] Kathleen O'Connor affirms that "The real subject of the Book of Job and the crux of the human problem for Israel is not human suffering, but human relationship with God in the midst of suffering."[31] Job does not apply himself directly to the problem of innocent suffering or the ambigu-

24. Archer, *A Survey of Old Testament Introduction*, 503.

25. Hinson, *The Books of the Old Testament*, 104.

26. Schultz, *The Old Testament Speaks*, 279.

27. Dillard and Longman, *An Introduction to the Old Testament*, 199.

28. John Gibson, *Job*, 3.

29. Habel, *The Book of Job*, 60.

30. Von Rad, *Wisdom in Israel*, 221.

31. O'Connor, *The Wisdom Literature*, 104.

ity of God's justice. These are questions better asked and wrestled with from a safe distance when the crisis has passed and the need is less immediate. Job is confronted with a crisis of trust; trust in the goodness of God, trust in the orderliness of his created world, trust that God is, in fact, trustworthy. Thus, the more immediate question is not "Can I understand this God?" but rather "Can I still trust this God?"[32]

Job's friends, on the other hand, are engaged in the defense of a theological position. They do not, however, bear the central message of the book and in the end prove to be little more than a conventional foil for Job's words. Job's speech is characterized less by argument and reason than by lament. Thus, like ships passing in the night, the resulting conversations between Job and his three friends draw near to, but ultimately miss one another. While the former is expressing his pain and experience of abandonment, the latter are concerned with maintaining a doctrinal position that is insulated from the impact of experience.

> The most important element in the speeches of the friends is something quite different. They alone advance arguments in their speeches; in Job's speeches—except for one at the end, as we shall see—the lament stands in the place of the argument. This incongruity between the speeches of the friends and the speeches of Job is the most noticeable and also the most important structural clue in the book . . . Throughout the whole dialogue section there is this juxtaposition of doctrine and lament. The doctrine, which comes directly out of tradition but is now rigidified, stands over against the burning lament, which arises directly out of an existential anguish. The lament finds no hearing and elicits no consolation; the doctrine ricochets off the reality of pain. Thus the disputation must run its course without resolution; only the high court can decide.[33]

Ironically, many traditional readings of Job have allowed the speeches of the friends, rather than those of Job, to set the agenda and determine the central meaning of the book. To approach the book of Job as a detached doctrinal treatise dressed up in a colorful story is to misinterpret its core message. Job is not concerned with a doctrinal contradiction, but rather with a fundamental betrayal of trust.

---

32. See Charry, "May We Trust God and (Still) Lament?" 95–108.

33. Westermann, *The Structure of Job*, 5.

> If we ignore the fact that these complaints embody a man's tor-
> ment, if we make them into general, timeless, abstract statements
> about God, we shall have misunderstood them fundamentally.
> This is what Job's friends do. They are putting forward a time-
> less, abstract teaching about God. According to this teaching,
> what Job says about God in his complaints is wicked. They must
> condemn him. But nothing of what Job says in his complaint
> to God about his suffering can be torn from its context without
> radically altering its meaning.[34]

Whereas Job's friends seek to insulate their understanding of God from
experience, Job is able, through the practice of lament, to re-examine
his most deeply held beliefs about God in light of new experiences of
God and to explore places in his relationship with God that his friends
are unwilling and unable to enter. Job is able to press forward into the
heart of God's silence and hiddenness. As with lament in the Psalms,
the root problem here is not the circumstance per se, for circumstances
can change, but the threat to relation posed both by God's silence and
by his culpability. Much more forcefully than in the Psalms, Job exam-
ines the notion of God as enemy.[35]

André Neher has explored the generally overlooked use of silence
in scripture. Silence, he argues, communicates as much and sometimes
more than does speech. He distinguishes between dialogue and other
kinds of speech, noting that dialogue is characterized by both speech
and silence. It requires both an act of aggression and an act of surrender
as each party speaks and then falls silent while the other speaks. "Every
dialogue, then, implies an aggression, an [sic.] renunciation, a death
to oneself, and an absolute silence, which are attitudes preliminary to
opening up, to communication, to dialogue, to life-within-dialogue, and
to love."[36] Dialogue also offers the prospect of new speech as two distinct
individuals offer their own contributions and move toward a synthesis
that exceeds the sum of its parts. "'Then true dialogue would be not
only the interchange of two consciousnesses, the inter-communication
of two mental worlds, it would be the sacrifice of two partners ready

34. Westermann, "The Two Faces of Job," 19.

35. Crenshaw states it even more plainly: "What all this adds up to is easily expressed in a single sentence: Job thinks God has become a personal enemy." *A Whirlpool
of Torment*, 68.

36. Neher, *The Exile of the Word*, 48.

to throw themselves open to the creation."[37] The silence of God in the book of Job, then, far from indicating that God is disengaged and un-interested, carries with it an invitation to genuine dialogue. The silence of God makes room for and invites Job to offer authentic expression, an invitation that Job accepts, reluctantly at first, but then with increasing passion as the narrative progresses and God's silence is prolonged. Job's friends, on the other hand, are not engaging in dialogue, for they already know the "right answers" before they speak and are not open to genuine exchange or to the possibility of change. Consequently, there is no need for them to address God as Job does. Neher calls this type of speech declaration, rather than dialogue. Declaration implies both a mindless repetition and a guaranteed outcome.

> And this is just how theologians and catechetical—or dare I say clerical and petty-bourgeois—readings interpret dialogue in the Bible. Covenant between the divine Word and the human may indeed pass through dangerous phases, know critical moments, and even suffer the agonies of dying and even death itself; but all this is only a passing episode, a piece learned by rote, whose narrators know that it will be followed, through an absolute inner necessity, by a celebration for which all was prepared in advance and which will compensate death by resurrection, suffering by beatitude, and this present world by the next.[38]

Job is engaged in real dialogue. He both offers and experiences silence,[39] he sacrifices himself, i.e., his comfortable, established understanding of the world, and he is open to the possibility of newness and change. By desiring to engage God in dialogue, Job opens himself to the possibility that those things that he has believed and declared about God might be changed or even lost entirely. Job's great courage is manifest in his unwillingness simply to declare the expected and accepted answers in light of a new experience of God, allowing faithful speech to degenerate into blind dogma. He refuses simply to read from the prepared script, as

---

37. Raymond Carpentier, "L'échec de la communication," cited by Neher, *The Exile of the Word,* 49.

38. Neher, *Exile of the Word,* 49.

39. Job's silence is most easily seen in the wordlessness shared with his friends for the first seven days of their visit, but Job also grows increasingly silent toward God after his speech reaches a climax of invitation in chapter 13.

his friends are doing, and he does not know ahead of time how the story will end. Lament grants Job admission to a dialogue with God.

Job Spoke What Was Right to God

The book of Job is predominantly about speech. Job's sufferings have tempted him to silence, not in the sense that he would stop talking, but in the sense that he would abandon truthful dialogical and join his friends in making declarative statements about Yahweh that sound right but, as the reader knows already in the first chapter, prove to be false. In his first speech responding to his friend, Job is forced by the precariousness of his circumstance to abandon such declarative affirmations. If he does not speak the truth soon, it will be too late.

> Remember, that my life is a breath . . .
> As the cloud fades and vanishes,
> > so those who go down to Sheol do not come up; . . .
> Therefore I will not restrain my mouth;
> > I will speak in the anguish of my spirit;
> > I will complain in the bitterness of my soul. (Job 7:7, 9, 11)

In his second speech, he acknowledges that honest communication is restrained by his fear of Yahweh's punishment.

> If he would take his rod away from me,
> > and not let dread of him terrify me,
> then I would speak without fear of him,
> > for I know I am not what I am thought to be. (Job 9:34–35)

But eventually his suffering becomes so wearisome that he no longer cares that God may castigate him for his candor.

> I loathe my life;
> > I will give free utterance to my complaint;
> > I will speak in the bitterness of my soul.
> I will say to God, "Do not condemn me;
> > let me know why you contend against me." (Job 10:1–2)

It is in his third speech, though, when each of his friends have had their say, that Job gains the boldness to demand of Yahweh a true conversation. Pierre van Hecke points out the sharp contrast here between Job and his friends. Job knows the same things that they know (13:1–2), but is not satisfied simply with knowledge. "Job then goes on to show in what respect he and his friends *are* different: it is not knowledge, but the way in which they involve God in their respective speeches that sets them apart."[40]

> But I would speak to the Almighty,
>   and I desire to argue my case with God.
> As for you, you whitewash with lies;
>   All of you are worthless physicians. (Job 13:3–4)

Job foreshadows here God's ultimate condemnation of the friend's speech at the close of the book. He seeks a direct encounter with God and an open discussion of his circumstances. Faced with the reality of Job's innocent suffering, it is blasphemous for the friends to speak the truth *about* God, rather than addressing truth *to* him. [41]

> Will you speak falsely for God,
>   and speak deceitfully for him?
> Will you show partiality towards him,
>   will you plead the case for God? (Job 13:7–8)

Ellen Davis identifies the friend's blasphemy specifically with the second commandment. They seek to detach God's name from his person, so that he becomes simply the cosmic rubber stamp for their theology.

> If blasphemy is taking God's name in vain, invoking that power
> for validation of a position or action apart from any genuine
> encounter with God, then it is these garrulous theologians [Job's
> friends] and not Job who must be charged with that offense.[42]

Job counsels his friends to keep silent, lest they bring condemnation on themselves, while he offers God an invitation to full-blown conversation. "Let me have silence, and I will speak, and let come on me what may" (Job 13:13). In presenting his case, Job will "defend his ways," "declare his words," having "prepared his case." Hecke suggests that, having boldly invited God to enter a conversation on equal terms, there is little more for Job to say to him apart from waiting on God to respond. This,

---

40. Van Hecke, "But I, I Would Converse With the Almighty (Job 13:3)," 22.

41. Dale Patrick points out that throughout the entire dialogue between Job and his friends in chapters 3–27 the friends offer not a single word directed to God. Job, on the other hand, addresses 54 verses in the dialogue section. "Job's Address to God," 268–69, 272.

42. Davis, "Job and Jacob," 105.

says Hecke, is the reason there is little in the way of direct address to God by Job after chapter 13.[43]

When Yahweh does appear and enter the conversation with Job, it is noteworthy that his final words turn to the speech used throughout by Job and his friends. "The LORD said to Eliphaz the Temanite: 'My wrath is kindled against you and against your two friends; for you have not spoken of me what is right, as my servant Job has'" (Job 42:7). Here God casts aside the words of Job's friends as worthless and even sinful. The problem, though, is that the content of those words is a fair summary of the theological perspective that God, being just, rewards the righteous and dispenses judgment against the wicked. How is it, then, that proverbial wisdom is found not on the lips of Job, but on those of his friends? And how are we to understand Job's speech as being "what is right" when he challenges directly doctrines that are so broadly attested to elsewhere in scripture? In short, what has led to this theological reversal?

Gustavo Gutiérrez locates the apparent contradiction offered in the book of Job in the friends willingness to separate belief from experience. He argues that theological language that is cut off from experience, particularly the experience of suffering, cannot accurately reflect truth. "The language we use depends on the situation we are in. Job's words are a criticism of every theology that lacks human compassion and contact with reality; the one-directional movement from theological principles to life really goes nowhere."[44] Gutiérrez argues that a theology of pure words and ideas must finally exhaust itself in endlessly repeated and fully inadequate formulas when faced with experiences that do not fit with the theological framework. This is the position in which Job's friends find themselves as the are finally reduced to repeating doggedly their arguments over and over again while remaining closed to any experience of suffering that might qualify, or even disqualify, those arguments. Gutiérrez identifies Job 16:2–6 as a center piece of the book, rejecting as it does any theology of suffering that is disconnected from experience.

> I have heard many such things;
>> miserable comforters are you all.

---

43. Hecke, "But, I Would Converse With the Almighty," 23.

44. Gutiérrez, *On Job*, 30.

Have windy words no limit?
　　Or what provokes you that you keep on talking?
I also could talk as you do,
　　if you were in my place;
I could join words together against you,
　　and shake my head at you.
I could encourage you with my mouth,
　　and the solace of my lips would assuage your pain.
If I speak, my pain is not assuaged,
　　and if I forbear, how much of it leaves me?

"This is a key passage," says Gutiérrez. "It is a rejection of a way of theologizing that does not take account of concrete situations, of the sufferings and hopes of human beings."[45] For Gutiérrez theology that does not arise from and remain open to reflect on experience becomes a false theology. Authentic "God-talk" includes the experience of suffering. When experience is separated from reflection, a detached and intellectual theology results, which is a mere shadow and mockery of genuine God-talk.

The book of Job compels us to concede that content alone cannot constitute truthful speech. A propositional construct, lifted from any relational context, settles for a meaningless half-life. It gains logical integrity but looses relevance. Speech that ignores experience, dismisses context, and neglects direct address cannot offer truth about God, regardless of its content.

Rickie Moore identifies the meeting point of theological truth and religious experience with Job's practice of prayer, arguing that the book of Job is fundamentally about prayer. The book opens with Job's intercession offered on a regular basis for his children and closes with him praying for the restoration of his friends. Job's speech is laced throughout the book with prayers addressed to God. For Moore, God's concluding statement about right speech provides a key for understanding both the message of the book as a whole and the tendency among biblical scholars to identify more readily with theological, rather than with experiential questions. He asserts that the standard translation of Job 42:7c, "for you have not spoken of me what is right, as my servant Job has," ignores both the context of what is happening in the chapter and what is by far the most common translation of the Hebrew prepositional phrase *elay*,

45. Ibid., 29.

translated "of me." The immediate context of Yahweh's commendation is a circumstance of prayer. "Seeing "right prayer" as the decisive issue here fits well with the immediate context of 42:7, for in the very next verse and in consequence to what God has just said, God tells Eliphaz and his friends to go with sacrificial offerings and 'let my servant Job pray for you.'"[46] Moore points out that, while this phrase with its pronominal suffix can be translated "of me" or "about me," in the vast majority of its approximately 300 uses in the Old Testament it is rendered "to me."[47] The problem, then, with the friends' speech is not its content, but that they spoke about but not to God, as Job had done.

More recently Pierre Hecke has suggested additional arguments in favor of reading this prepositional phrase "toward me." First of all, when Job uses *el* and *dabar* in combination elsewhere, it is always translated "towards" (2:13; 13:3; 40:27; 42:7, 9). Secondly, when the cognate *amar* is used in Job with *la*, it is also always translated "toward" (1:7, 8, 12; 2:2, 3, 6, 10; 9:12; 10:2; 34:31). Most compelling for Hecke, though, is the observation that on the one other occasion in Job when God is the object of this phase in 13:3, the accepted translation is "toward." Additionally, Heck observes that God is only rarely the object of *dabar el*, with only Abraham, Joshua and David appearing as the subject of this particular phrase.[48]

Job, Moore argues, is commended not for the content of his speech as much as for the fact that he directs his speech to God. Moore goes on to suggest that the choice of the translation "about me" rather than "to me" is shaped by the theological decision that the book of Job is about a right theology of suffering, rather than a right response to God in the midst of suffering.

> Specifically, modern scholars approach the book as a theoretical "discussion of a problem," without giving weight to the claims of particular, existential experience; . . . Which is the more fundament truth?: (1) that the wisdom categorization of Job has influenced its modern interpretation, or rather (2) that modern

46. Moore, "Raw Prayer and Refined Theology," 41.

47. Ibid., 39.

48. Van Hecke, "From Conversation about God to Conversation With God," 119–20.

interpretation has influenced the wisdom categorization of Job?
I submit it is the latter.[49]

If Moore is correct, the problem is not with the content of the friend's
speech or, as Guitiérrez has argued, simply with the fact that it is di-
vorced from the context of Job's suffering, but rather that whereas Job's
friends speak with him about the problem, Job addresses the problem
to God in active lament. "Right speech" in the context of innocent suffering is lament offered to God. In the extremity of Job's suffering, lament became the right way, the only way forward in his relationship
with God. While Job's friends tried to insulate and distance God (and
themselves) from Job's pain by speaking correctly about God, Job spoke
what was right to God, with the result that he received not an answer to
his questions, but a fresh encounter with his creator.

This raises the intriguing possibility that *right speech* may, in certain contexts, include *wrong content* from a theological perspective.
Theological concerns, though present, are certainly secondary and
derivative in Job. What really matters is Yahweh's response to Job's invitation to dialogue. The book of Job offers a guide to the integration
of theology and experience. The writer asserts firstly that theology that
has been severed from its existential roots can become at best irrelevant
and at worst blasphemous in the face of suffering. Secondly, the silence
of God in the presence of innocent suffering should not be understood
as callous rejection, but as an invitation to dialogue. Finally, Job demonstrates for us that, in the face of overwhelming suffering and loss, lament is faithful speech. Indeed, lament offers Job the only way forward
in his relationship with Yahweh.

In which World Does God Live?

Stephen Hawking opens his book *A Brief History of Time* with the story
of an astronomer delivering a lecture to a group of lay persons:

> After carefully explaining the movement of the earth around
> the sun, the nature of solar systems, and the movement of gal-
> axies through the universe, an elderly woman stood to her feet
> and explained "What you've told us today is all rubbish. In fact,
> the earth rests upon the back of a giant turtle." The lecturer, not
> wanting to be offensive or condescending asked the woman, "If

49. Moore, "Raw Prayer and Refined Theology," 44.

the earth rests on the back of a giant turtle, on what is the turtle standing?" The woman replied, "On the back of another larger turtle." Wanting still to answer the woman from within her own understanding the scientist replied, "Ah, but what does that turtle stand on?" "It's no use young man," responded the woman in triumph, "it's turtles all the way down."[50]

There is something tremendously comforting about having the world figured out, with everything explained, catalogued, and put in its proper place. Any construct that we use to describe the universe, whether in terms of turtles or solar systems, will be adequate to explain some, perhaps even many, of the structures and relationships that we observe around us, but no construct can capture perfectly that which it seeks to model. There is always a degree of slippage, of uncertainty and extrapolation, of apparent paradox and contradiction, and of data that simply will not fit the construct. Hopefully solar systems are a closer approximation of the observable cosmos than are giant turtles, but even our most careful observations about our world are incomplete and, to a degree, inaccurate, so that they must be periodically updated and changed. Add to this the complexities that arise when we attempt to comprehend and represent not a physical phenomenon but a growing, dynamic relationship and the degree of uncertainty is multiplied. Relationships bring with them the possibility for growth, unique combination, change, and endless newness. Inevitably we come to gaps in our understanding where we most gloss over uncertainties, turn a blind eye to odd bits of rogue data, and affirm with as much confidence as we can muster, "It's turtles all the way down."

Job is caught between two worlds or more accurately between two ways of construing the world. He is forced by his circumstances to risk the loss of a familiar world -- one that is well ordered and predictable. In that world God punishes the wicked and prospers the righteous so consistently that we need merely to observe the external state of a person in order to see into their soul. Such a world rests, at least in part, on giant turtles and as Job discovers no system, not even a "right" system, can exhaustively describe the divine/ human relationship. But Job is also invited to risk gaining a new world, with a new set of freedoms and terrors. In this world God and his creatures are guided by, but are not tied slavishly to, a set of principles that describe the moral order of

50. Hawking, *A Brief History of Time*, 1.

the world. God may act according to revealed standards of justice or he may choose to strike down the innocent or show mercy to the wicked for no discernable reason, so that humanity must learn to accept both good and evil from his hand. Both worlds have their risks and rewards but the former is by far the most comfortable, so that only the most extreme of circumstances can compel Job to exchange one set of turtles for another. It is a testimony to Job's greatness that he is willingness to take such a risk.

The constructedness of the world that Job and his friends share at the opening of the book becomes apparent as soon as he is willing to have his attention directed to the seams and cracks in the cement, that is, to data that has heretofore gone unnoticed. Once he starts looking for them, inconsistencies in his understanding of God's justice and the moral order of the world are not difficult to find. Job counsels his friends that to see the weakness in their understanding they need do nothing more arduous than step out of the sheltered lives that their wealth provides for them (assuming, of course, that rich men like to have other rich men as their friends) and speak to those who have a wider acquaintance with the world.

> Have you not asked those who travel the roads,
>   and do you not accept their testimony,
> that the wicked are spared on the day of calamity,
>   and are rescued on the day of wrath?
> Who declares their way to their face,
>   and who repays them for what they have done?
> (Job 21:29–31)

The startling reality of these words is that neither we nor Job nor Job's friends require a continuance in the proceedings in order to go to the nearest airport, begin interviewing passengers, and discover with dismay the truth of Job's statement. We already know that there is truth, or at least some truth, to his words. Everyone has this data to hand in one form or another, but the world that we choose to construct will determine how we interpret it and, indeed, if we will choose simply to ignore it completely. A central feature of Job's use of lament is the way that it serves as a vehicle for exploring, exploding, and rebuilding the worldview in which God is both just and involved in the world. The prayer of lament is instrumental to Job's exploration, being ideally suited to sustain the growing dissonance between the two worlds that

Job is considering and the data that both confirm and contradict them. Job uses lament to search out the uncertain moral order of a world that is newly unfamiliar to him.

One reality that Job confronts is that God does not simply react to human moral decisions, but can choose to work outside of our understanding of moral order. A human judge may be compelled to accept testimony, evidence, and argument, but such reasoning does not guarantee a successful outcome in the heavenly court, for "how can a mortal be just before God?" (Job 9:2b). Yahweh can even turn a witness' own tongue against them, so that their words become his evidence to convict and condemn them.

> Though I am innocent, my mouth would condemn me;
>   though I am blameless, he would prove me perverse.
> I am blameless; I do not know myself;
>   I loathe my life.
> It is all one; therefore I say,
>   he destroys both the blameless and the wicked.
> When disaster brings sudden death,
>   he mocks at the calamity of the innocent.
> The earth is given into the hand of the wicked;
>   he covers the eyes of judges—
>   if it is not he, who then is it? (Job 9:20–24)

Right words and right actions will not guarantee God's response. Job's experience of God simply will not fit seamlessly within a retributive framework of reward and punish. Indeed, the narrator is at pains to tell us in the opening chapters that Job has not gotten it wrong, that God is afflicting him for reasons other than his guilt or innocence. God may choose to lift up or to destroy for other reasons or, as God himself says in 2:3, for no reason at all. Job discovers that the system of retributive justice alone is inadequate to model God's dealings with his creation and so he is obliged to consider other possibilities and other explanations.

Job's experience leads him initially to conclude that God has become his enemy. In chapter 16, Job says that God has "worn me out," "made desolate," "shriveled me," "torn me," "hated me," "gnashed his teeth at me," "sharpened his eyes against me," "gaped at me," "struck me," "gives me up," "casts me into," "broke me," "seized me," "set me up as a target," "slashes my kidneys," "shows no mercy," "pours out my gall," "bursts upon me," and "rushes at me." A similar cascade of verbs follows in chapter 19. Yahweh has "not answered," "walled up," "set in darkness," "stripped," "taken," "breaks," "uprooted," "kindled wrath," and "counted as an adversary." This leads Job to conclude that God is set on destroying the innocent without justification and without giving Job the opportunity to defend himself. This causes Job to question his bedrock belief in the justice of God. In three successive speeches Job uses lament to examine the belief that God destroys the wicked, while upholding the cause of the righteous.

Beginning with chapter 21, Job considers the shape of a world that is the opposite of the one the he has always accepted as being authentic, a world in which God does not act to maintain justice. Verse 7 states the question with which he struggles; "Why do the wicked live on, reach old age, and grow mighty in power?" In the verses that follow, Job pictures the life of the wicked as being filled with prosperity and blessing. Every breeding of human and of beast in their households produces offspring, they are kept safe from fear, and their life is a continual celebration filled with dancing and joy. What is more, they give God credit for none of their prosperity.

> They say to God, "Leave us alone!
>   We do not desire to know your ways.
> What is the Almighty, that we should serve him?
>   And what profit do we get if we pray to him?"
> Is not their prosperity indeed their own achievement?
> (Job 21:14–16a)

Here Job turns the accusation of the satan on its head. The satan demands of God, "Does Job fear God for nothing?" But Job denies any profit, any advantage in the fear of the Lord. In vv. 19–21, Job overturns the spurious argument of his friends that judgment will eventually catch up with the children of the wicked, balancing the scales of justice. The weakness of such an argument is obvious. "For what do they care for their household after them, when the number of their months is cut off?" Like the writer of Ecclesiastes, Job also recognized the absolute barrier that death places on the working of God's justice. "One dies full of prosperity . . . Another dies in bitterness of soul . . . They lie down alike in the dust, and the worms cover them" (Job 21:23–26). To postpone the justice of God beyond the death of the individual who suffers injustice is to deny it. In the remainder to the chapter, Job offers the evidence of those who travel about in the world and see on a daily basis miscarriages of justice. Job finally rejects all the traditional arguments and explanations offered by his friends. "How then will you comfort me with empty nothings? There is nothing left of your answers but falsehood?" Having examined the traditional mechanisms for dealing with the slippage in God's administration of justice in the world, all are found wanting.

In the speech that follows, Job takes up once more the prosperity of the wicked in chapter 24. "Why are times not kept by the Almighty, and why do those who know him never see his days?" In the verses that follow, Job catalogues a steady litany of oppression by the wicked against the widow, the orphan, the poor, the needy, the naked, the hungry, and the thirsty. Here Job challenges directly and explicitly the teachings of the Torah. The wicked routinely, even systematically, break Torah, yet when the oppressed appeal to him for deliverance, "God pays no attention to their prayer" (Job 24:12b). By contrast, God attends solicitously to the needs of the wicked.

> Yet God prolongs the life of the mighty by his power;
>   they rise up when they despair of life.
> He gives them security, and they are supported;
>   his eyes are upon their ways. (Job 24:22–23)

In the midst of his description, though, Job introduces a counter-testimony to his own arguments. Verses 18–20 proclaim that the wicked are cursed and are quickly snatched away. "The womb forgets them and the worm finds them sweet." They are not remembered and are broken. In a similar vein, vv. 24–25 attest that the exaltation of the wicked is but for a little while. Soon they will wither, fade, and be cut off.

Chapter 24 has provoked a great deal of controversy among biblical scholars because of Job's seemly schizophrenic shifting back and forth between opposing views. A frequently offered explanation is that the text of this chapter has been fragmented or corrupted, so that what we have today is a rather incompetent attempt to put the pieces back together in some semblance of logical order. James Wharton, for example, concludes that "the entire block of material from 24:18 (perhaps from 24:9) through 27:23 has been rather hopelessly scrambled, whether deliberately or inadvertently, somewhere in the process of copying, preserving, editing, and transmitting the text."[51] In a similar vein, John Gibson suggests that a number of fragments of Job's thought have been collected without particular concern for order or original context.[52] The problem with this explanation, though, is that it fails to address the question of why the author or editor of the book of Job would present such a carefully reasoned and developed argument elsewhere, only to degenerate into a haphazard cut-and-paste approach here. And why would such an irrational reconstruction of a corrupted text be both accepted and preserved, presumably even after it had been brought into contact with other, less corrupted copies of the narrative? Robert Gordis points to a unified style throughout chapter 24 suggests that 24:18–24 present Job's restatement of his friend's views. This restatement was originally followed by a rebuttal of those views which was subsequently lost.[53] These solutions assume a corrupted text and raise more questions than it answers.

Carol Newsom argues that the seeming mixed message of chapter 24, with its resulting dissonance, is an intentional device to reflect the tension that Job himself is experiencing.

> His language can only be the language of radical dissonance, a mimetic embodiment of the rent in the heart of the world. Job does not simply wish to *say* that life is experienced as contradiction. He forces those who listen to him into a painful cognitive dissonance, a loss of mastery, that is an echo, however, faint, of what Job has experienced of the world.[54]

John Hartley suggests that the apparent tension in chapter 24 reflects the nature of the prayer of lament. Lament leads to and is able to sustain a tension between conflicting views. It is in the nature of lament, says Hartley, to draw the person praying to God, even in the act of protesting against him.

> Job's concern for injustice leads him to challenge the theology of his day, but at the same time, because of his profound faith in God, his lamenting drives him to God for an answer. He is

---

51. Wharton, *Job*, 111.
52. Gibson, *Job*, 188.
53. Gordis, *Book of Job*, 533–34.
54. Newsom, *The Book of Job*, 167.

anxious that God curse the wicked, holding them accountable
for their evil deeds.[55]

Thus, it is typical of lament both to question God and, at the same time,
to challenge him to respond as he should. Examples of this type of sustained tension can be found among the Psalms. Psalm 74, for example,
asks of God the question "How long will you just stand there with your
hands in your pockets doing nothing?" and then challenges him to defend himself.

> How long, O God, is the foe to scoff?
>   Is the enemy to revile your name for ever?
> Why do you hold back your hand;
>   why do you keep your hand in your bosom? . . .
> Rise up, O God, plead you cause;
>   remember how the impious scoff at you all day long.
> (Ps 74:10–11, 22)

Job ends his speech with a challenge, "If it is not so, who will prove me
a liar, and show that there is nothing in what I say?" But what exactly
is Job asserting? Is he saying that the wicked prosper throughout their
long lives? Or does he suggest that their happiness is fleeting and will
come to a quick and inevitable end? Perhaps it is the basic contradiction
itself that Job is affirming; the beliefs both that "God prolongs the life
of the mighty by his power" and that "they are exalted a little while, and
then are gone." Job rejects as inadequate any picture that seeks to reduce
the moral order of the world to a mechanical certainty.

Because lament is offered in a context of sustained dissonance,
fluctuating and seemingly erratic moves between doubt, challenge, despair, and renewed confidence, such as are apparent in chapter 24 of Job,
are not unusual. Gisela Fuchs maintains that "a state of constant flux,
swaying between the extremes of impassioned despair and trust-filled
confession to God is, for lament, a typical tension."[56] Fuchs points to the
presence of such radical shifts of mood in the lament Psalms and the
prophecies of Jeremiah, as well as in Job's laments. Walter Baumgartner
understands the repeated shifting back and forth between complaint
and expressions of trust in some psalms of lament to reflect the emotional state of the one praying.

---

55. Hartley, *The Book of Job*, 254.
56. Fuchs, "Die Klage des Propheten," 223; trans. mine.

> To our differently trained sense of style, a song like this neces-
> sarily creates an impression of great disorder: instead of a strict
> progression of ideas there is a restless to-ing and fro-ing of
> ideas. But it would be quite wrong to try to introduce some or-
> der by always placing similar ideas together. The apparent dis-
> order corresponds to the psalmist's excited state of mind. It is an
> attempt, albeit a schematized one, to express the ups and downs
> of his mood, his wavering between dark hopelessness and firm
> confidence, timorous petition and victorious assurance.[57]

The seeming reversals in Job's laments are not, in and of themselves, evidence for a corrupted text. Such seeming inconsistencies only become irreconcilable when we assume emotional detachment and objective distance on the part of the writer.

In Job's next speech, he appears to have reversed completely his original position. In chapter 27 Job expresses complete confidence in the eventual working out of justice by God.

> This is the portion of the wicked with God,
>   and the heritage that oppressors receive from the Almighty:
> If their children are multiplied, it is for the sword;
>   and their offspring have not enough to eat. (Job 27:13–14)

This chapter echoes the conclusion reached by the Psalmist in Psalm 73, that the prosperity of the wicked, though real, is precarious and temporary.

> Truly you have set them [the wicked] in slippery places;
>   you make them fall to ruin.
> How they are destroyed in a moment,
>   swept away utterly by terrors!
> They are like a dream when one awakes;
>   on awaking you despise their phantoms. (Ps 73:18–20)

Many biblical scholars, including Hartley, consider chapter 27 to be a misplaced and mislabeled speech of one of Job's friends, most likely Zophar.[58] James Wharton is representative of another direction taken by scholars. He suggests that Job is here parroting the kinds of things that his friends have been saying about the wicked, so that "the third

---

57. Baumgartner, *Jeremiah's Poems of Lament*, 38.

58. Gordis, *The Book of Job*, 291; Westermann, *The Structure of the Book of Job*, 133; Habel, *The Book of Job*, 385; and Janzen, *Job*, 185–86.

cycle ends on a shrill note of despair, edging toward madness, signaling the end of any possible resolution of the issue between Job and his friends."[59] Such a solution, though, would signal a sharp change in Job's challenging and abrasive speech to his friends in the rest of the book.

As we have seen earlier, both David Penchansky and Bruce Zuckerman argue that dissonance is a key factor in interpreting the book of Job. Both authors, though, see this dissonance as evolving over time as successive contributors add discordant notes to what was originally a homogeneous narrative. Carol Newsom's recent commentary has taken the important step of recognizing that a single author is capable of bringing together dissonant elements and sustaining an ongoing tension between them.

> [T]he heuristic fiction I wish to employ is that a single author wrote the book of Job (except for the Elihu speeches). But he wrote it by juxtaposing and intercutting certain genres and distinctly stylized voices, providing sufficient interconnection among the different parts to establish the sense of the "same" story but leaving the different parts sharply marked and sometimes overtly disjunctive.[60]

As John Hartley has pointed out, there is a single genre, the lament, that by its very nature can articulate and sustain the kind of dissonance that Newsom sees between genre. But whereas Hartley confines his observation to chapter 24 of Job, Claus Westermann's argument that the book as a whole can be characterized by Job's use of lament suggests that this tension between moral worlds runs throughout the book. Lament permits Job to question and challenge the moral order of the world, even as he affirms that order. In lament Job draws together what is and what should be, offering both to God in prayer.

Speaking to God in a Changing World

The voice of Job has no real parallel in scripture. With stark honesty and fearlessness, Job both acknowledges the loss of one world and seeks to build another. There is a very real sense in which, having experienced both catastrophic loss and the seeming betrayal by God, things can never again be as they were before. Job's relationship with God is

59. Wharton, *Job*, 111.
60. Newsom, *Book of Job*, 16.

forever transformed by the divine test. Throughout this process, lament is his principal means of navigation and his prayers illustrate for us a number of the functions served by lament. First of all, Job learns to extend and deepen his understanding of God's justice. He acknowledges that God's involvement in our lives cannot be neatly catalogued and is not infallibly predictability. Our every understanding of God is limited and, therefore, if we attend to our relationship with God with open eyes, we cannot help but notice gaps, inconsistencies, and unanswered questions. Lament, then, is the language of those gaps, pressing for dialogue when God is silent.

Secondly, the book of Job is characterized by a sustained dissonance between belief and experience. Attempts by various scholars to resolve this dissonance have resulted in a dissecting of the book and a somewhat condescending attitude toward the final editor(s) of the text. The prevailing attitude among biblical scholars is that ambiguity cannot be intentional, but must reflect textual corruption, and that those who formulated the book were not up to the task of "fixing" the problems in the text. A discomfort with dissonance and the willingness to pay a substantial premium for a flatly consistent interpretation of Job's experience, though, resonates more faithfully with Job's friends than with Job. Lament allows Job to sustain the multiple tensions active in the narrative, while pressing toward the God who is found in the midst of dissonance. Job's understanding of God throughout defies closure, reductionism, and an easy answer.

Thirdly, Job underscores the reality that God's justice is essentially relational rather than propositional in nature. Indeed, to be concerned with finding an answer to suffering is to find ourselves once more on the side of Job's friends, speaking about God rather than to him. Certainly Job would very much like to have such answers, but not at the expense of his integrity. When Job asks the question "Why?" in the midst of his suffering, he is not seeking clarification regarding the mechanical workings of the cosmos, but is giving voice to a betrayal of trust. Job does not want to have his theology clarified, for he already knows all the right answers. Rather he desires to discover anew a God who can be trusted in the midst of unexplainable and irreplaceable loss.

Fourthly, this emphasis on the relational over the informational helps Job to offer correct speech. Correct speech seeks to engage and not merely to describe. Furthermore, authentic God-talk is not purely intellectual, but includes experience. Any speech that attempts to bracket out the experience of suffering in the name of objectivity and dispassion is false speech. False speech surrenders dialogue in favor of declaration and divorces proposition from experience. This separation makes it possible for Job's friends to offer right content that results in wrong speech. Any theology resulting from such separations is blasphemous.

Finally, the book of Job reveals and explores a basic truth about all of our lives, namely, that we live between worlds. With regard to our relationship with God, we live between the worlds of how we encounter God and how we conceive of him, that is, between experience and construct. Experience exposes the reality that our every construct is plagued by cracks in the sidewalk. Speaking historically, we also live between worlds in the sense that the world we experience is constantly changing. Indeed, change is the quintessential attribute of this moment in human history. As we are forced by loss to recognize the inadequacies of current models of meaning, lament offers a means of speaking to God even as the foundations beneath our feet shift. Lament is the language of change. It allows us to address God with a foot in each of two worlds, both the world that is passing away and the world that is being birthed. Lament both sustains us in loss and makes room for the creation of a new vision of the world around us. In the course of his laments, Job is able both to turn loose of God and to draw near to him though the experience of loss.

In the next chapter we will consider the functioning of lament in the prophetic tradition. Jeremiah offers the broadest representation of the lament tradition among the prophets. He is tasked with speaking on God's behalf in a season of death and new birth. The old covenant is being dismantled and the Exodus experience reversed, while room is being sought for a new covenant and a transformed understanding of God. Jeremiah does not simply offer his own lament, but he embodies the lament of God. Just as Job places at risk the accepted moral order of God's world, Jeremiah's laments risk the understanding of covenant derived from Sinai and explore the impact that suffering has had on Yahweh, the covenant maker.

5

Jeremiah and the Vocation of Shared Suffering

In what respects do we mirror God? In our knowledge. In our love. In our justice. In our sociality. In our creativity. These are the answers the Christian tradition offers us.

One answer rarely finds its way onto the list: in our suffering. Perhaps the thought is too appalling. Do we also mirror God in suffering? Are we to mirror him ever more closely in suffering? Was it meant that we should be icons in suffering? Is it our glory to suffer?[1]

Shared Suffering and Prophetic Vocation

JEREMIAH HAS LONG BEEN CALLED THE WEEPING PROPHET FOR THE SUF-fering that he experiences and expresses in his message. His prophecies are set amidst the conquest and subsequent destruction of Judah by the Babylonians. He has been given by God both a clear vision of the unfold-ing desolation and a means by which the people of Judah can limit that destruction and escape with their lives, namely by recognizing the hand of God in the invading army and by surrendering to the encroaching Babylonians. However, Jeremiah's proclamations are offered in a culture of institutional and societal denial. He is called to prophesy to a people who will reject his message. "Hear this, O foolish and senseless people, who have eyes, but do not see, who have ears, but do not hear" (Jer 5:21). "To whom shall I speak and give warning, that they may hear? See, their ears are closed, they cannot listen. The word of the LORD is to them an object of scorn; they take no pleasure in it" (Jer 6:10). Like the prophet Isaiah, Jeremiah is called to speak, knowing before he even

1. Nicholas Wolterstorff shares with his readers new experiences of faith created by his journey into unrelenting pain as the result of his son's death in a climbing accident. *Lament for a Son*, 83.

opens his mouth that his breath is wasted.[2] But much more than in the case of Isaiah, the resistance that Jeremiah encounters to his word is both energetic and violent. This is so because he offers his warning with the enemy already at the gate. Whereas Hezekiah has the luxury of giving mere lip service to Isaiah's warning ("Then Hezekiah said to Isaiah, 'The word of the LORD that you have spoken is good.' For he thought, 'There will be peace and security in my days,'" Isa 39:8), the people to whom Jeremiah speaks confront the immediacy of Yahweh's judgment, so that the maintenance of their denial is more costly and leaves little room for voices of dissent. The ferocity of Jeremiah's rejection is fueled by the people's fear and by the increasing energy required to perpetuate an illusion in order to believe the lies of the false prophets who proclaim "'Peace, peace,' when there is no peace" (Jer 6:14; 8:11). The people pin their hopes on the belief that safety lies in the possession of a divine talisman against evil, the presence of the temple in Jerusalem, and there is a frantic edge to their repeated incantation, "This is the temple of the LORD, the temple of the LORD, the temple of the LORD" (Jer 7:4). The religious and political institutions that Jeremiah's prophecies jeopardize are vigorously defended not because there is substantial evidence for their validity, but because they provide a temporary levee against the rising chaos that threatens to inundate and overwhelm Judah.

At the heart of prophetic ministry in the exilic period is an awareness of the suffering that the covenant relationship with humanity has occasioned in God. "This notion that God can be intimately affected, that He possesses not merely intelligence and will, but also pathos," says Heschel, "basically defines the prophetic consciousness of God."[3] The primary task of the exilic prophets is first to experience and then to express the anguish and anger of God caused by his relationship with an unfaithful people. As we discussed in chapter two, the tears of God exist alongside and are often mingled with Jeremiah's tears.[4] The pain

2. The message which Isaiah is given in 6:6–13 proclaims that this people will "not comprehend," "not understand," "not look," "not listen," and "not comprehend." God calls on the prophet to "make minds dull," "stop ears," and "shut eyes," so that the people may not "look," "listen," "comprehend," "turn," and "be healed."

3. Heschel, *The Prophets*, 2:4.

4. Roberts, for example, argues that the passages in Jeremiah which cause Jeremiah to be identified as the weeping prophet (Jer 4:19–21; 8:18–9:3; and 14:17–18) refer not to the weeping of the prophet, but to the weeping of God. "The Motif of the Weeping God." See also O'Connor, "The Tears of God and Divine Character in Jeremiah 2–9."

and persecution that Jeremiah experiences at the rejection of his message, and his sense of being betrayed by a God who neither adequately defends his prophet nor acts swiftly in order to validate his message, are tied to the suffering of God. "The suffering of Jeremiah," says Mark Smith, "is a dramatic symbol in the laments. Yet, beyond the pain of Jeremiah over Israel sent in exile lies the torment of the one who sent the prophet."[5] Heschel maintains that:

> Israel's distress was more than a human tragedy. With Israel's distress came the affliction of God, His displacement, His homelessness in the land, in the world. And the prophet's prayer, "O save us," involved not only the fate of a people. It involved the fate of God in relation to the people.[6]

Each attempt by Yahweh to reach out to his people is met with rejection and, in spite of ceaseless provocation, he fails adequately to protect himself from those rebuffs with decisive action. Divine hesitation adds to the prophet's misery. Like the prophet Jonah, Jeremiah pays the price for serving a God who is "merciful, slow to anger, and abounding in steadfast love, and ready to relent from punishing" (Jonah 4:2).[7]

While in the book of Jeremiah prophetic lament reflects and is fueled by divine pathos, in Lamentations the prophet takes up a cry on behalf of Yahweh's covenant partner.[8] In Lamentations prophetic lament

There has been a long-standing debate among scholars as to whether the laments of Jeremiah are autobiographical (Skinner, Bright, Muilenburg, Blank, Nicholson, Clements), reflecting the prophet's personal experience, or are symbolic of God's rejection and the nation's suffering (Reventlow). It seems neither possible nor desirable, though, to make a clear distinction between the two. To the extent that Jeremiah's sufferings are personal experiences, they nevertheless embody the panoramic suffering of the failed relationship between Yahweh and his people. Likewise a prophet or prophetic tradition that proclaims such a message and yet remains personally disengaged from it ceases to be prophetic, becoming instead merely scribal, passively recording the passions of others. See Walter Brueggemann, *Jeremiah 1–25*, 109.

5. Mark S. Smith, *The Laments of Jeremiah in Their Contexts*, 64.

6. Heschel, *The Prophets*, 1:112.

7. For the prophet Jonah this declaration is not an expression of praise, but an accusation brought against God. God sets up his messenger to fail by sending him with a word of judgment that he, Yahweh, is all to ready to abandon. Jeremiah's suffering is tied to God's hesitancy to follow through on his threats of judgment.

8. There is a general consensus among biblical scholars that the author(s) of Lamentations is not the same person that penned the book of Jeremiah. Bracke, *Jeremiah 30–52 and Lamentations*, 183; Dobbs-Allsopp, *Lamentations*, 5; O'Connor,

is tasked with raising a protest on Israel's behalf. Punishment for sin has become extreme and the prophet cries out as God's chastening of Judah threatens to become abusive. Here the prophet negotiates Israel's future with God, speaking on behalf of a people who are devastated and cannot speak for themselves. It is the fate of the prophet in Jeremiah to experience and report on the pathos of God as he struggles with his decision finally to terminate his long-estranged marriage to Israel. It is the place of the prophet in Lamentations to suffer with God's people and to call God to account, lest the execution of justice should overwhelm all claims to mercy. Finally it is the task of the exilic prophet to negotiate between estranged partners in the covenant marriage, while taking on himself the suffering of both.

A Broken Covenant

A central theme of Jeremiah's prophecy is the judgment that Israel has provoked by breaking the terms of the Sinai covenant. Jeremiah 11 ties Yahweh's impending judgment directly to the curses pronounced in Deuteronomy 27–28 against those who break the covenant.

> Thus says the LORD, the God of Israel: Cursed be anyone who does not heed the words of this covenant, which I commanded your ancestors when I brought them out of the land of Egypt . . . So I brought upon them all the words of this covenant, which I commanded them to do, but they did not . . . they have gone after other gods to serve them; the house of Israel and the house of Judah have broken the covenant that I made with their ancestors. Therefore, . . . though they cry out to me, I will not listen to them. (Jer 11:3–4, 8, 10–11)

> "Cursed be anyone who makes an idol or casts an image, anything abhorrent to the LORD, the work of an artisan, and sets it up in secret." All the people shall respond, saying, "Amen!" (Deut. 27:15)

Chapter 11 refers repeatedly to Israel's covenant with Yahweh (11:2, 3, 6, 8, and 10), identifying specifically the Sinai tradition: "Hear the

---

Lamentations and the Tears of the World, 15. Without taking up the question of authorship, I would simply note the effect of pairing these two prophetic writings. In Jeremiah the prophet's laments are occasioned by the sufferings of one covenant partner, while in Lamentations they are occasioned by that of the other.

words of this covenant and do them. For I solemnly warned your ancestors when I brought them our of the land of Egypt, warning them
persistently, even to this day, saying, Obey my voice."

Scholars have long observed the similarities between the Sinai
covenant formula and the Suzerain covenant form used to solemnize
the relationship between a conquering king and a vassal state. Applying
this parallel more directly, Meredith Kline has argued that the outline
of the book of Deuteronomy follows this same structure of a Suzerain
covenant, with its adoption of: a preamble (Deut 1:1–5), a historical
prologue providing a covenant history (Deut 1:6—4:49), the main
terms and conditions of the treaty (Deut 5–26), a covenant ratification,
including a list of curses and blessings (Deut 27–30), and arrangements
for preserving and publicly reading the covenant (Deut 31).[9] Yahweh's
judgment of the people, then, is seen as the execution of the terms of the
covenant that defines the nature of the relationship between God and
his vassal state Israel.

As the prophecy of Jeremiah unfolds, though, we discover that
Yahweh is not simply the God of Mounts Gerizim and Ebal, that is, the
God who blesses and curses as a mechanical, dispassionate response
to the actions of his people. Rather, the understanding of covenant
presented by the prophets has moved on from that found in the deuteronomic tradition. The writer of Jeremiah both borrows from the
innovations of other prophetic writers that have gone before and introduces the notion of a new covenant that extends beyond the limits of
the Sinai covenant.

Walter Brueggemann has called attention to the dependence of
Jeremiah on the earlier writings of Hosea. Hosea's principal contribution to the notion of covenant is to re-imagine it no longer in terms of
a contract between political powers, but rather in terms of a marriage
covenant.

> While Hosea seems to be immersed in and faithful to that
> [Ephraimite] tradition, it is equally clear that the tradition of
> Hosea exhibits remarkable innovation that will subsequently

9. Kline, *Treaty of the Great King*, 28. Kline developed the hypothesis first put forward in Mendenhall, *Law and Covenant in Israel and the Ancient Near East*. Wenham,
in his dissertation, "The Structure and Date of Deuteronomy," has argued that while
the covenant form in Deuteronomy is similar to the Hittite form in many respects, it is
nevertheless a distinct form.

be taken up by Jeremiah. Most spectacularly, Hosea articulates the covenant of Sinai in terms of deep interpersonal imagery of marriage, divorce, and remarriage.[10]   .

The metaphor of marriage, divorce, and remarriage provides space for a key distinction that is not apparent in the original Sinai tradition as it is recorded in the Pentateuch, namely, the pathos of God as he suffers from the infidelity of his covenant partner. As we shall see, the laments of Jeremiah and the book of Lamentations center on the recognition of God's pathos, so that he can no longer be expected to respond to Israel with objectivity and detachment in the execution of judgment for covenant unfaithfulness. This acknowledgment of God's suffering provokes in the prophet a re-visioning of the nature of covenant that exceeds the limits placed on relationship by the Sinai covenant.

Jeremiah shares with Hosea the use of the images of a failed marriage and a faithless spouse in the expression of his message.[11] "I remember," say Yahweh, "the devotion of your youth, your love as a bride, how you followed me in the wilderness, in a land not sown" (Jer 2:2). Soon enough the honeymoon ends and the nature of the relationship changes. So vile is the comportment of Yahweh's bride that the only course open to him, should he wish to keep his honor intact, is a swift divorce. "If a man divorces his wife and she goes from him and becomes another man's wife, will he return to her? Would not such a land be greatly polluted? You have played the whore with many lovers; and would you return to me?" (Jer 3:1). The marriage has been marked by Yahweh's constant humiliation and betrayal at the hands of his people. It is the vocation of Jeremiah first to experience that humiliation and rebuff, and then to pronounce Yahweh's rejection of his people. The weeping prophet, though, must linger long in his message, for Yahweh is finally a reluctant spouse who despite extreme provocation, cannot bring himself to sign the divorce papers.

Related to this prophetic re-imagining of the dynamics of the covenant in terms a marriage relationship is a vision by the prophet of

---

10. Brueggemann, *The Theology of the Book of Jeremiah*, 15. Wilson offers a careful analysis of the distinctive features of the Ephraimite and Judean prophetic traditions in his study *Prophecy and Society in Ancient Israel*.

11. The metaphor of Israel as a faithless spouse is also an important one in Ezekiel's message (Ezek 16:15–16, 28, 31, 41; 23:5, 19, and 44) and is the centerpiece of Hosea's prophecy.

a new understanding of covenant, one that transcends the limits of the Sinai covenant. It is not the case that Jeremiah merely thinks about the old covenant in new ways, but rather that, in light of his shared experience of God's pain at Israel's faithfulness, he comes to realize that a new covenant is called for.

> The days are surely coming, says the LORD, when I will make a new covenant with the house of Israel and the house of Judah. It will not be like the covenant that I made with their ancestors when I took them by the hand to bring them out of the land of Egypt—a covenant that they broke, though I was their husband, says the LORD. But this is the covenant that I will make with the house of Israel after those days, says the LORD: I will put my law within them, and I will write it on their hearts; and I will be their God, and they shall be my people. No longer shall they teach one another, or say to each other, "Know the LORD," for they shall all know me, from the least of them to the greatest, says the LORD; for I will forgive their iniquity, and remember their sin no more. (Jer 31:31–34)

The prophet speaks of this new covenant as enabling an obedience that the old could not. "I will make an everlasting covenant with them, never to draw back from doing good to them; and I will put the fear of me in their hearts, so that they may not turn from me" (Jer 32:40). Also, in Jer 33:20–21, 25, the prophet reaffirms the eternal nature of his covenant with the house of David. Under this new covenant, Yahweh's humiliation and suffering will finally end, and it is precisely the awareness of God's pathos by the prophet that drives this vision of transformed covenant. The laments prayed by Jeremiah both give expression to divine pathos and, in doing so, create space for the notion of covenant to be conceived of in new ways. It is Jeremiah's unique contribution to see in divine suffering the basis for a new covenant that embraces personal relationship rather than political attachment as its basis.

The Confessions of Jeremiah:
The Prophet's Suffering with God

The first twenty-eight chapters of the book of Jeremiah focus on the coming judgment that Yahweh has pronounced on his people for the dual sins of idolatry and oppressing the powerless. In particular it is the leaders of the people, the prophets, priests, and kings, who have led the way in drawing the hearts of the people away from the Lord. Amidst these oracles of impending judgment, though, we find a contrasting note of lament offered by Yahweh himself, by the people of Judah, and by the prophet.

The divine laments in 4:19–21 and 8:18—9:3 set the tone for the announcements of judgment that both precede and follow them. Even as Yahweh pronounces the destruction of his people he weeps: "My anguish, my anguish! I writhe in pain! . . . My joy is gone, grief is upon me, my heart is sick . . . O that my head were a spring of water, and my eyes a fountain of tears, so that I might weep day and night for the slain of my poor people." The execution of judgment exacts a price from the judge who passes sentence and it is this suffering on Yahweh's part that is the foundation of Jeremiah's laments. It is important to recognize that Yahweh is the first to suffer and the first to lament. The laments of both the people and the prophet that follow relate directly to this divine anguish.

In 14:7–9 and 14:19–22 we find two prayers of community lament that acknowledge the people's sin and seek the Lord's forgiveness "for your name's sake." In both instances, though, Yahweh rejects their appeals. "Do not pray for the welfare of this people. Although they fast, I do not hear their cry, and although they offer burnt-offering and grain-offering, I do not accept them, but by the sword, by famine, and by pestilence I consume them" (Jer 14:11–12). "Though Moses and Samuel stood before me, yet my heart would not turn towards this people. Send them away out of my sight and let them go! . . . I am weary of relenting" (Jer 15:1, 6). Evidently these prayers do not constitute the genuine repentance called for in the surrounding passages (Jer 3:11—4:4; 17:19–27; 18:5–11; and 22:1–5).

Interwoven with Jeremiah's pronouncements of the coming judgment of God are a series of personal laments which have been labeled his "confessions" (11:18–23; 12:1–6; 15:10–14, 15–21; 17:14–18; 18:19–23; 20:7–18).[12] These expressions of personal suffering by the prophet seem almost an interruption to the unfolding message, switching atten-

---

12. Walter Baumgartner's classic study, *Jeremiah's Poems of Lament*, observes numerous parallels in form between the confessions of Jeremiah and the laments found in the Psalter, and his conclusion that the confessions are prayers of lament has gained general acceptance among scholars, although discussion continues as to the extent to which the author of Jeremiah adapts the lament form for the prophetic task.

tion as they do from the content of Jeremiah's prophetic proclamation to his personal suffering as a result of declaring that message, and yet they are integral to both the structure and the content of his prophecy.[13] The suffering of Jeremiah reflects his experience of being rejected as the messenger of God and, by extension, shares in and testifies to God's own experience of rejection.

> In the book of Jeremiah, the prophet above all else speaks for the Lord. Jeremiah's words reveal God. Because in the book so much similarity exists between laments that are the direct speech of God and the laments spoken by the prophet, it seems likely that the laments of Jeremiah need to be heard as reflecting God's hurt and pain.[14]

The prophet both shares directly in the experiences of God's rejection and suffers as a result of standing between God and the cause of his pain.

> As a prophet he makes the astounding claim to have felt what God feels as well, however. "But I am full of the wrath of the LORD; I am weary of holding it in" (Jer. 6:11) . . . Since he spoke both for the people and for God, Jeremiah is also depicted as one who found both the people and God to be his enemies, so in addition to participation a part of his work led to isolation.[15]

Like a marriage counselor, the prophet is frequently caught in the cross-fire as the relationship deteriorates. Even as he seeks to empathize with both partners, Jeremiah is regularly the target of both the people's and Yahweh's displeasure. Pronouncements of the coming divine judgment

---

13. Scholars have long debated the origin of Jeremiah's confessions. While there is a significant consensus of opinion that the confessions existed originally as a separate collection of material (Mihelic, "Dialogue with God," 43; Mark S. Smith, *The Laments of Jeremiah in Their Contexts*, 32), more recently scholars have pointed out that they are so integral to the message of the prophecy in its current form as to be inseparable from it (O'Connor, *Confessions of Jeremiah*, 1988, 3, 101). While the confessions may originally have existed as a separate collection, the message of the book of Jeremiah as we now have it has been dramatically shaped by these laments, so that they can in no sense be considered as ancillary. Fretheim states "However much these laments may be grounded in the experience of the prophet, they have become something more than that in the canonical process. They are no longer (auto)biography—if they ever were—but proclamation; in and through which readers hear the voice of God." *Jeremiah*, 189.

14. Bracke, *Jeremiah 1–29*, 8.

15. Gowan, *Theology of the Prophetic Books*, 107.

against Judah are repeatedly punctuated by expressions of the torment that their unfaithfulness occasions in both God and the prophet alike. "When one considers the prophet's laments alongside the divine laments," says Terence Fretheim, "readers can see that the prophet does not simply mirror the laments of God but incarnates that divine word."[16] The laments of Jeremiah add the element of shared pathos to his proclamations of the coming devastation, and underscore the extent to which God has left himself vulnerable to his covenant partner Israel.[17] The pain that the proclamation of God's word occasions in the prophet is a mirror of what it costs God to pronounce such a word against one that he loves, so that Yahweh can be the agent of Judah's destruction and yet weep for that destruction: "For the hurt of my poor people I am hurt, I mourn, and dismay has taken hold of me" (Jer 8:21).

The laments of Jeremiah are provoked by his calling and by a promise from Yahweh which accompanies it.[18] Jeremiah is called to proclaim the words of God and promised divine protection from those who will reject that word. The calling is given in Jeremiah 1:5, 7.

> Before I formed you in the womb I knew you,
>   and before you were born I consecrated you;
> I appointed you a prophet to the nations . . .
> Do not say, "I am only a boy";
>   for you shall go to all to whom I send you,
>   and you shall speak whatever I command you.

The content of his message is introduced in Jeremiah 1:10 and is reiterated throughout the book.

> See, today I appoint you over nations and over kingdoms,
>   to pluck up and to pull down,
> to destroy and to overthrow,
>   to build and to plant.[19]

---

16. Fretheim, *Jeremiah*, 189. See also Bracke, *Jeremiah 1–29*, 164.

17. "Nevertheless, they [the confessions] yield insights into new developments within the office of prophecy that were occasioned by the experience of Jeremiah. Here for the first time the prophetic task becomes identified with the suffering of the one filling that office." Crenshaw, *A Whirlpool of Torment*, 37.

18. Mihelic goes so far as to argue for the inclusion of Jeremiah's calling narrative as part of his confessions. "Dialogue with God," 43.

19. This refrain reappears in Jer 18:6–10 (the potter's house); 24:4–7 (two baskets of figs); 31:27–30 (the new Covenant and individual responsibility); and 42:9–10 (the offer

Jeremiah is tasked with announcing the loss of the old and the birth of the new.[20] Furthermore, the prophet is to turn a deaf ear to any and all prayers that would seek to hinder this death and thereby postpone rebirth. He is repeatedly forbidden by Yahweh to intercede for the people (Jer 14:10–13; 7:17; and 11:14).

The promise of protection that stands behind the prophet's laments follows hard on the heels of his calling.

> Do not be afraid of them, for I am with you to deliver you, says the LORD . . . Do not break down before them, or I will break you before them. And I for my part have made you today a fortified city, an iron pillar, and a bronze wall, against the whole land—against the kings of Judah, its princes, its priests, and the people of the land. They will fight against you, but they shall not prevail against you, for I am with you, says the LORD, to deliver you. (Jer 1:8, 17–19)

The laments that Jeremiah offers arise both from his calling to speak God's words and the doubts that plague him when God's promised protection is too long delayed. His laments are in the context of the threatened loss of the established, the familiar, and the safe through the event of the Exile, but do not deal directly with that loss. The book of Lamentations, as we shall see, utilizes prayers of lament to explore the threat of such a loss, but Jeremiah laments the apparent failure of Yahweh to keep his promise to shield his prophet from the consequences of speaking the word he has been given. He laments that he is compelled to speak a word that will cost him dearly and that the God who promised to protect Jeremiah cannot even adequately protect himself from the people's rejection. Terence Fretheim observes:

> . . . as we turn to the suffering of the prophet, it is wise to remember that it is as a servant of God that he suffers. The suffering emerges because of the service undertaken; hence the

---

of restoration under the king of Babylon). See also Jer 2:21; 11:17; 12:2; and 32:40–41. Brueggemann sees in these six verbs the articulation of the prophet's two-part message of judgment and hope. *Theology of the Book of Jeremiah*, 35–38.

20. This is not a new theme among biblical writers. Dennis Olson has argued that the book of Numbers can be divided structurally into two parts, each of which opens with a census of the people. The first half of the book (chaps. 1–25) is centered on the death of the old generation that had witnessed the Exodus events, while the second part of the book (chaps. 26–36) focuses on the new generation of hope. *Numbers*.

prophet is not the suffering representative of the people, but one who embodies the suffering of God.[21]

It is in this embodiment of God's suffering that prophetic lament is given meaning. It is worth noticing that Jeremiah's role in the exercise of Yahweh's judgment is fundamentally different from that of Abraham or Moses. Hard on the heals of Yahweh's covenant making, Abraham and Moses are invited to discuss and dispute with God the meaning of his judgment. Yahweh says to Abraham regarding his plans to destroy Sodom, "Shall I hide from Abraham what I am about to do" (Gen 18:17), whereupon Abraham reasons with God regarding what is and is not a worthy expression of his judgment. When Israel sins by worshipping the image of a calf, Yahweh says to Moses "Now leave me alone, so that my wrath may burn hot against them and I may consume them" (Exod 32:10), whereupon Moses decidedly does not leave God alone, but persuades him to relinquish his plans. But Jeremiah does not simply advice or admonish God concerning his plans for Israel. Rather he shares with God in the cost of such counsel. God's suffering is prolonged by his unwillingness to enact judgment and by entering into God's suffering, the significance of Jeremiah's experience is transformed. He is not the victim of a tyrant's capriciousness, but a partner with God in his pain.

The persecution that Jeremiah experiences is stirred up by the prophetic word that he has been charged to proclaim. In reflecting on the origins of his ministry, Jeremiah recalls, "Your words were found, and I ate them, and your words became to me a joy and the delight of my heart; for I am called by your name, O LORD, God of hosts." (Jer 15:16). And yet the prophet's joy is short-lived as he finds that the prophetic commission sets him apart from those who rejoice, filling him instead with indignation. Joy turns to "pain unceasing," so that the Jeremiah feels betrayed by God. In Jeremiah's fourth confession, he is rebuked by Yahweh for the words that he speaks and Yahweh's promise of protection depends upon the prophet mending his speech.

---

21. Fretheim, *The Suffering of God*, 154. Part of the significance of pairing Lamentations with the prophecies of Jeremiah is that together that present a balanced understanding of the prophet's role in shared suffering. In Jeremiah the prophet's suffering represents the divine partner, while in Lamentations it is Israel's suffering that the speaker embodies and reveals.

Therefore, thus says the LORD:
If you turn back, I will take you back,
    and you shall stand before me.
If you utter what is precious, and not what is worthless,
    you shall serve as my mouth.
It is they who will turn to you,
    not you who will turn to them.
And I will make you to this people
    a fortified wall of bronze;
they will fight against you,
    but they shall not prevail over you,
for I am with you
    to save you and deliver you. (Jer 15:19–20)

In Jeremiah's fifth confession, 17:14–18, the prophet appeals to God for deliverance, offering as a motivation his faithful service and faithful speech in vv. 15–16. Here Jeremiah comes to the realization that the bearing of the word of Yahweh has been his undoing. By the time he reaches his final confession Jeremiah concludes; "For the word of the LORD has become for me a reproach and derision all day long."

This failure on Yahweh's part to insulate his messenger has occasioned for Jeremiah a crisis of trust.[22] He begins his prophecy by mocking the people's stupidity.

For my people have committed two evils:
    They have forsaken me, the fountain of living water, and dug
    out cisterns for themselves,
    cracked cisterns that can hold no water. (Jer 2:13)

But as his ordeal unfolds, Jeremiah changes his view. Faithfulness to Yahweh no longer seems a guarantee of life and sustenance. "Truly," the prophet accuses Yahweh, "you are to me like a deceitful brook, like waters that fail" (Jer 15:18b). Samuel Balentine sees here evidence of a fundamental conflict in the prophet's understanding of God. He points out that in 17:17 God is both a terror and a refuge to the prophet.

God had promised his presence; of this Jeremiah was certain. But the way in which God would be present is not given. God's presence could not be manipulated: it could only be expected.

22. Crenshaw, *A Whirlpool of Torment*, 48. Fuchs identifies the constant fluctuation between trust and doubt as a key component of the lament prayer in "Die Klage des Propheten," 223.

The way in which Jeremiah addresses God suggests that he understood this fundamental characteristic of God even if, at times, it was an understanding painfully hard to live with (e.g., 4:19; 10:19; 12:1–3; 15:10; 20:14–18).[23]

The problem for the prophet is one of distance. It is not that Yahweh has removed himself and is far away, as in the case of the lament Psalms, but rather that he is too near and too involved. He has joined himself with his people, indeed married them, and in so doing has lowered his guard and become vulnerable. Jeremiah suffers not because God is absent, but because the divine partner is exposed and at risk.

Jeremiah's crisis of trust reaches its crescendo in the final confession. In 20:7 Jeremiah accuses God of deceiving and attacking him.

> O LORD, you have enticed [deceived] me, and I was enticed;
>   you have overpowered me, and you have prevailed.
> I have become a laughing-stock all day long;
>   everyone mocks me.

Yahweh, it seems, has failed to make good on his promise to be a wall of protection for the prophet.

Finally, though, we should not seek to understand Yahweh's apparent faithlessness apart from the prophet's calling to enter into the woundedness of God. Unlike Job, Jeremiah takes up the suffering of another. He finds himself abused and abandoned precisely because he accepted the calling to take up God's offense and weep with him. Jeremiah stands in a new place, heretofore only hinted at in the Psalter. The pain that brings a protest to Jeremiah's lips is the pain of God. It is this burden that shapes the prophetic lament.

Answers Devoid of Comfort

One of the more unusual features of Jeremiah's confessions compared with those found in the Psalter is the frequency with which Yahweh responds directly to the prophet's prayers.[24] This underscores the distinct nature of Jeremiah's problem. God has not hidden his face so that he does not see and cannot hear, as is so often the case in the Psalms and Job. On the contrary, Yahweh is quick to answer his prophet.

23. Balentine, "Jeremiah, Prophet of Prayer," 337.

24. Among the lament Psalms, only 12:5 records a direct divine response to the prayer.

Following the direction suggested by Baumgartner of liken-ing Jeremiah's confessions to the laments found in the Psalter, Ernest Nicholson has seen in these divine answers to prayer evidence of the liturgical functioning of Jeremiah's laments.[25] It has long been observed that many of the psalms of lament contain an abrupt shift from lament to praise, so that while they begin by crying out to God, they finish up praising him for deliverance. Joachim Begrich has suggested that the stimulus for this sudden shift was a *"priesterliche Heilsorakel"* or "priestly salvation oracle" pronounced by the priest as part of a liturgy, but not included in the prayers themselves.[26] Thus the "answer" that the lamenter receives, causing him or her to move from complaint to praise, is a liturgical one, rather than a change in outward circumstances or a more direct experience of encounter with God in prayer. Although Begrich's hypothesis has gained wide acceptance among Psalms schol-ars, there are a number of fundamental problems with his suggestion, not the least of which is the absence of any clear example of a salva-tion oracle anywhere in the Psalter to mirror those that Begrich finds in the prophecy of Isaiah.[27] In the context of Jeremiah's confessions, two additional objections can be made to offering this as a model for un-derstanding the divine responses to Jeremiah's laments. First of all, the content of the God's response only initially promises deliverance from his condition of suffering. Such promises are only offered as long as the prophet confines himself to expressing his own suffering and disappear as soon as he moves to questioning and accusing Yahweh. Secondly, the divine responses to Jeremiah's laments are not followed, as they are in the Psalms, by a shift from lament to praise, but rather by a renewed complaint from the prophet, a return to prophetic oracles against Judah, and a promise of further hardship for the prophet.[28] God's responses to

25. For examples, see Nicholson, *Jeremiah 1–25*, 112.

26. Begrich, "Das priesterliche Heilsorakel."

27. Conrad has offered a compelling critique of Begrich's hypothesis, pointing to numerous weaknesses in his arguments. At the heart of Conrad's critique is the observa-tion that this solution borrows a reassurance formula from Second Isaiah without any evidence either of corresponding prayers of lament in Isaiah or of a similar assurance formula in the psalms of lament. "Second Isaiah and the Priestly Oracle of Salvation."

28. Bright has pointed out that God's response to the prophet in 15:19–21 does not fit the recognized form for a *Heilsorakel* or salvation oracle and should be understood as a rebuke and a conditional promise. "Lament and Its Answer: Jeremiah 15:10–21." See also Diamond, *The Confessions of Jeremiah in Context*, 74–75.

Jeremiah cannot be understood as a liturgical device intended to transform his lament. The divine responses to Jeremiah's prayers do not put an end to his complaints which in fact intensify as a result of Yahweh's promises to deliver.

The first four confessions of the prophet occur in pairs, with each pair following a similar pattern. The pair of confessions in both 11:18–12:8 and 15:10–21 consist of two prayers of lament by the prophet, each followed by a divine response. In the first part of each pair of confessions, Jeremiah voices his suffering and/or a desire for vindication.

> But I was like a gentle lamb led to the slaughter . . .
> But you, O LORD of hosts, who judge righteously,
>   who try the heart and the mind,
> let me see your retribution upon them,
>   for to you I have committed my cause. (Jer 11:19a, 20)

"Woe is me, my mother, that you ever bore me, a man of strife and contention to the whole land!" (Jer 15:10). To these Yahweh responds with a promise to punish the prophet's enemies. "Therefore thus says the LORD of hosts: I am going to punish them; the young men shall die by the sword; their sons and their daughter shall die by famine; and not even a remnant shall be left of them" (Jer 11:22–23a). "Your wealth and your treasures I will give as plunder, without price, for all your sins, throughout all your territory" (Jer 15:13). This pattern of complaint followed by an expression of confidence that the Lord will deliver and vindicate is familiar from the Psalms of lament, although the recording of Yahweh's answer is not.

In both instances, though, the prophet follows the first divine response with a return to lament. This second confession in each pair is marked by a change of tone and subject. In 12:1–4 Jeremiah calls God to appear in court so that he may answer for allowing the wicked to prosper. The prophet's tone is respectful, but he nevertheless seeks to put God on the defensive. In 15:15–18, the prophet thinks back on his initial calling and reflects on the fact that, while he has kept his end of the bargain and faithfully proclaimed his assigned message, Yahweh has failed to keep his promise to protect his chosen mouthpiece. "Why is my pain unceasing, my wound incurable, refusing to be healed? Truly, you are to me like a deceitful brook, like waters that fail" (Jer 15:18). This change of attitude on the part of the prophet elicits in both instances a shift in Yahweh's response. To the questioning of his justice in chapter 12, Yahweh gives an answer reminiscent of the questions that Yahweh puts to Job in response to his complaints, querying the prophet's ability even fully to understand the scope of the question that he is posing.

> If you have raced with foot-runners and they have wearied you,
>   how will you compete with horses?
> And if in a safe land you fall down,
>   how will you fare in the thickets of the Jordan? (Jer 12:5)

Far from offering to relieve the prophet's anguish, Yahweh promises that what he has experienced to date is just a foretaste. Yahweh's restraint in judging the wicked runs deeper than the prophet yet realizes. To the accusation in chapter 15 that the "reliable cistern" and the "fountain of living water" has become a deceitful brook, Yahweh responds that it is the prophet's speech that has gone astray. He demands that his prophet repent and cease for speaking what is worthless rather than what is precious.

> Therefore, thus says the LORD:
> If you turn back, I will take you back,
>   and you shall stand before me.
> If you utter what is precious, and not what is worthless,
>   you shall serve as my mouth.
> It is they who will turn to you,
>   not you who will turn them. (Jer 15:19)

The questions that Jeremiah's affliction has provoked meet with sharp rebuke rather than explanation or justification. As in the case of Job, Yahweh's answers are overpowering, even bullying. They seem to confuse and evade the issues at hand rather than responding to them.

The key to comprehending these exchanges between God and his prophet lies in correctly understanding the prophetic task.[29]

> A distinction between prophetic office and ordinary worshiper may be the clue to understanding this divine response.

---

29. Von Rad has argued that in the act of lament Jeremiah has stepped away from his prophetic office. "Yet he differs from all his predecessors in that with him the prophetic office—which in the case of Amos was still a monolithic whole – breaks apart at a decisive point, and through that rift an ominous gloom rushes in, devoid of light." Von Rad fails to take account, though, of the laments of Yahweh that are such a prominent feature of the book. Nor does he give adequate consideration to the representational nature of Jeremiah's suffering. Von Rad, "The Confessions of Jeremiah," 88–99, 97.

If Jeremiah proceeds with his charges against God, he can no longer function as an extension of the divine utterance. In short, he cannot serve as God's mouth if the words he proclaims undermine the speaker and place the deity's trustworthiness in doubt.[30]

Jeremiah is called not simply to proclaim God's words, but to share in the divine experience of rejection. The suffering that the prophet experiences as a result of judgment delayed reflects not a cruel capriciousness on Yahweh's part, but rather a conflict within God himself between the desires for judgment and mercy. Terence Fretheim suggests that we can best understand the roughness of God's answers to Jeremiah by realizing that they reveal an essential tension in his nature.

> The tension in God over what to do with the people whom he loves has its earthly counterpart in the prophet . . . It is in this context that the two instances of God's rebuke of Jeremiah (12:5; 15:19–20) are to be understood. Jeremiah seeks to be relieved of this tension (15:18a); he has had enough of weariness (12:5). God continues to bear up under this tension, but Jeremiah cannot keep up with God, and so wants it all to end for the wicked right now, not least so that the land will cease to mourn (12:1–4; cf. 23:10) . . . Thus, to be a true prophet is to be willing to stand in the same tension-filled situation as God himself and to endure weariness as long as God does.[31]

Jeremiah's confessions arise from and are grounded in divine suffering and it is this which distinguishes them from the laments found in the Psalter or Job. The closest parallel are those lament psalms which affirm that the people suffer because of their relationship with Yahweh.

> All this has come upon us,
>   yet we have not forgotten you,
>   or been false to your covenant . . .
> Because of you we are being killed all day long,
>   and accounted as sheep for the slaughter. (Ps 44:17, 22)

But we find in Jeremiah that which is lacking in the Psalter, namely, a clear sense that the one praying suffers not for himself, but both for and with another.

---

30. Crenshaw, *A Whirlpool of Torment*, 49.

31. Fretheim, *The Suffering of God*, 159. See also Balentine, "Jeremiah, Prophet of Prayer," 337; and Heschel, *The Prophets*, 108.

Not surprisingly, some scholars have discerned a direct dependence on Jeremiah's confessions in the portrayal of the suffering servant
in Second Isaiah. Sheldon Blank concludes; "The prophet-servant figure
so resembles the prophet Jeremiah in one particular after another that
without a doubt the Second Isaiah chose, as paradigm for the servant,
the life and work of Jeremiah."[32] Kathleen O'Connor suggests that "the
suffering of Jeremiah serves as a paradigm of the innocent suffering of
believers."[33] This element of shared suffering and suffering on behalf of
another marks an essential change in the practice of prophetic lament.

The confessions of Jeremiah are a direct product of the prophetic
call. His suffering is occasioned by the rejection of his message, but he
does more than simply suffer for representing God to the people; he
participates directly in the divine experience of rejection. It is this identification with God's pathos that prolongs Jeremiah's anguish until it
threatens to become unjust. It seems pointless for God to postpone his
divorce and the same hesitation on God's part that fills him with inner
conflict spills over onto the prophet. Jeremiah is called on to endure and
to linger in his pain because Yahweh endures and lingers.

Faith in Tension

In the remaining confessions of Jeremiah, the prophet describes with
increasing urgency and despair his experience of being Yahweh's
mouthpiece. In doing so, he draws heavily on classic elements of lament
prayers. In Jeremiah 17:14–18, for example, he reports the enemy's
taunts; "Where is the word of the LORD? Let it come!" Derision by
the psalm writer's enemies is a common element in psalms of lament;
"As with a deadly wound in my body, my adversaries taunt me, while
they say to me continually, 'Where is your God?'" (Ps 42:10; cf. 35:21,
25; 40:14–15; 70:2–3; and 71:11). Jeremiah also makes a conventional
protestation of innocence in the face of his enemy's attacks; "But I have
not run away from being a shepherd in your service, nor have I desired
the fatal day." Such pronouncements set the tone of the lament as one of
bewilderment, frustration, and even outrage.

32. Blank, "The Prophet as Paradigm," 111–30, 126.

33. O'Connor, *The Confessions of Jeremiah*, 169. See also Polk, *The Prophetic
Persona*, 129.

> They beset me with words of hate,
>> and attack me without cause.
> In return for my love they accuse me,
>> even while I make prayer for them.
> So they reward me evil for good,
>> and hatred for my love.
> (Ps 109:3–5; cf. 7:3–5, 8; 26; 35:7; 44:17–22; and 59:3–4)

A third element in Jeremiah's confession in chapter 17 that is common to the psalms of lament is the two-part prayer of for deliverance and vindication that essentially says; "save me, but destroy them." Verse 18 expresses this desire:

> Let my persecutors be *shamed*,
>> but do not let me be *shamed*;
> let them be *dismayed*,
>> but do not let me be *dismayed*;
> bring on them the day of *disaster*;
>> destroy them with *double destruction*.

The three-part parallelism presents a contrast that sharply distinguishes the prophet from his enemies, "shamed // not shamed; dismayed // not dismayed," and an intensification, wishing for the adversary "disaster // double destruction."

Jeremiah's sixth confession in 18:19–23 is reminiscent of Psalm 109. In both laments the one praying wishes that his of her enemies would suffer eternal destruction, that is, that all their males of child-bearing age and all their children that would keep alive hope for a future would meet with destruction, so that the very memory of them would cease to exist.

> May the iniquity of his father be remembered before the
> LORD,
>> and do not let the sin of his mother be blotted out.
> Let them be before the LORD continually,
>> and may his memory be cut off from the earth.
> (Ps 109:14–15)

> Do not forgive their iniquity,
>> do not blot out their sin from your sight.
> Let them be tripped up before you;
>> deal with them while you are angry. (Jer 18:23b)

Jeremiah 20:7–18 brings the prophet's lament to a climax. There is a disjointed three-part vacillation as the passage unfolds. Verses 7–10 are marked by bitter accusation against God and a sense of the prophet being trapped by his calling.

> O LORD, you have enticed me, and I was enticed;
>> you have overpowered me and you have prevailed.
> I have become a laughing-stock all day long;
>> everyone mocks me . . .
> If I say, 'I will not mention him,
>> or speak any more in his name,'
> then within me there is something like a burning fire
>> shut up in my bones;
> I am weary from holding it in,
>> and I cannot.

Scholars have frequently pointed to the graphic nature of the violence suggested in this verse. Samuel Balentine asserts:

> The Hebrew text is embarrassingly plain: the word for "deceived" (*pathah*) is that which is used elsewhere to describe the seduction of a virgin for the purpose of having sexual relations with her (Ex 22:16; cf. Judg 16:5; Job 31:9; Hos 2:14) . . . The language employed here refers in other places to sexual assault, more particularly to the force exercised by a man in seducing a young woman (cf. Deut 22:25; 2 Sam 13:11). The reference in verse 8 to Jeremiah's cry, "Violence and destruction," may also carry a sexual connotation, perhaps suggesting the cry of one who has been sexually violated (cf. Deut 22:27).[34]

A. R. Diamond points out, however, that prophetic use of the verb *pathah* elsewhere does not carry with it sexual connotations, so that "it is not likely that such sexual connotations exert a dominant influence in the present passage."[35] Kathleen O'Connor observes that of the many uses of *pathah* in the Old Testament, only three require a translation that carries with it sexual connotations and she concludes that "A close reading of these shows that the sexual meaning emerges from the contexts and not from the verb itself."[36] David Clines and David Gunn argue for a

---

34. Balentine, "Jeremiah, Prophet of Prayer," 338. See also Heschel, *The Prophets*, 113; Crenshaw, *A Whirlpool of Torment*, 38.

35. Diamond, *The Confessions of Jeremiah in Context*, 110.

36. O'Connor, *The Confessions of Jeremiah*, 70.

softer reading, "you tried to persuade me," pointing to uses of *pathah* in which there is no connotation of deception. Clines and Gunn, however, do understand the prophet to be protesting against being dominated by Yahweh. "The persuasion has only been God's means to the end of achieving domination (*tûkal*) over the prophet, and it is against that domination that Jeremiah is protesting."[37] The distinction, though, is one of degree and not character. Whether the metaphor is one of sexual assault or violent betrayal or forced domination, clearly Jeremiah sees in his rejection and suffering the destructive hand not just of his enemies, but of Yahweh who called him and then failed to protect him.

And yet in vv. 11–13, the prophet shifts abruptly to an expression of confident trust in Yahweh. "Sing to the LORD; praise the LORD! For he has delivered the life of the needy from the hands of evildoers." Such a movement from lament to praise is typical of the prayers of lament in the Psalter, so that the original unity of vv. 7–13 on form-critical grounds has gained substantial support among scholars.[38]

Form critical parallels with laments in the Psalter do not, however, prepare the reader for the abrupt shift in vv. 14–18. Having just expressed confidence in God, Jeremiah now curses the day of his birth in a manner reminiscent of the third chapter of Job.[39]

> Cursed be the day on which I was born!
>   The day when my mother bore me, let it not be blessed!
> Cursed be the man who brought the news to my father saying,
>   "A child is born to you, a son," making him glad.
> (Jer 20:14–15)

> Let the day perish on which I was born,
>   and the night that said, "A man-child is conceived." (Job 3:3)

Here scholarly consensus judges vv. 14–18 to be affixed by the editor of the book to a psalm of lament that had a previous existence as an independent unit. This raises the question of the function of the curse in vv. 14–18 in the finished text of chapter 20. Clines and Gunn have argued that it is not part of the final confession of Jeremiah, but serves rather to express Jeremiah's distress not for his own rejection, but for that of

37. Clines and Gunn, "'You Tried to Persuade Me,'" 26.

38. Clines and Gunn, "Form, Occasion and Redaction in Jeremiah 20"; and O'Connor, *The Confessions of Jeremiah*, 67–69.

39. See O'Connor, *Confessions of Jeremiah*, 77–78.

Israel that is to be described in chapters 21–24. "Read in this context, the self-curse and the 'why' question (v. 18) are naturally understood as representing the prophet's personal reaction to impending destruction that he will share with his people."[40] This explanation, though, pays little attention to the focus of Jeremiah's confessions. The source of his distress has consistently been the burden of God's message and the resistance that it has occasioned in its hearers. The human enemies that compel the prophet to seek divine help are not located outside the city gate, but within.

By contrast, Walter Brueggemann sees in the abrupt movement from lament to trust to cursing an expression of the turmoil experienced by the prophet. "We must be aware of the odd (and, I judge, deliberate) juxtaposition of Jer 10:7–13 and 14–18. There two poetic units are utterances of faith in tension . . . Such faith as Jeremiah's has seasons of trustful resolution and of bitter alienation."[41] For the community that preserved the prophet's writings, says Brueggemann, it is not the personal suffering of the prophet in this confession that is valued, but the way that his "faith in tension" reflects the tension experienced by the nation. "The two moods here in juxtaposition perhaps echo God's way with Jerusalem, which also knows about judgment and promise, about alienation and resolution."[42]

The reluctance of some scholars to grant to Jeremiah's prophecies a degree of ambiguity or to his character a measure of complexity smacks of condescension. The assumption suggested by limiting the confessions to the familiar form-critical patterns found in the lament psalms is that the writer and/or editors of Jeremiah's prophecies are incapable of adapting a familiar form to a new context or of portraying Jeremiah as anything other than a flat, one-dimensional character. Whether the dissonance expressed in Jeremiah's vacillation between complaint and praise reflects the prophet's personal experience or the complexity of his literary character, that dissonance replicates the tension that is expressed first by Yahweh.

Whether the juxtaposition of vv. 7–13 and vv. 14–18 is a feature original to the prophet's expression of consternation or the product of

40. Clines and Gunn, "Form, Occasion and Redaction in Jeremiah 20," 408.

41. Brueggemann, *Jeremiah 1–25*, 179.

42. Ibid.

a later editor's hand, in its present role it serves to bring to a climax the portrait of the prophet created for the reader by Jeremiah's confessions. In Jeremiah confident trust in God and fidelity to his calling is continually undermined and threatened by the suffering that his obedience continues to occasion. The bitter irony of Jeremiah's message is that, even as he calls Israel back to covenant faithfulness as a means of escaping the impending judgment, his own faithfulness to God's calling both occasions and perpetuates his pain. The word that Yahweh has placed in the prophet's mouth is a consuming fire that threatens to devour the speaker. The prophet was "known," "consecrated," and "appointed" before he was even born and though he stops short of cursing God, Jeremiah curses the moment of his birth that marks the beginning of his indenture to the word and to the suffering of God.

When Judgment Becomes Abusive: The Prophet's Suffering on Behalf of the People in Lamentations

The book of Lamentations is a companion piece for the laments of Jeremiah and marks a pivotal change in the role of the prophet. In the book of Jeremiah the prophet personifies the anguish of a God who has been made a cuckold and has endured lengthy humiliation. In Lamentations, though, the prophet takes up the cause of the cast off remnant of Israel who have experienced the full weight of God's wrath. A defining assumption of the book of Lamentations is that, regardless of the nature of the nation's sin, all judgment must finally be tempered with mercy and forgiveness. Once again the prophet fulfills his calling by embodying the pain of a covenant partner, but this time he represents the exiled survivors, the scope of whose loss now borders on the abusive.

Although ancient tradition generally attributes authorship of Lamentations to the prophet Jeremiah, there is widespread reluctance among contemporary scholars to identify the author of Lamentations with the writer of Jeremiah.[43] Kathleen O'Connor's conclusion is representative; "Lamentations' author or authors are unknown"[44] For our purposes, though, authorship is less relevant than the complementary function of the prophetic laments that these two books together create.

---

43. Provan offers a concise discussion of the range of views held by modern scholars with regard to the authorship and dating of Lamentations. *Lamentations*, 7–9.

44. O'Connor, *Lamentations and the Tears of the World*, 15.

In both writings the prophetic task is to enter into, expose, and express the suffering of another. Together they explore the devastation that this relationship has wrought on both partners, for there can be no "winner" when the marriage ends and neither party escapes unscathed. The two books together fulfill the representational function of prophetic lament.[45]

Although the prayers in Lamentations share much in common with the lament form familiar from the Psalter, sufficient differences of form exist to raise questions about the genre of Lamentations. [46] Claus Westermann rightly rejects Gunkel's classification of the dominant genre as a funeral dirge, pointing out that a dirge proper lacks any sense of trying to motivate God or move him to respond.[47] Dirges express the pain of permanent loss, without the hope of salvation or resurrection, while even at the extremes of suffering, the prayers of Lamentations manifest continued hope. Adele Berlin, attending to the centrality of "daughter Zion," suggests a specialized form, the "Jerusalem lament."[48] Bo Johnson classifies the poems as a *Mischgattung* or mixed form that draws together elements of both the individual and the community lament.[49] The lack of a clear division between individual and community underscores the prophet's role as mediator and fellow-sufferer. Although an exact classification proves challenging, the prayers in Lamentations carry forward the prophetic concerns for the suffering of others and for the tempering of judgment with mercy.

Numbers of scholars have commented on the highly structured nature both of the five individual prayers and of the book as a whole. The first four chapters each form nearly perfect acrostics, while the fifth chapter, though not an acrostic, contains twenty-two verses, the number of letters in the Hebrew alphabet. Until recently a loose consensus

45. The lack of uniform agreement in the tradition regarding the canonical function of Lamentations is reflected by the fact that in the Septuagint it is paired with the prophecy of Jeremiah, which in the Masoretic text it is found in the five "festival books" of the *megilloth* (Ruth, Song of Solomon, Ecclesiastes, Lamentations, and Esther). The prophetic office of lament provides a unifying theme for the two books which is underscored by the placement of Lamentations in the Septuagint.

46. C. W. Miller provides an excellent overview of the discussion of genre in Lamentations. "The Book of Lamentations in Recent Research," 12–15.

47. Westermann, *Lamentations*, 94–95.

48. Berlin, *Lamentations: A Commentary*, 24–25.

49. Johnson, "Form and Message in Lamentations," 60.

among scholars identified chapter three as the focal point of the book on both structural and theological grounds. Alan Mintz typifies this perspective.

> Chapter Three is the monumental center of the Book of Lamentations. It is three times the length of the chapters that flank it on either side; its triple alphabetical acrostic spreads over sixty-six verses. The chapter also contains the most regular use of the distinctive *kinah* meter, the limping, mourning rhythm of 3 + 2 stresses per line. The chapter is also the theological hub of Lamentations.[50]

By identifying the third chapter as its theological center, the book is given an essentially positive tone, in spite of the many expressions of extreme suffering. The move from complaint to confident trust is not linear in Lamentations, as it most often is in the Psalter, but concentric, suggesting a tentative move toward resolution that remains as yet uncertain.

More recent Lamentations scholarship, however, has witnessed a shift in thinking with regard to the overall message of the book. Tod Linafelt reads the book as a collection of "survivor prayers." For the survivor of an atrocity submissive repentance or supplication are inappropriate. Linafelt understands Lamentations to center not on a theological resolution to suffering, but on an expression of pain and protest that seeks to keep the memory of suffering alive.

> Emerging from this reading is an ancient text that, contrary to the consensus of biblical scholars, is more about the *expression* of suffering than the meaning behind it, more about the vicissitudes of *survival* than the abstractions of sin and guilt, and more about *protest* as a religious posture than capitulation or confession.[51]

Linafelt offers three objections to the focus on chapter three as the theological center of the book.

> The focus in nineteenth- and twentieth-century Lamentations scholarship on the suffering man of chapter 3 is variously motivated. There are at least three perceivable biases at play in such

---

50. Mintz, "The Rhetoric of Lamentations," 10. See also Johnson "Form and Message in Lamentations," 60; and Miller, "The Book of Lamentations in Recent Research," 14.

51. Linafelt, *Surviving Lamentations*, 4.

a focus: (1) a male bias toward the male figure of chapter 3;
(2) a Christian bias toward the suffering man of Lamentations
based on a perceived similarity to the figure of Christ; and (3)
a broader emphasis on reconciliation with God rather than
confrontation.[52]

I do not find Linafelt's assumption of a male bias to be compelling. While
there is a male bias in the cultures that have both produced and traditionally interpreted the biblical text, numerous examples can be offered
in the biblical text where a male image provides a negative example,
while a female association is positive. Also Linafelt's assumption that
the modern interpreter will automatically gravitate to the male image
as the defining one, even if that reading is against the grain of the text,
is assumed rather than demonstrated. With regard to the second perceived bias, the prophetic emphasis on innocent suffering for another
is amply attested to in prophetic writers without the need to reference
New Testament theology for support. The argument for the centrality
of the message of chapter three rests on the concentric structure of the
book and not simply on the content of its five chapters. Linafelt's third
suggested bias is, however, more convincing. There is, among modern
readings of the biblical text, a resistance both to prolonged ambiguity and to extended articulations of pain,[53] and Linafelt is right to be
suspicious of an excessive emphasis being placed on the book's third
chapter. Even if chapter three does represent the theological core of
Lamentations, the movement of the book is not a linear one from crisis
to resolution, but rather a circular one that sustains the tension between
expressions of hope and despair. A "happy ending," though very much
hoped for, is still decidedly in doubt.

Linafelt has sought to redress the theological imbalance of the
book by noting that an awareness of sin and guilt, though present in
Lamentations, is deemphasized in favor of the articulation of pain. The
author, though not denying Israel's guilt, "nevertheless saw fit to shift
the focus of these poems away from the issue of guilt and toward the experience of pain and suffering, regardless of guilt."[54] Linafelt's reading of
Lamentations as survival prayers, however, has led him to lean toward

---

52. Ibid., 5.

53. See Brueggemann, "The Costly Loss of Lament."

54. Linafelt, *Surviving Lamentations*, 46.

dissolving the tension between guilt and suffering that the writer of Lamentations has sought to sustain. In his comparison of Lamentation with the holocaust death camp story "The Shawl," for example, Linafelt does not so much counter-balance questions of guilt as bracket them out entirely.

Katheen O'Connor, drawing on Linafelt's reading of Lamentations as "survivor prayer," abandons completely questions of guilt or righteous judgment, drawing on the analogy of the wholly innocent suffering of an abused spouse.

> His merciless battering leaves her faint and she cannot get up. Her words create a scene of domestic violence in which a powerful, angry man beats his wife, hurls her about, and leaves her for dead. The recognition that God is the batterer compounds her pain . . . Like a woman in an abusive relationship, she agrees that YHWH is justified in his treatment of her because she has "rebelled against his word" (1:18a).[55]

The problem with this analogy is that it changes fundamentally the question being addressed in Lamentations from "Does righteous judgment have an end?" to "Can God ever be justified in his acts of violence?" O'Connor's choice of analogies provides the answer for us, as the perpetrator of domestic violence can never be justified. Thus, while recognizing in Lamentations the threat that judgment may become abusive were it to continue, O'Connor's reading of the book makes no attempt to keep alive the struggle to balance divine judgment with divine mercy.[56]

---

55. O'Connor, *Lamentations and The Tears of the World*, 26–27.

56. Dobbs-Allsopp adopts a more balanced view that reflects the tenor of Lamentations more accurately. He argues that "There is genuine acknowledgment of sin in Lamentations, but that is not the whole story, or even the most important part of the story. Whatever Judah's sin may have been—in light of the catastrophe its exact nature is no longer important, it in no way can justify the extent and degree of suffering she has experienced." Dobbs-Allsopp, "Tragedy, Tradition, and Theology in the Book of Lamentations," 37. Blumenthal's application of the metaphor of an abusive spouse to God in the context of the holocaust seems less inappropriate because he offers it in the context of innocent suffering, rather than justice that is deserved, but excessive. "Moments of abuse are characterized not only by deep human suffering but, most importantly, by the innocence of the victim . . . *The innocence of the victim, not the depth of the suffering or the cruelty of the perpetrator, is what makes abusive behavior 'abusive.'*" Blumenthal, *Facing the Abusing God*, 248.

Throughout the five prayers of Lamentations there is movement from acknowledged guilt, to a confession that the debt of that guilt has been paid, to a claim of innocent suffering as the punishment threatens to exceed the crime. The prayers of Lamentations do not deny Israel's guilt and some acknowledgment of sin can be found in each of the five chapters (1:5, 8, 9, 14, 18, 20, 22; 2:14; 3:39–42; 4:13; and 5:7, 16). It should be noted, though, that such confessions predominate in the first chapter and are far less numerous as the book unfolds. Chapter four in particular asserts that God's wrath has been fully poured out, so that if suffering were to continue for Israel, it would no longer be justified.

> For the chastisement of my people has been greater than the punishment of Sodom . . . The LORD gave full vent to his wrath; he poured out his hot anger . . . The punishment of your iniquity, O daughter Zion, is accomplished, he will keep you in exile no longer. (Jer 4:6, 11, and 22)

Should Yahweh fail finally to respond with mercy, then and only then would judgment become abusive.

A further indicator that God's continued punishment can no longer be seen as a just punishment for sin is the repeated call to judge Israel's enemies who have persecuted the nation without cause. In Lamentations 1:21–22, even as Israel's guilt is acknowledged, the prophet prays that her enemies will receive a similar punishment.

> Let all their evildoing come before you;
>   and deal with them as you have dealt with me
> because of all my transgressions;
>   for my groans are many and my heart is faint. (1:22)

Lamentations 3:52–66 contains an extended curse against "those who were my enemies *without cause*," while the last two verses of chapter four warn Edom of impending judgment. The cup from which Zion was forced to drink will now be passed to Edom and while Zion's chastisement is fully accomplished, Edom's has yet to begin.

Chapter three describes the unfailing mercy and faithfulness of Yahweh.

> But this I call to mind,
>   and therefore I have hope:
> The steadfast love of the LORD never ceases,
>   his mercies never come to an end;

> they are new every morning;
>> great is his faithfulness . . .
> For the Lord will not
>> reject for ever.
> Although he causes grief, he will have compassion
>> according to the abundance of his steadfast love;
> for he does not willing afflict
>> or grieve anyone. (Lam 3:21–23, 31–32)

What the prophet learned to his detriment and expressed in the Confessions is now put to good use in calling an end to Israel's punishment. The compassion of Yahweh consistently qualifies his judgment and must inevitably place limits on his wrath. It is in this context that the closing verses of the book should be understood.

> Restore us to yourself, O LORD, that we may be restored;
>> renew our days as of old—
> unless you have utterly rejected us,
>> and are angry with us beyond measure. (Lam 5:21–22)

In a move reminiscent of Abraham's challenge "Shall not the judge of all the earth do what is just?" in Genesis 18:25, these prayers suggest that God's wrath has burned too long and that he has forgotten to be merciful. For Yahweh to continue to do so would be for him to abandon his own name. Exodus 34:5–7 names Yahweh as one who lives within the tension of compassion and judgment.

> The LORD descended in the cloud and stood with him there, and proclaimed the name, "The LORD." The LORD passed before him, and proclaimed, "The LORD, the LORD, a God merciful and gracious, slow to anger, and abounding in steadfast love and faithfulness, keeping steadfast love for the thousandth generation, forgiving iniquity and transgression and sin, and yet by no means clearing the guilt, but visiting the iniquity of the parents upon the children and the children's children, to the third and fourth generation."

Having reminded God of his nature, the lament of the prophet calls Yahweh to act like himself. Yahweh is not, as O'Connor has suggested, an abusive spouse, but should he fail to respond to the prayer of lament that is precisely what he would become. The continued pursuit of wrath would lead to the denial of the divine name.

A New Covenant Born from Tears

The prophecies of Jeremiah, which are so defined by the prophet's immersion in the suffering of God, also look ahead to newness. In Jeremiah 31 the prophet speaks of a new covenant; "The days are surely coming, says the LORD, when I will make a new covenant with the house of Israel and the house of Judah." The central message of the prophet announced in 1:10 is reiterated in 31:28, as the prophet looks beyond judgment to a new beginning; "And just as I have watched over them to pluck up and break down, to overthrow, destroy, and bring evil, so I will watch over them to build and to plant, says the LORD."

Of interest to our study is the inclusion in this chapter of both human lament and the pathos of God. The promise of newness is given in the context of Rachel's tears.

> A voice is heard in Ramah,
>   lamentation and bitter weeping.
> Rachel is weeping for her children;
>   she refuses to be comforted for her children,
>   because they are no more. (Jer 31:15)

We will give further attention to Rachel's tears as a foundation for the new covenant in the next chapter with a look at the function of the prayer of lament in the New Testament. As Jeremiah has learned through his own experience as God's prophet, in the face of Israel's sin newness is only possible when it is accompanied by loss. God will only build and plant after he has plucked up, pulled down, destroyed and overthrown.

But chapter 31 contains another element that is also fundamental to the message of the book, namely the pathos of God.

> Is Ephraim my dear son?
>   Is he the child I delight in?
> As often as I speak against him,
>   I still remember him.
> Therefore I am deeply moved for him;
>   I will surely have mercy on him, says the LORD. (Jer 31:20)

The suffering of both covenant partners accompany the vision of a new covenant. Jeremiah's laments are more than merely an expression of his personal pain. Nor are they simply the postmortem on a covenant relationship that has reached its end. They embody the suffering of both spouses, of both Rachel and Yahweh, as the bonds of the marriage covenant are first broken and then restored. The cry of lament prepares the ground for the renewal of life and covenant.

It is tempting to suggest that such renewal would not be possible in the deuteronomic reading of the covenant, where the God of Mount Gerizim and Mount Ebal speaks only of blessing and cursing, of the reward for obedience and the cost of rebellion. But it is the prophet's discovery that Yahweh is not just a lord to whom obedience is due, but also a spouse who loves beyond reason. Without the suffering of God and God's prophet, divorce might well be the final word in the Sinai covenant, so that Rachel's tears would find no comfort.

Risking Injustice

At risk in the confessions of Jeremiah is the assumption that God is clearly and unambiguously committed to the unqualified execution of justice. The great irony of the prophecies of Jeremiah is that, even while calling Israel back to covenant obedience, Yahweh proves to be highly reluctant to enforce the terms of that covenant. Yahweh both announces the judgment of divorce and pronounces the impossibility of repentance once that divorce is finalized.

> If a man divorces his wife
>   and she goes from him
> and becomes another man's wife,
>   will he return to her?
> Would not such a land be greatly polluted?
> You have played the whore with many lovers;
>   and would you return to me? (Jer 3:1)

God lingers long in his suffering, to the point of provoking in his prophet questions of his justice and faithfulness. He has become to Jeremiah a deceitful brook not because of his capricious cruelty, but because when the time comes to finalize the divorce, he hesitates. At risk in the prophecies of Jeremiah is the God of sure, swift justice. Even though Yahweh plucks up and pulls down in order to later build and plant, he nevertheless is reluctant to begin the process. Having decreed the divorce, it is Yahweh himself who threatens to pollute the land by taking back the wife that has abandoned him for other lovers.

And yet it is precisely this vulnerability in God that the prophet appeals to in Lamentations. God's wrath, though long delayed, has finally been fully poured out. But the prophet's prayers center on his commitment to a core belief, that God's compassion will inevitably limited his wrath. The confessions of Jeremiah arise from and testify to a God divided within himself, whose compassion makes every exercise of judgment uncertain and open-ended.

In the next chapter we will explore the use of lament in the New Testament. Though far less common in the second covenant, prayers of lament follow the trajectory set for them by the prophet Jeremiah. His promise that the new covenant must be accompanied by the weeping of Rachel comes to fruition with the birth of Messiah.

6

Can Messiah Come Without a Cry?

Lament in the New Testament

Elements of the gospel which I had always thought would console did not. They did something else, something important, but not that. It did not console me to be reminded of the hope of resurrection. If I had forgotten that hope, then it would indeed have brought light into my life to be reminded of it. But I did not think of death as a bottomless pit. I did not grieve as one who has no hope. Yet Eric is gone, here and now he is gone; now I cannot talk with him, now I cannot see him, now I cannot hug him, now I cannot hear of his plans for the future. That is my sorrow. A friend said, "Remember, he's in good hands." I was deeply moved. But that reality does not put Eric back in my hands now. That's my grief. For that grief, what consolation can there be other than having him back? . . . Though I shall indeed recall that death is being overcome, my grief is that death still stalks this world and one day knifed down my Eric.[1]

Seeking Lost Lament

TWO DECADES AGO WALTER BRUEGGEMANN WARNED THE CHURCH of the perils of "The Costly Loss of Lament."[2] Prayers of lament, he suggested, expose tears in the fabric of society and community that a wealthy, triumphalistic church is often unwilling to acknowledge. Having argued persuasively that the language of lament must be recovered, Brueggemann's observations invite us to take up the task of reinvesting in the practice of lament. One obstacle to the fresh own-

---

1. Wolterstorff, *Lament for a Son*, 31–32.
2. Brueggemann, "The Costly Loss of Lament."

ing of lament in a Christian context, though, is the New Testament itself, which includes little in the way of lament and which has been interpreted theologically by some as actively discouraging prayers of lament among Christians.[3] In this chapter we will examine the use of lament in the New Testament, with particular attention to the ways that it functions and the roles that it fulfills. Our discussion will fall into four parts: the extent to which the lament prayer form is found in the New Testament, a consideration of the New Testament doctrine of our shared suffering with Christ that appears to invalidate the prayer of lament under the New Covenant, observations on the function of lament within the structure of the Revelation of John, and an exploration of the canonical function of lament in Matthew.

References, Fragments, and Allusions to Lament in the New Testament

Intact prayers of lament that contain a significant number of the elements typical to the form as it is used in the Old Testament are almost entirely absent from the New Testament.[4] Characteristically, lament prayers contain such elements as a cry or invocation addressed to God, a complaint describing the problem, a plea both for deliverance and for the destruction of one's enemies, motives offered why God should save, a recollection of past experiences of God's salvation, a confession of trust, a vow of praise, and a transition from lament to praise once the person praying has experienced or is fully confident of deliverance. While it is unusual to find all of these elements in any single example, we can identify an example of the lament form when a reasonable number of these elements are present and when the overall context of the prayer is a crisis or circumstance of need.

3. Claus Westermann suggests the influence of Greek stoic philosophy on western Christian thought as an explanation for the disappearance of lament from prayer and worship in the West; *The Praise of God in the Psalms*, 265.

4. As Douglas Moo's excellent study demonstrates, many of the New Testament's borrowings of laments from the Old are in the form of indirect allusions, and when a writer does quote an Old Testament lament directly, the quotation is fragmentary and there is no attempt to apply the intact form. *The Old Testament in the Gospel Passion Narratives*, 225–300. The same point is illustrated in a more focused way by John H. Reumann's study of the use of Psalm 22 with reference to the crucifixion. The psalm as a unit is essentially ignored as individual verses are quoted or alluded to in widely varied contexts. "Psalm 22 at the Cross."

While not appearing fully formed in the New Testament, prayers of lament do occur expressed as references, fragments, and allusions. References are made to laments being offered without the reader being told their content. So, for example, we read in Matthew:

> A voice was heard in Ramah,
>   wailing and loud lamentation,
> Rachel weeping for her children;
>   she refused to be consoled,
>   because they are no more. (Matt 2:18)

The content of that lament is not revealed and we cannot even be certain that it transcended raw cries of anguish to find expression as coherent prayer. On other occasions we glimpse the central content of the lament prayer, though the full prayer is not recorded. This is the case of Jesus' prayers in Gethsemane (Matt 26:36–46; Mark 14:32–42; Luke 22:39–46) in which hours of anguished prayer are summarized for us with the core petition, "My Father, if it is possible, let this cup pass from me." This may also be the case when Jesus weeps over the city of Jerusalem (Matt 23:37–39; Luke 13:34–35). The parable of the Widow and the Unjust Judge in Luke 18:1–8 is more concerned with the fact of ongoing, persistent lament as a model of faith-filled prayer than it is with the content of such prayer. In a similar vein, three times Paul offers a prayer for deliverance from his thorn in the flesh (2 Cor 12:8–9) and while we know the answer that he receives, "My grace is sufficient for you," the specifics of his prayers are not recorded. Again the emphasis appears to be on the fact of lament rather than its content.

Lament fragments, isolated petitions that are self-contained and stand alone, are also common. Cries that demand to know "Why?" and "How long?", though a hallmark Old Testament prayers of lament, are almost completely absent from the New Testament.[5] More common are lament fragments found in healing and deliverance stories, often consisting of a simple invocation and plea, such as the cry of blind Bartimaeus, "Jesus, Son of David, have mercy on me!" (Mark 10:46–52; cf. Matt 8:1–4; 17:14–16; 20:29–34; Mark 10:46–52; Luke 18:35–43). They are also tied to Jesus' working of miraculous signs that reveal and

---

5. The only occurrence of "Why?" directed to God is Jesus quotation of Ps 22:1 on the cross in Matt 27:46 and Mark 15:34. The question "How long?" appears only as a prayer of lament on the lips of Christian martyrs awaiting God's judgment of the wicked in Rev 6:10.

advance his messianic mission. The disciples, for example, fearing that their boat is about to be swamped manage a quick invocation, plea, and complaint all in one breath: "Lord, save us! We are perishing!" (Matt 8:25, 27; cf. Matt 8:1–4; 14:29–33; Mark 1:40–45; 4:37–41; Luke 5:12–16; 8:22–25; 9:37–43; 17:11–14). The result of their brief prayer and Jesus' response is renewed wonder as to "what sort of man this is."

Christ upon the cross makes a direct allusion to the lament prayers in Psalm 22, "My God, my God, why have you forsaken me?," and Psalm 31, "Father, into your hands I commend my spirit."[6] Such allusions point quite naturally beyond themselves to the complete prayers.[7] Though an allusion to every element of the content of both psalms may not be intended, nevertheless, they tap into the lament tradition of Israel in a way that cannot be accidental.

This observation provides the foundation of William Johnson's rejection of Jürgen Moltmann's claim that Jesus' cry on the cross signals the actual abandonment of Christ by the Father.[8] Johnson points to the many parallels between the gospel's account of Jesus' crucifixion and the content of Psalm 22 to support his contention that Jesus' cry is, in fact, an intentional allusion to and utilization of the entire psalm

6. Matt 27:46; Mark 15:34; and Luke 23:46. Although the verse cited expresses a confident trust in God, Psalm 31 is a lament to God that turns eventually to an expression of trust, just as Psalm 22 does.

7. Reumann, "Psalm 22 at the Cross," 49; and Mays, "Prayer and Christology," 322.

8. Moltmann dismisses the many additional allusions to Psalm 22 as being later interpretive additions by the church and sees in the cry of Christ recorded by Mark the most historically reliable element of the narrative. He chooses to ignore the interpretive direction taken by the early church of understanding Jesus' cry in the context of the larger psalm, opting instead for the context of Jesus' ministry as the Son of the Father. Jesus' expression of abandonment refers to an ontological change in the divine nature that sets up an enmity of "God against God" that is then resolved in the resurrection. "The cross of the Son divides God from God to the utmost degree of enmity and distinction. The resurrection of the Son abandoned by God unites God with God in the most intimate fellowship." *The Crucified God*, 152. This understanding begs the question of why Jesus would cite Psalm 22 in the first place and lends credence to Johnson's belief that Moltmann is ignoring the textual context "in the service of a rather extreme theology of creation, a theology that alleges the world stands under complete and unrelenting alienation, darkness, and despair." Johnson, "Jesus' Cry, God's Cry, and Ours," 84. By loosing Jesus' citation from its immediate context both in its original setting in the Psalter and in its application in the gospels, Moltmann creates a great deal of latitude for introducing a theological model that is not broadly attested to in the wider biblical text. His application of this single verse, while ignoring questions of context, leans heavily toward prooftexting.

and not, as Moltmann maintains, the recasting of a single verse in an wholly new context with an entirely new meaning. As a result, Johnson contends, we must understand the crucifixion event not in terms of God-abandonment, but rather of God's presence to deliver. "Jesus, in lifting up the lament from Psalm 22, is situating himself directly within that long line of servants who have suffered unjustly for God's sake and whom God will *not* abandon."[9] Allusions to the laments in the Old Testament point both to the fuller text of specific laments and to the broader lament traditions.

These references, fragments, and allusions all point to the presence of lament embedded in the fabric of the New Testament. They do more than simply adopt a familiar form of prayer, incorporating the broader significance of that form. Lament in the New Testament communicates in a type of shorthand that carries with it an excess of meaning. As we shall see, lament in the New Testament provides a source of continuity with the traditions and perspectives of the first covenant.

Though much less common in the New Testament, lament is nevertheless present throughout its writings. This does not, however, address the questions "Why do we find so few prayers of lament in New Testament writings?" and "Has the death and resurrection of Christ invalidated the practice of lament under the new covenant?"

The New Testament Theology of Shared Suffering

One of the principal arguments against adopting the practice of lament in the Christian context is a pronounced doctrine of the believer's participation in Christ's suffering, which has led some to conclude that expressions of lament are contrary to New Testament practice and faith.[10] Typical of Paul, for example, are such statements as "We know that all things work together for good for those who love God, who are called according to his purpose" (Rom 8:28); and "For this slight momentary affliction is preparing us for an eternal weight of glory beyond all measure" (2 Cor 4:17). For Peter, suffering calls for rejoicing, rather than plea or protest.

9. Johnson, "Jesus' Cry, God's Cry, and Ours," 84.

10. I am aware of presenting a somewhat one-dimensional picture of the New Testament writer's understanding of suffering. Barry D. Smith, for example, has argued for no less than seven Pauline understandings of the cause and function of suffering among godly persons. *Paul's Seven Explanations of the Suffering of the Righteous.*

> In this you rejoice, even if now for a little while you have had to suffer various trials, so that the genuineness of your faith—being more precious than gold that, though perishable, is tested by fire—may be found to result in praise and glory and honor when Jesus Christ is revealed." (1 Pet 1:6–7)

Luke, in describing the flogging of the apostles, reports that, "As they left the council, they rejoiced that they were considered worthy to suffer dishonor for the sake of the name" (Acts 5:41). Similarly James admonishes us; "My brothers and sisters, whenever you face trials of any kind, consider it nothing but joy" (Jas 1:2). Suffering is seen as the mark of our participation in the crucifixion of Christ and is, therefore, to be greeted with joy and thanksgiving, rather than complaint and protest.

Patrick Miller associates the disappearance of lament from the New Testament with an emerging theology of the cross. As a result, in circumstances of suffering, the response of the one in crisis is not a prayer of protest, but one of submission to the will of God and the affirmation that suffering in this present life is of little importance, apart from the representation which it provides of the suffering of Christ. The tone is set already, says Miller, in the Lord's prayer, which affirms in its second line "Your kingdom come. Your will be done, on earth as it is in heaven" (Matt 6:10). He points also to the prayer of Jesus in the garden of Gethsemane in which he pleads "My Father, if it is possible, let this cup pass from me; yet not what I want but what you want" (Matt 26:39; cf. Mark 14:36; Luke 22:42). The Johannine account omits Jesus' prayer in the garden, but includes a statement not found in the Synoptic Gospels; "Now my soul is troubled. And what should I say—'Father, save me from this hour?' No, it is for this reason that I have come to this hour. Father, glorify your name" (John 12:27–28a). In the Pauline writings, Miller points to Paul's thrice repeated prayer that his "thorn in the flesh" should be removed, with God's answer that "My grace is sufficient for you, for power is made perfect in weakness" (2 Cor 12:9). Thus, says Miller, "The *appeal for help* 'for your name's sake' has moved in Paul to an *acceptance of the trouble* 'for the sake of Christ.'"[11] For Miller, the crucifixion of Christ has fulfilled ultimate suffering. New Testament

---

11. Patrick D. Miller, *They Cried to the Lord*, 323.

lament, Miller argues, consists in our taking up of Christ's intercessory lament for the world.[12]

Douglas Hall's vision of a theology of the cross, I believe, leaves greater space for the continued function of lament. By "theology of the cross" Miller refers to participating in the suffering of Christ, so that one's pain and will are subordinated to the larger plan and purpose of God. Hall, on the other hand, offers a broader understanding of suffering as inherent to the very nature of creation, being present in the experiences of loneliness, finitude, temptation, and anxiety. He sees in the cross an acknowledgment that life still carries with it limits and the prospect of failure. Suffering serves a positive role in the Church, says Hall, as a part of human becoming and as participation in the transformative suffering of Christ.[13] Of relevance to our study, though, is the distinction that Hall makes between the suffering that is necessary for human becoming and that which is destructive, detracting from life.[14] While Hall focuses on the former, arguing against a triumphalism in the Church that would seek to bracket out suffering from Christian expectations of life, it seems to me that his second category acknowledges the ongoing place of lament along side of transformative suffering with Christ. Central to the challenge of continuing the practice of lament under the shadow of the cross is a clear distinction between suffering with leads to life and that which diminishes life.

Kathleen Billman and Daniel Migliore have suggested that the acceptance of suffering as part of Christian witness and identification with Christ is often tied directly to the acceptance of a specific vocation:

> It is important to note that in the case of both Jesus and Paul the consent to God's will in the midst of suffering was connected to a specific vocation. It was for the sake of faithfulness to this divinely given vocation that consent was given. Consent was not a result of some general principle of acquiescence governing every instance of suffering.[15]

Vocational suffering that shares in the suffering of Christ does not do away with the cry of lament and even those who have such a vocation

---

12. Patrick D. Miller, "Heaven's Prisoners," 20–23.

13. Hall, *God and Human Suffering*, 128–42.

14. Ibid., 67–68.

15. Billman and Migliore, *Rachel's Cry*, 37.

continue to seek God's deliverance and the working out of his justice against the enemy.

The problem, though, is that personal suffering and vocational suffering may not be as easy to distinguish as Billman and Migliore seem to suggest. Paul's prayer concerning his thorn in the flesh can be seen as an instance of personal suffering that, with God's answer, takes on a vocational significance so that the power of Christ can be revealed. It seems, however, neither possible nor desirable to make a clear distinction between our personal and our vocational lives as Christians. The vocation to follow after Christ and to share in his sufferings cannot, I suggest, be cleanly compartmentalized into personal and vocational aspects.

Nicholas Wolterstorff bases his call for the persistence of lament under the new covenant on the divine benediction in Genesis, "be fruitful and multiply." In what he calls the "each and every principle," Wolterstorff argues that fullness of life and length of days are God's intended desire for his creation. "God desires that each and every human being shall flourish as an animalic person until full of years, and he desires of you and me that we desire that end for ourselves and for our fellow human beings as well."[16] The fact that suffering and death are seen in both testaments as a distortion of creation that will eventually be set right lends credence to Wolterstorff's contention. In God's new heaven and new earth, "no more shall there be in it an infant that lives but a few days, or an old person who does not live out a lifetime; for one who dies at a hundred years will be considered a youth, and one who falls short of a hundred will be considered accursed" (Isa 65:20). In the New Jerusalem God "will wipe every tear from our eyes. Death will be no more; mourning and crying and pain will be no more, for the first things have passed away" (Rev 21:4). As with Hall's understanding of the theology of the cross, though, the problem arises when we try to distinguish clearly between suffering that ultimately promotes life and that which thwarts it.

Though God responds to and works within suffering and death, that is not to say that suffering and death are his desired end for humanity. While the new covenant and Christ's example of suffering for others creates a call for Christians to share in Christ's suffering, that does not negate the fact that sickness and death are a distortion of creation that

16. Wolterstorff, "If God is Good and Sovereign, Why Lament?" 50.

Messiah is overcoming with the advent of his kingdom. Alongside of transformational suffering in the New Testament we still find cries for deliverance, shouts of protest, and even calls for vengeance, all of which characterize the prayer of lament.

Certainly the meaning of suffering and the function of lament are changed in light of the death and resurrection of Christ. Prayers of lament, though, form a backdrop for the unfolding messianic mission attested to in the New Testament. The weaving of lament into the fabric of John's Revelation at a surface level and the more programmatic utilization of lament by Matthew point to the use of lament to provide canonical structure and theological continuity. As such, lament can be understood as instrumental to the expression of the new covenant.

Lament as a Frame for the Revelation of John

We have seen that prayers of lament, though much less common, persist in the New Testament. Certainly, though, the function served by prayers of lament is noticeably different in the New Testament and, for at least two New Testament writers, laments are fundamental to the shape and content of their messages. In the Revelation of John we find lament fragments, including the only New Testament instance of the common lament interrogative "Sovereign Lord . . . how long?" John's use of the lament fragment is significant for two reasons. First of all, it is consistent with the overall message of his vision of travail and tribulation, as the evil powers of this present age seem for a time to be truly unstoppable. Secondly, the placement of lament fragments in Revelation suggests their use in forming a structural *inclusio* for the book as a whole.

The Revelation of John uses lament fragments to provide brackets for God's unfolding judgment on the wicked. In Revelation 6:10 the martyrs cry out from beneath God's altar, "Sovereign Lord, holy and true, how long will it be before you judge and avenge our blood on the inhabitants of the earth?" Both the cry "How long?"[17] and the call for judgment on the wicked[18] are characteristic of the lament form. Also, laments often include a marked shift from lament to praise as the one praying receives an answer. In Revelation 16:5–7 the answer to the martyr's cry is given,

17. Pss 13:1–2; 35:17; 62:3; 74:9–10; 79:5; 80:4; 90:13; 94:3; Jer 4:21.

18. Pss 9:16; 10:15; 31:17; 94:13; 109; 141:10.

And I heard the angel of the waters say,
"You are just, O Holy One, who are and were,
   for you have judged these things;
because they shed the blood of saints and prophets,
   you have given them blood to drink.
It is what they deserve!"
And I heard the altar respond,
"Yes, O Lord God, the Almighty,
   your judgments are true and just!"

The reference to the saints of God slain in his service, to the altar of God, and to the call for judgment against the enemies of God's people in both chapter 6 and 16 of Revelation suggest that the two should be read together as lament and response.[19] Furthermore, in 19:1–2 we find another characteristic lament feature, a move from lament to a hymn of praise: "Hallelujah! Salvation and glory and power to our God, for his judgments are true and just; he has judged the great whore who corrupted the earth with her fornication, and he has avenged on her the blood of his servants." The placement of the cry "How long?" in chapter six, the transition from lament to praise in chapter sixteen as the prayer receives its answer, and the hymn of praise offered in chapter nineteen because "he has judged and avenged" lend to the book of Revelation as a whole the tone of a lament prayer as the unfolding vision moves from a cry in the midst of suffering to a shout of triumph as God answers the prayer of lament. Lament forms part of the fabric of Christ's victory over the power of anti-Christ in the world, shadowing the movement of the book as a whole from the apparent triumph of evil and the delay of salvation to the final victory of God and the destruction of those deserving of judgment. It is also interesting to note that one of the most problematic features of lament prayers in the Old Testament, the cry for God to take vengeance on the enemies of the one praying, figures so prominently in John's vision of the age of the Church leading up to Christ's return to establish his kingdom.[20] The cry of vengeance against those who destroy the innocent is fundamental to John's apocalyptic vision.

19. I am indebted to John Christopher Thomas for first directing my attention to the way that these lament fragments are woven into the structure of the Apocalypse.

20. Zenger has argued that the prayers for vengeance in the Psalms reflect not a personal vindictiveness on the part of the one praying, but rather a more general call for God to restore justice in the face of human violence. Erich Zenger, *A God of Vengeance?* 84–85. Zenger's argument seems better suited for the Revelation of John

The appearance of lament fragments in Revelation, though, is at most suggestive of a backdrop against which the book is to be read. It is in the Gospel of Matthew that we find a clear, programmatic use of lament as an integral part of the overall message of the book.

The Canonical Use of Lament in Matthew

I would like now to focus on Matthew's use of lament at key points in his gospel as a means of heralding and propelling the unfolding of Jesus' messianic ministry. For Matthew lament is programmatic. His account of the birth of Messiah contains not an account of Mary's joy, as in Luke's Gospel, but a report of Rachel's tears. Mary's song of rejoicing in Luke 1:46–55 finds its counterweight in the bitterness and weeping of Rachel: "A voice was heard in Ramah, wailing and loud lamentation, Rachel weeping for her children; she refused to be consoled, because they are no more" (Matt 2:18). Often Rachel's cry is overlooked in our remembrance of the Christmas story. Most of the narrative can be drawn from Luke, although a foray into Matthew must be made in order to recover the story of the three wise men. Why is it, though, that we rarely if ever remember the place of Rachel's lament in the Christmas story?[21]

Kathleen Billman and Daniel Migliore have pointed out the need to balance the prayers of Mary and Rachel.

> Rachel and Mary are thus bound together as sisters of faith in the biblical tradition. Even though the church has often remembered Mary but forgotten Rachel, the two belong together in the prayer and practice of Christian faith. Together they remind us that the danger of praise without lament is triumphalism, and the danger of lament without praise is hopelessness . . . Christian prayer is whole and strong only when it includes both Rachel's cry of sorrow and protest and Mary's cry of joy and praise.[22]

The balancing of Rachel's cry and Mary's song remind us of the fundamental tension that defines life lived in the in-between time. We live

---

than it does for the Psalms, as Revelation clearly intends to address the cosmic implications of evil and God's response to it. In the context of the lament psalms, though, Zenger's solution has the effect of depersonalizing the crisis by making it about violence and injustice in general, rather than about specific experiences that seek immediate and concrete resolution.

21. See Sehested, "A Voice Was Heard in Ramah," 28–29.

22. Billman and Migliore, *Rachel's Cry*, 4.

between the coming of Messiah, with the breaking in of his kingdom, and his return when "he will wipe every tear from their eyes. Death will be no more; mourning and crying and pain will be no more, for the first things have passed away" (Rev 21:4). Rachel weeps with the coming of life that has, nevertheless, not yet fully vanquished death.

Frederick Niedner considers Matthew to be casting the birth of Messiah in terms of a new Exodus, with a new Joseph to dream dreams, a new Pharaoh to slaughter babies, and a single child who escapes to become savior. "By sounding Rachel's lament at the beginning, Matthew makes certain no part of Jesus' story, no piece of the church's narrative tradition regardless of how sweet or apparently innocent, escapes the shadow of the cross."[23] If Niedner is right, then the cry of Rachel is also crucial to Matthew's story for another reason. The Exodus salvation begins with just such a cry.

> The Israelites groaned under their slavery, and cried out. Out of the slavery their cry for help rose up to God. God heard their groaning, and God remembered his covenant with Abraham, Isaac, and Jacob. God looked upon the Israelites, and God took notice of them. (Exod 2:23–24)

Just as the cry of Israelite slaves initiated God's deliverance in the Exodus, so too the initiation of his Exodus of all creation through the birth of Emmanuel finds its genesis in the tears brought about by innocent suffering, obscene corruption, and inconsolable loss. Matthew, though, insists on reminding us that, just as with the Exodus so too with the coming of Messiah, the first word in God's salvation is not a shout of joy, but a cry of pain.

This is not the first place in scripture, though, that we find Rachel weeping and with this reference Matthew draws the Old Testament into the New. In Genesis Jacob's last child is born to him and through that birth he loses his beloved Rachel. Though she has experienced the joy of seeing her barrenness ended, her happiness turns to bitterness as she hemorrhages to death. She names her child Ben-oni or "son of my sorrow." Jacob, though, would not endure so poignant a reminder of the price paid for new life and overrode his dying wife's final wish, renaming the child Benjamin or "son of the right hand" (Gen 35:18). Just as

---

23. Niedner, "Rachel's Lament," 412.

in our reading of the Christmas story, here too the tears of Rachel are unwelcome, even offensive.

But Rachel's tears are remembered again in the prophecy of Jeremiah. In chapter 31 the prophet announces the return of Israel from Exile and the coming of a new covenant. In the midst of such a positive message, though, once again we find Rachel weeping (Jer 31:15), and it is this passage that is cited in Matthew. Emil Fackenheim points out that for Christians the center of Jeremiah 31 is the new covenant, but for Jews it is the weeping of Rachel. More specifically, it is the return from Exile that will finally put an end to that weeping.[24] Matthew's placement of lament at the inception of his gospel sets the tone for what follows. The tears of Rachel herald the coming of Messiah just as surely as does the prophecy of Simeon or the worship of the shepherds in Luke. The advent of Messiah calls us to Exodus. Journeying through the wilderness in the in-between time, there remains a place for lament in our prayers alongside of our praise. Both are faithful prayers. Both result from being in a state of becoming.

But there is a second instance of Matthew's use of lament to provide canonical shape to his message. In Matthew's account of Jesus' encounter with the Canaanite woman, we find the most structurally complete prayer of lament in the New Testament[25] and see most clearly the canonical function of lament as a means of advancing the unfolding of the messianic ministry. Matthew's account reads as follows:

> Jesus left that place and went away to the district of Tyre and Sidon. Just then a Canaanite woman from that region came out and started shouting, "Have mercy on me, Lord, Son of David; my daughter is tormented by a demon." But he did not answer her at all. And his disciples came and urged him, saying, "Send her away, for she keeps shouting after us." He answered, "I was sent only to the lost sheep of the house of Israel." But she came and knelt before him, saying, "Lord, help me." He answered, "It is not fair to take the children's food and throw it to the dogs." She said, "Yes, Lord, yet even the dogs eat the crumbs that fall from their masters' table." Then Jesus answered her, "Woman,

24. Fackenheim, "The Lament of Rachel and the New Covenant."

25. The prayer of the church in Acts 4:24–31 contains an address, complaint, and petition, but its citation of Psalm 2 and general sense that God is sovereign and active, even predestining the persecution experienced by the apostles, prevents our classifying this as a prayer of lament.

great is your faith! Let it be done for you as you wish." And her daughter was healed instantly. (Matt 15:21–28)

The first thing to consider in looking at the passage is its context. Immediately preceding Jesus' discourse with the Canaanite woman is his discussion with the Pharisees and Scribes concerning what is clean and unclean. Promptly following this, Jesus removes himself to Gentile territory (the only time in Matthew), placing himself in the path of the Canaanite woman. Assuming Marcan priority, Matthew makes numerous changes to the version found in Mark 7:24–30. Matthew deletes Mark's explanation, "Let the children be fed first," which served to soften Jesus' rebuff. Matthew adds the initial petition, address, and complaint of the woman, the observation that Jesus responded initially with silence, Jesus' statement to his disciples that "I was sent only to the lost sheep of the house of Israel," and the commendation for the woman's great faith when he finally responds to her prayer. Only Matthew includes the title "Son of David," which has particular messianic significance in his gospel (see Matt 9:27; 21:9, 15; and 22:42), and it is noteworthy that he should place this address on the lips of a Gentile woman at this juncture, as the gospel gradually shifts from being closed to the Gentiles to beginning actively to endorse outreach to the nations.

Jack Dean Kingsbury has pointed out that the title "Son of David" in Matthew's Gospel is never found on the lips of Jesus, his disciples, or prominent religious leaders, but is spoken by those in society who are without position or prestige. "As Matthew tells it, then, it is 'no-accounts' in Israel who 'see' and 'confess' that Jesus is the Son of David, Israel's Messiah. But except for them, Matthew contends that Jesus, Son of David, is neither recognized nor received by Israel as its Messiah."[26] Coupled with this is Terence Mullins's observation that the title "Son of David" is more than a messianic designation for Matthew. Each time it is used the title is accompanied by some reference to blindness and by conflict with the religious leaders.[27] The use of this messianic title here accents the sense of movement in Matthew's Gospel as the long awaited "Son of David" is rejected by the religious leaders who are unable to

26. Kingsbury, "The Title 'Son of David' in Matthew's Gospel," 599–600.

27. Mullins, "Jesus, the 'Son of David,'" 117. See also Loader, "Son of David, Blindness, Possession, and Duality in Matthew"; and Kingsbury, "The Title 'Son of David,'" 601–2.

see, only to be accepted by the outcasts of society and by the Gentile outsiders.

James Kugel has called attention to the role of the cry of the victim in inciting God to establish justice. He argues that we can find in Exodus 22:21–24 a pattern that is repeated in numerous places throughout the Old Testament.[28]

> You shall not wrong or oppress a resident alien, for you were aliens in the land of Egypt. You shall not abuse any widow or orphan. If you do abuse them, when they cry out to me, I will surely heed their cry; my wrath will burn, and I will kill you with the sword, and your wives shall become widows and your children orphans.

Kugel notes that it is not the practice of injustice, but the cry of the victim which sets into motion God's response.

> It is interesting, however, that the prohibition and the punishment for its violation are not quite contiguous: the text does not say, "Do not do this, and if you should do it, then this will be your punishment." Instead, an intermediate element is evoked. If you abuse people who are in this weak, exposed position, "then they will certainly cry out to Me, and I will just as certainly hear them." It is the oppressed human's cry, in other words, that will unleash the chain of events that will ultimately result in your being punished. I am powerless *not* to react, God seems to say, once the abused party cries out to Me.[29]

The fact that Matthew portrays Jesus as initially unwilling to respond to the cry of a Canaanite woman, so that it is her continued cry that finally initiates deliverance, suggests a similar understanding on the part of the gospel writer regarding the role of the victim's cry in provoking divine response.

Kingbury's and Kugel's observations point us in an interesting direction. Just as we can speak of a calling to suffer with Christ that demonstrates his strength in human weakness, so too we can speak of a calling to lament and protest among and on behalf of the powerless in society. It becomes the vocation of the blind, the woman, the Gentile,

---

28. Kugel, *The God of Old*, 109–36. Kugel includes as additional examples Exod 15:24–25; Num 20:16; Judg 10:12; Isa 19:20; Pss 12:5; 34:17; 79:11; 88:1-3; 102:19-20; 145:18-19; Job 34:28; and Neh 9:27.

29. Kugel, *God of Old*, 110.

the widow, and the martyr to hasten the fulfillment of the coming of the kingdom of God. In no sense does this negate the personal element of lament. Those whose babies were slaughtered by Herod, Blind Bartimaeus, the ten lepers, the disciples in the midst of the storm, and the Canaanite woman were no doubt concerned first and foremost about their own need and the expression of their own pain, but for the gospel writers their cries are integrally linked to the coming of Messiah and the proclamation of his gospel. A tension does exist in the New Testament between the call to rejoice in shared suffering with Christ and the continued presence of lament as a voice of protest. As part of the gospel, lament continues to make a claim against those forces that deny dignity, justice, prosperity, and life.

Gail O'Day observes that Matthew's version of the story of the Canaanite woman is cast in the form of a prayer of lament. The Canaanite woman's appeal to Jesus includes four elements common to lament: an address or invocation, a complaint, a plea, and a motivational statement expressing why she should be heard. To this list can be added the divine contribution to lament, namely, the silence of God. Just as the acute crisis in the prayer of lament is the silence of God, so too here we are told explicitly that Jesus "did not answer her at all." But beyond even the form, the woman's approach to Jesus mirrors the persistence and fearlessness demonstrated by Israel's prayers of lament. "The very boldness of the woman's stance before Jesus has it roots in Israel's bold stance before God in the laments."[30] The Canaanite woman holds Jesus to a higher standard of godhood than he initially wishes to meet. She demands that he respond to the prayer of lament, even though it is offered by one who is outside the covenant. The unclean outsider takes the lament of Israel on her lips to address Israel's Messiah and through it forces entrance into the community of the clean for whom God acts to save.

Mark Shipp points out that Matthew's gospel is directed to Jews and yet touches repeatedly on Jesus' mission to the Gentiles.[31] He also describes a tension inherent in the gospel. On the one hand there are a

30. O'Day, "Surprised by Faith," 294.

31. Shipp offers the following list of references in Matthew to Gentiles, the Gentile mission, and the inclusion of Gentiles in the kingdom; 2:1–2; 4:12–17; 6:7, 32; 8:5–13; 10:5, 18; 11:10–22; 12:18–21, 41–42; 15:21–28; 20:25; 21:33–43; 22:1–10; 24:14; 25:32–46; 26:13; and 28:19. "Bread to the Dogs? Matthew 15:21–28 and Tensions in Matthew's Understanding of the Gentiles," 121.

number of passages that indicate that the Gentiles are to have no part in the kingdom, while at the same time Matthew incorporates several traditions that emphasize Gentile inclusion in Jesus' gospel.[32]

In sending out the twelve in Matthew 10:5–6, Jesus commands them expressly to "Go nowhere among the Gentiles, and enter no town of the Samaritans, but go rather to the lost sheep of the house of Israel." In Matthew 15, having just declared to the Pharisees, Scribes, and the multitude that nothing outside a person can make them unclean, Jesus removes himself to Gentile territory. When confronted with the Canaanite woman's lament, he seems at first to contradict what he has just been saying in the previous dialogue. He first responds with silence, the accustomed divine contribution in circumstances of lament. He then repeats his instruction to the twelve; "I was sent only to the lost sheep of the house of Israel," apparently as an explanation to them for his seeming callousness. The prayer of lament, though, is tailor-made to assault the silence of God. In this instance it breaks through Jesus' objection. Like an interrogating police officer, the woman first breaks the barrier of silence, getting Jesus to speak to her. Once she has Jesus talking, the process of changing his position can begin in earnest. Jesus responds sharply—even cruelly—calling his inquisitor a dog, but she beats him at his own game with the insightful "yet even the dogs." By the end of the exchange, lament has claimed the prize and a Gentile now sits at the table of blessing alongside the lost sheep of the house of Israel.

By the end of Matthew, the Great Commission sends the disciple to "all nations." Jesus' mission to the Gentiles is now fully actualized. Of interest to our study is the role played by the Canaanite woman's lament in Matthew's Gospel. As the gospel transitions from an exclusive to an inclusive proclamation, it is the prayer of lament that "breaks through," pushing Jesus into active ministry to a Gentile.

It is true that the centurion in Matthew 8:5–13 also receives a healing for his servant and is commended for his faith prior to this account. In Luke's account, though, he is presented as a "God-fearer" with significant standing in the Jewish community (Luke 7:4–5). Matthew's gospel

32. Shipp, "Bread to the Dogs?" 126. Ulrich Luz explains this apparent tension by located the Matthean community in Syria after the destruction of the temple in A.D. 70. "It [Matthew's gospel] *seeks to provide a new perspective for the Jewish Christian communities in Syria in the name of the exalted Lord, calling them to mission to the Gentiles now that their mission to Israel has failed." Studies in Matthew,* 11.

follows a progression similar to that found in Acts. The first Gentile convert in Acts is also a Roman centurion who is a God-fearer with strong ties to the Jewish community and faith. Both Matthew and Luke choose to transition in stages from an exclusive to an inclusive proclamation of the gospel message. The centurion in Matthew's account is not rebuffed by Jesus, as the woman is, nor does he offer a lament. Indeed, in the account of the centurion's servant, Jesus goes so far as to speak of a future time when "many will come from east and west and will eat with Abraham and Isaac and Jacob in the kingdom of heaven." But the time is not yet. The Canaanite woman refuses, however, to wait for the opportune season. Taking up Israel's most powerful weapon for attacking divine silence, she unleashes lament on a silent Christ and insists that *today* is the day when those who come from afar will no longer have to crawl under the table for scraps, but can sit down with Abraham and Isaac and Jacob and share in the feast of the Lord's table.

The Changing Role of Lament in the New Testament

We can make a number of observations and draw a number of preliminary conclusions from our observations. First of all, prayers of lament, though grounded in specific experiences of loss, transcend the historical context of their origin to serve a theological function. They both herald loss and call for newness. The tears of Rachel, the cry of the disciples in the midst of the storm, and the protest of the Canaanite woman all point beyond the immediate circumstance to a growing awareness of the dawning of the messianic kingdom. Rachel's cry announces the coming of Messiah. The cry of the disciples lead to a deeper understanding of Christ's identity and mission. The lament of the Canaanite woman forces open (prematurely ?) the door on inclusion in the kingdom by the outsiders. The theological function that lament serves in the New Testament is decidedly different from that in the Old Testament. Instead of seeking for a hidden God in the midst of suffering, the New Testament lament accompanies, and even impels, the coming of God's response to suffering, the ministry of Messiah.

Secondly, lament accompanies the proclamation of the gospel and is inseparable from it, both in the announcement of the arrival of God's kingdom and in waiting for that kingdom to be fully manifest. The weeping of Rachel and the cries of the martyrs beneath God's throne testify to both.[33]

Thirdly, the crucifixion of Christ has transformed suffering for the Christian. Suffering can now be seen in the context of active participation in Christ's suffering. The calling to shared suffering, though, does not do away with the need to lament for two reasons. First and foremost, lament remains the language all who suffer in the face of God's silence. Neither the persistent widow nor Blind Bartimaeus nor the Canaanite woman would accept silence and being ignored as a final answer. Each continued to cry out until they were heard and answered. But also, as we have seen in both Revelation and Matthew, it is possible to speak of a vocational lament that transcends the immediate need and seeks to hasten the fulfillment of messianic ministry. In the Gospel of Matthew, lament serves a canonical function both initiating the messianic ministry to Israel and driving its transformation into a mission to all nations. In the Revelation, lament underscores the reality that the victory of Christ awaits fulfillment.

Fourthly, there is a fundamental tension in the New Testament between the "vocation of shared suffering" and "vocation of lament."[34] In one sense the significance of some suffering has been transformed, as it becomes a testimony to the strength of Christ exercised through weakness. But there is also a continued need for cries and protests in the in-between time, in the now-but-not-yet of the unfolding Kingdom of God. As we await the return of Christ, lament cries out impatiently, urging that *someday* would become *this day*. As long as we live in the now-but-not-yet of this life, we can and should cry out to God for the suffering of the innocent and protest God's silence in the face of need.

As we consider the ways in which lament has shifted in both form and function in the New Testament, it is fair to ask whether the guiding metaphor for this study remains useful when talking about New Testament lament. In what sense do those who call out to God in the

---

33. Though it is not possible, I think, to speak of a canonical shape lent by prayers of lament to the New Testament as a whole, I find it nevertheless provocative to note that both the first and last book of the New Testament canon incorporate lament into the fabric of their messages.

34. Westermann points out that the doctrine of bearing suffering patiently is not developed in Jesus' teaching, but rather in the apostolic writings that seek to interpret and apply the gospel message to the church; *Praise and Lament*, 265.

New Testament "risk truth"? Certainly the laments of the New Testament require that notions of faithful speech continue to make room for both cries and protests. Even the call to share in Christ's suffering, a vocation that appears with the exilic prophets, but which is generalized in the New Testament to include the Church as a whole, does not negate either the possibility or the continued necessity for lament. The continued presence of lament qualifies every theology that tries to guarantee deliverance, healing, and safety if we simply have sufficient faith.

A more basic risk run by the continuation of lament in the New Testament, though, is the risk of the loss of hegemony by the established church. Prayers of lament fail to observe the niceties of due process. They are jarring, even violent in their assault on decency and order. They are the language of the nobody, the outsider, and the foreigner. Rachel's cry reminds the prosperous Western church that a gospel proclaimed without tears is a distortion and a mockery. The protest of the Canaanite woman will not accept Gospel hand-me-downs, but demands a place at the table and a voice among the children of Israel. Blind Bartimaeus will not lower his voice, speak civilly, and wait his turn. The poor widow will not settle for what is legal, but demands what is just from the judge who has lost all concern for the defenseless in society. The continued presence of lament in the New Testament not only suggests that the "nobodies" of society have a place at the table, but that those who weep may take precedence over a Church that is committed to the avoidance and denial of pain.

7

The Shapes of Lament

According to the South African Department of Health, the scale of the HIV/AIDS epidemic in that country has reaching alarming proportions. It is estimated that 1 in every 10 adults is HIV positive and that 3 women in every 10 who attend public antenatal clinics test positive for the virus. While there is some indication that the rate of infection is stabilizing, the rate of AIDS related deaths continues to climb.[1]

GERALD WEST REPORTS ON THE CRISIS IN SOUTH AFRICAN SOCIETY among the large HIV/AID positive population. He says that it is usual at the funeral of a person whose death is AIDS related to avoid any mention of the infection. Furthermore, a favored biblical text among Reform pastors who preach at such funerals is Job 1:21, "Naked I came from my mother's womb, and naked shall I return there; the LORD gave, and the LORD has taken away; blessed be the name of the LORD." In support groups for persons who have tested positive for HIV, though, the laments of Job are being introduced to challenge the theological monolith suggested by Job 1:21. Persons struggling both with the infection and with their subsequent rejection by their families, their communities, and often by the church are learning to voice the laments of Job and to offer their own laments to God.[2]

Perhaps most significant in this application of lament prayer to this foundational crisis in South Africa is that unsophisticated "non-experts," when they take up the practice of lament, seem to understand intuitively that lament is not about replacing Job 1 theology with Job 3

1. Geffen, "What Do South Africa's AIDS Statistics Mean?"
2. West and Zengele, "Reading Job 'Positively' in the Context of HIV/AIDS in South Africa."

theology, but is in fact a wrestling with the tension created by accepting both to be true. West offers an example of a lament written by a lay person who participated in a study of Job's laments.

> God you have allowed me to feel this painful experience. I don't not know whether this is because I am a bad person in your eyes, or because of my sinfulness. You have taken away my husband; I am left alone with four young children to look after and I am unemployed. My prayer is: please help me to raise these children under your guidance, let them do good in your eyes like Job. I am begging you to keep me alive for a longer time so that I can be there for my children. Give me strength to come closer to you, more than before God. I curse the family (my in-laws) I stay with, they are horrible to me![3]

As with the lament of Job himself, these prayers are characterized by their ability to sustain an excruciating tension as they explore the intersection between belief and experience.

Living with Dissonance

Western society is, I suspect, less comfortable with dissonance than are other cultures that have not been so indelibly marked by the precepts of the Enlightenment. Continuing in the direction set by Isaac Newton's description of the mathematics of gravity, truth in the West has often been characterized in terms of mathematical precision, objective detachment, and rational cohesion rather than with the categories of mystery, uniqueness, and uncertainty. Within such a model of knowing, cognitive dissonance becomes something negative that results from flawed reasoning and insufficient data, rather than being understood positively as an essential descriptive of reality. The application of principles deriving from the Enlightenment are, however, of limited use in describing phenomenon in which a degree of uncertainty is inherent, such as relationships between people. Enlightenment thinking is better suited for explaining objective phenomenon rather than subjective relationships. It has been a central assumption of this study that Israel's encounters with God are described in relational rather than propositional

---

3. West, "The Poetry of Job as a Resource for the Articulation of Embodied Lament in the Context of HIV and AIDS in South Africa."

terms and that the drawing together of two distinct beings in a close relationship results inevitably in a persistent dissonance and discord.

The essence of the prayer of lament is captured in the tension between belief and experience. The first step in a practice of lament that mirrors the lament prayers in the Bible is a willingness to entertain such a dissonance. There must be both a belief in the normalcy of divine response and the experience that God has unexpectedly stepped back from his relationship with the one praying. Were that tension to be resolved, the practice of lament would alter fundamentally. Without the belief that there is a God who is loving and good, who hears and answers prayer, who speaks and acts in the world, lament becomes little more than complaint for its own sake, with no expectation that change could be effected. Apart from such beliefs, all prayer becomes simply a monologue, a speaking into the emptiness. In short, the Enlightenment influenced conviction that God neither speaks nor acts in history must change the shape and function of lament. Without the addition of fresh experiences of encounter with God, belief is saved from uncertainty, but only at the cost of a growing irrelevance. Lament as it is practiced in the Bible sustains the dissonance between belief and experience, revitalizing both.

Having established this dissonance, the cultures that produced biblical lament are better equipped to abide in its continued presence. Though it is true that belief cannot endure forever in the face of contradictory experience, nevertheless those who prayed the laments seemed to recognize the importance of persisting in the tension.

Inherent in the insistence that both belief and experience be entertained is the element of risk that provides a central thesis for this study, that risk is intrinsic to the prayer of lament. It requires that we acknowledge openly a breakdown in the system of beliefs that provide our lives with structure, stability, and security. It demands an open acceptance of the alternate reality that the emperor really is naked, even when it would be so much easier to pretend with those around us that we too "see" the emperor clothed and everything else as it should be in an ordered and secure world. Lament must often go against the majority voice and in so doing leads to a deeper isolation for the one who prays it. Lament compels us to turn loose of support systems and the framework that we use to make sense of our world, for though they offer a degree of security, in the extreme moments of life such systems prove to be dysfunctional.

Lament is also, though, an act of hope. In a courage born of desperation, those who lament create a space for the possibility of newness. Such newness is not achievable as long as denial is maintained and the status quo guarded. Lament is offered in the conviction that the silence of God can be broken.

When God Gets Close Enough to Suffer

A sharp dissonance also marks the ways that God is portrayed in scripture. He is both the God who suffers for and with us, and the God who judges and even destroys for no reason. He is experienced as both deliverer and enemy. He is spurned lover and avenging judge. God experiences suffering, remains silent as his people suffer, and at times causes the suffering of the innocent. God's suffering is integral to his nature and expressions of his mercy, wrath, forgiveness, and judgment are shaped and qualified by his pathos.

The cause of God's suffering lies in his initiative for relatedness. Whereas God the judge may be able to remain dispassionate, God the rejected spouse cannot. The nature of Yahweh's commitment to Israel has brought with it his vulnerability, his openness to being wounded and changed, so that the prophets speak of God being constrained and directed by what he feels.

In the context of judging Israel, God both suffers and takes up laments. The practice of lament, when placed on the lips of God, gives shape to his wrath and offers the promise of restoration. When spoken by God, lament is a re-creative act, keeping alive the prospect that, when wrath has spent itself, a return to the land and a new beginning are possible.

Human prayers of lament also provide clarity when God is experienced as an enemy. Though God is identified as one who sends innocent sheep to be slaughtered, who destroys without cause, who is a deceitful brook, and who treats foreigners like dogs, nevertheless speech continues. The persistence of prayer in the face of God's silence and even his open rejection suggests that "God as enemy" is at best a partial and imperfect descriptive. Lament assumes a level of trust that is ultimately incompatible with true malevolence on God's part.

In the prayers of lament God is addressed by those who are "insiders," with the right not simply to plea, but to protest and demand. Insiders are different. Family can make demands that a stranger cannot. In Psalm 143, the writer seeks from God a double standard.

> Do not enter into judgment with your *servant*,
>   for no one living is righteous before you, . . .
> In your steadfast love cut off my enemies,
>   and destroy my adversaries,
>   for I am your *servant*. (Ps 143:2, 12)

To be God's servant means being able to pray in the same breath forgive my sins, for no one is innocent, but in your steadfast love (*ḥesed*) hold my enemies accountable without mercy. The Canaanite woman in Matthew 15 recognizes that even the dogs under Israel's table have a claim on the Son of David and in pressing that claim she is able to break through every pretense of God as enemy. Ultimately the prayer of lament will not accept the animosity of God.

A Story to Tell

Israel's story defines them as a people. Beginning with Abram's calling and the promise that he would be the father of a great nation, Israel's identity has been drawn from their relationship with Yahweh. Such elements as the Exodus deliverance, the Sinai encounter, the wilderness wandering, the conquest of the land, and the eternal Davidic monarchy shape the praying community's understanding of God and their expectations regarding his dealings with his people.

There is, of course, a substantial difference between the recital of history and the remembering of story. The writers of Scripture were not engaged in historiography in the modern sense, nor should the appeals to story that anchor so many of the lament psalms be categorized as history in the modern sense of that term. The very nature of the psalm writer's appeals, though, attests to their understanding of the story as resting in some sense on concrete historical referents. Israel's military victories in the conquest of the land are appealed to as a basis for requesting of Yahweh his intervention in an ongoing campaign in the present. The psalmists' primary focus is not on a substantiation of the past, but on an *inbreaking* in the present. A fresh encounter with Yahweh is the only acceptable confirmation that the story is true.

Appeals to story will always be more oriented to the present than is history. Through the twin acts of remembering and testifying, the praying community steps once more into the flowing river that is Israel's story. That story invites participation and the question with which many of the lament psalmist struggle is, "Am I still a participant in Israel's story?"

I have suggested that the offering of testimony to a fresh encounter with God is, for the lament psalmist, an act of traditioning. It is that constant renewal that prevents Israel's story from becoming extinct, that is, from becoming the history of historiography. Testimony to an encounter with God is more than a confirmation of the past, it is a denial that Israel's story can be confined to the past. While history may only be recalled, Israel's story is to be lived.

Prayer without Ceasing

One of the striking features of the lament is the writer's refusal to abandon the conversation. Regardless of the expressions of pain and anger, the accusations of injustice on God's part, and even the suspicion that God has become the enemy of the one praying, speech continues. The amazing thing about Job is, after all that he experiences, he simply will not shut up. Nor will he back away from the uncertainty of dialogue and join his friends in safe, stable declarations about God.

The book of Job is decidedly about speech, both the right speech of Job and the foolish speech of Job's friends. In the context of relationship, truthful speech is not determined by content alone. The power of Job's words rests not simply in what he says, but in who he addresses. When faced with a crisis of relationship, it is the passionate verbalizing of pain and not the detached propositional description of justice that is finally authentic. As anyone who has been involved in a long standing and intimate relationship with another person can attest, it is possible to say something that is technically accurate and still be wrong.

The book of Job also explores a foundational insight into Yahweh's practice of justice, namely that, like Job's speech, it is essentially relational rather than mechanical. God suspends the practice of retributional justice in Job's case, intervening actively in the flow of reward and punishment in his life. It is even possible to speak of the injustice of God, if by injustice we mean that God "breaks the rules," bringing into Job's life that which he has not earned. The book of Job adds an important qualifier to the deuteronomic understanding of divine justice. Yahweh's practice of justice is both relational and contextual, so that he will not respond as Job's friends say that he must. Job testifies to the reality that God's justice can never be reduced to a mechanical certainty.

Even more so than in the lament psalms, lament in Job is geared toward engaging change. Job is forced to abide in the gap between two worlds, each of which offers a distinct vision of moral order. The moral construct offered by each of these worlds is in the end simply that, a construct, so that each can offer at best only a partial understanding of reality. Just as the poetic body of the book does not negate the vision of God's justice offered by the friends, so too the prose frame with its blessed ending to Job's life does not nullify the prospect of future uncertainly and unpredictability in God's exercise of justice. Through the practice of lament Job finds a way to both honor his belief and own his experience.

Living as we do in a time of fundamental moral transition, Job's laments offer an especially suitable tool in the midst of change. Rather than cling dogmatically to a morality that does not always fit our experience or dispose of it out of hand as something that no longer seems relevant, lament offers us an avenue into fresh dialogue with God. Laments can sustain dissonance and adapt to change in part because they speak to God and not about him.

A Victim of God's Compassion

The reversal of the Sinai covenant which is embodied in the Exile requires of Israel a reexamination of their relationship with Yahweh. The description of Israel's relationship with Yahweh found in the writings of the exilic prophets is significantly different from that encountered in the Pentateuch. The prophecies of Jeremiah incorporate three substantial changes in the way that divine-human interaction is understood with regard to the covenant, to the nature of God's justice, and to the theological function of lament.

First of all, the exilic prophets have recast the image of covenant articulated in the deuteronomic tradition. Beginning with Hosea, the metaphor of a political treaty has been replaced by that of a marriage contract. The Suzerain lord of Deuteronomy who addresses Israel as a political entity has become the wounded spouse whose love for Israel battles with and threatens to overthrow his sense of what is "right."

This re-imaging of covenant by the prophet paves the way for the exploration of a second change, this time in the nature of God himself. It is the prophets who most clearly portray the pathos of God who suffers as a result of Israel's rejection. In God's pathos we see most clearly the impact that his relationship with Israel has made on his person. His heart recoils and his compassion grows warm, so that he relents of his decision to utterly destroy Israel. Yahweh remembers Ephraim and as he remembers he is deeply moved.

Jeremiah in particular also witnesses to a third change, this time in the function served by the prayer of lament. By taking upon himself the suffering of another and by suffering though he himself is innocent, the significance of the prophet's lament shifts. Lament as a prophetic vocation foreshadows both the role of Isaiah's suffering servant and lament's function in the New Testament as a prophetic word that both accompanies and propels the unfolding messianic proclamation.

The book of Lamentations attests to the power of lament to bring healing and to usher those who offer it into a new place in their relationship with Yahweh. Through the practice of lament, the national psyche of Israel advances from a confession of sin to an affirmation that God's righteous wrath has exhausted itself to a declaration that Israel's sin has been expunged, so that theirs is now an innocent suffering. This move is made in the process of offering lament. The orientation of the people changes, even though Yahweh has yet to respond to their prayer. Lament has moved the people from an exilic to a post-exilic orientation in their approach to Yahweh.

Laughter, Tears, and the Coming of Messiah

The writer of Matthew's gospel appears to have been decidedly influenced by the prophetic practice of lament. As in the case of Jeremiah, the prayer of lament in the New Testament is not offered to a hidden God, but to one who is experienced as present, and it has an impact that goes beyond the immediate needs of the person praying. For Matthew the prayer of lament accompanies and energizes the unfolding of the Kingdom of God. Matthew's use of lament to give structure to the message of his gospel points to a *vocation of lament*. Though personal suffering continues to elicit cries for deliverance, that suffering takes on a significance that transcends the needs of the individual praying.

Rachel's tears insure that lament will continue to be part of the message of the gospel. Her cries place a restraint on triumphalism and act as a reminder of the reality that the Church exists in the in-between time, in the now-but-not-yet when Mary's song is still accompanied by the cry of Rachel. Fullness of life and length of days have yet to be restored, so that pain and loss continue to be part of the fabric of the messianic kingdom.

This insistence that gospel proclamation does not bracket out, but embraces lament, together with the observation that it is the "nobodies" in society who recognize the Son of David in Matthew's gospel, serve to underscore an important shift in the twenty-first century Church. Though the prayer of lament remains a resource for all who experience a suffering that diminishes fullness of life, the vocation of lament is first and foremost the province of the foreigner, the widow, the deformed, and the destitute. The practice of this vocation challenges the hegemony of the Western church. The loss of the practice of lament in materialistic, wealthy cultures has signaled a shift away from a western, upper-middleclass, male control on the proclamation and interpretation of the gospel. Increasingly it is the "nobodies" of Western society and the long-silenced voices of the remainder of the world that challenge a Church that finds no place for lament.

Lament in the Bible serves a variety of functions. It reconnects those who pray it with a larger story and a more extensive community of faith. It offers a means of restoring trust in God when we are struck down for no reason. It challenges us to see our own pain in the context of the suffering both of God and of his creation, so that we are called to lament not just for ourselves, but for others. And it accompanies the proclamation of the good news as a constant reminder both that God's kingdom is revealed and that we are handed the vocation of crying out in plea and protest for the suffering of the weak and powerless.

The practice of lament embraces change and runs risks. It is constantly open to integrating belief and new experience. It does not hesitate to risk the loss of belief in order to keep that belief vital and growing. Prayers of lament willingly risk all in their pursuit of a fresh encounter with God.

Bibliography

Anderson, Bernhard W. *Creation versus Chaos: The Reinterpretation of Mythical Symbolism in the Bible.* 1967. Reprinted, Philadelphia: Fortress, 1987.

Andersen, Francis I. *Job.* Tyndale Old Testament Commentary. Downers Grove, IL: InterVarsity, 1976.

Archer, Gleason L. *A Survey of Old Testament Introduction.* Rev. and exp. ed. Chicago: Moody, 1994.

Balentine, Samuel E. "Jeremiah, Prophet of Prayer." *Review & Expositor* 78 (1981) 331–43.

———. *The Hidden God: The Hiding of the Face of God in the Old Testament.* Oxford: Oxford University Press, 1983.

———. *Prayer in the Hebrew Bible: The Drama of Divine-Human Dialogue.* Overtures to Biblical Theology. Minneapolis: Fortress, 1993.

Baumgartner, Walter. *Jeremiah's Poems of Lament.* Translated by David E. Orton. Decatur, GA: Almond, 1988.

Begrich, Joachim. "Das priesterliche Heilsorakel." *Zeitschrift für die alttestamentliche Wissenschaft* 52 (1934) 81–92.

Berkovits, Eliezer. *Faith after the Holocaust.* New York: Ktav, 1973.

Berlin, Adele. *Lamentations: A Commentary.* Louisville: Westminster John Knox, 2002.

Billman, Kathleen D., and Daniel L. Migliore. *Rachel's Cry: Prayer of Lament and Rebirth of Hope.* Cleveland: United Church Press, 1999.

Blank, Sheldon H. "The Prophet as Paradigm." In *Essays in Old Testament Ethics: J. Philip Hyatt, In Memoriam,* edited by James L. Crenshaw and John T. Willis, 111–30. New York: Ktav, 1974.

Blumenthal, David R. *Facing the Abusing God: A Theology of Protest.* Louisville: Westminster John Knox, 1993.

Bracke, John M. *Jeremiah 1–29.* Westminster Bible Companion. Louisville: Westminster John Knox, 2000.

———. *Jeremiah 30–52 and Lamentations.* Westminster Bible Companion. Louisville: Westminster John Knox, 2000.

Brenner, Athalya. "Job the Pious? The Characterization of Job in the Narrative Framework of the Book." *Journal for the Study of the Old Testament* 43 (1989) 37–52.

Bright, John. "Lament and Its Answer: Jeremiah 15:10–21." *Interpretation* 28 (1974) 59–74.

Brueggemann, Walter. *In Man We Trust: The Neglected Side of Biblical Faith.* 1972. Reprinted, Eugene, OR: Wipf & Stock, 2006.

———. "Psalms and the Life of Faith: A Suggested Typology of Function." *Journal for the Study of the Old Testament* 17 (1980) 3–32.

————. *The Message of the Psalms*. Minneapolis: Augsburg, 1984.

————. "The Costly Loss of Lament." *Journal for the Study of the Old Testament* 36 (1986) 57–71. Reprinted in Brueggemann, *The Psalms and the Life of Faith*, edited by Patrick D. Miller, 98–111. Minneapolis: Fortress, 1995.

————. *Jeremiah 1–25: To Pluck Up, To Tear Down*. Grand Rapids: Eerdmans, 1988.

————. "The Crisis and Promise of Presence in Israel." In *Old Testament Theology: Essays on Structure, Theme, and Text*, edited by Patrick D. Miller, 150–82. Minneapolis: Fortress, 1992.

————. "The Shape of Old Testament Theology, II: Embrace of Pain." In *Old Testament Theology: Essays on Structure, Theme, and Text*, edited by Patrick D. Miller, 22–44. Minneapolis: Fortress, 1992.

————. *Theology of the Old Testament: Testimony, Dispute, Advocacy*. Minneapolis: Fortress, 1997.

————. *The Prophetic Imagination*. 2nd ed. Minneapolis: Fortress, 2001.

————. *The Spirituality of the Psalms*. Facets. Minneapolis: Fortress, 2002.

————. *Praying the Psalms*. 2nd ed. Eugene, OR: Cascade Books, 2007.

————. *The Theology of the Book of Jeremiah*. Old Testament Theology. Cambridge: Cambridge University Press, 2007.

Buber, Martin. *I And Thou*. 2nd ed. Translated by Ronald Gregor Smith. New York: Scribner, 1958.

Carpentier, Raymond. "L'échec de la communication." In *Les hommes devant l'échech*, 13–30. Paris, 1968.

Charry, Ellen T. "May We Trust God and (Still) Lament? Can We Lament and (Still) Trust God?" In *Lament: Reclaiming Practices in Pulpit, Pew, and Public Square*, edited by Sally A. Brown and Patrick D. Miller, 95–108. Louisville: Westminster John Knox, 2005.

Clines, David J. A. "Deconstructing the Book of Job." In *What Does Eve Do to Help? And Other Readerly Questions to the Old Testament*, edited by David J. A. Clines, 105–23. Journal for the Study of the Old Testament Supplements 94. Sheffield: JSOT Press, 1990.

————. "The Shape and Argument of the Book of Job." In *Sitting With Job: Selected Studies on the Book of Job*, edited by Roy B. Zuck, 125–39. Grand Rapids: Baker, 1992.

Clines, David J. A. and David M. Gunn. "Form, Occasion and Redaction in Jeremiah 20." *Zeitschrift für die alttestamentliche Wissenschaft* 88 (1976) 390–409.

————. "'You Tried to Persuade Me' and 'Violence! Outrage!' in Jeremiah 20:7–8." *Vetus Testamentum* 28 (1978) 285–92.

Cohn-Sherbok, Dan. *Holocaust Theology*. London: Lamp, 1989.

Conrad, Edgar. "Second Isaiah and the Priestly Oracle of Salvation." *Zeitschrift für die alttestamentliche Wissenschaft* 93 (1981) 234–46.

Crenshaw, James. *A Whirlpool of Torment: Israelite Traditions of God as an Oppressive Presence*. Overtures to Biblical Theology. Philadelphia: Fortress, 1984.

Davis, Ellen F. "Job and Jacob: The Integrity of Faith." In *The Whirlwind: Essays on Job, Hermeneutics and Theology in Memory of Jane Morse*, edited by Stephen C. Cook, Corrine L. Patton and James W. Watts, 100–120. Journal for the Study of the Old Testament Supplements 336. Sheffield: Sheffield Academic, 2001.